FEAR LESS

FEAR LESS

How to envision
your future & create a
Brave New You

LOU HAMILTON

First published in Great Britain in 2018
by Orion Spring,
an imprint of The Orion Publishing Group Ltd
Carmelite House, 50 Victoria Embankment
London EC4Y 0DZ

An Hachette UK Company

1 3 5 7 9 10 8 6 4 2

A CIP catalogue record for this book
is available from the British Library.

ISBN (Trade Paperback) 9781409174707
ISBN (eBook) 9781409174714

Printed and bound by CPI Group (UK) Ltd, Croydon, CR0 4YY

MIX
Paper from
responsible sources
FSC www.fsc.org   FSC® C104740

For my children Sol and Ruby,
who keep pushing through fear
in order to do really awesome stuff.

You inspire me in every way.

Contents

Introduction

What is it to FEAR LESS?

You picked up this book because the title FEAR LESS somehow struck a chord with you. Fear has wormed its nose into your life and it's not doing you any favours. So you have been courageous enough to say to yourself, 'You know what, I don't think fear should rule the roost and I'm going to find out how to FEAR LESS.' Good for you. You have already taken the first few critical steps: (*a*) acknowledging that you don't feel as right as you might; (*b*) taking responsibility for learning how to feel better; and (*c*) deciding to read this book. You have proven some essential factors about yourself that will prepare you for a successful outcome; that you Care about yourself enough to do something about how you feel, that you are Curious about how you can do that, and that you have enough Courage to grab the reins of your life and take the required action. And since this book is about self-care, creativity (problem-solving requires curiosity) and transforming fear through action, you can feel comfortable in the knowledge that you've got what it takes.

Like Einstein! He'd see a problem, he'd get curious about it, he'd let his creative mind do its mulling, and then when a solution raised it's head he'd follow its lead. The act of getting this far has required you to do all those things. You have the gumption, and I'm going to help you build on that so that you can get to a place where fear no longer has its grip on you. A place where you have the tools and techniques to transform its energy into a powerful force for good, and where you can be at your own back in the face of anything the future holds.

This book will lead you through a series of eureka moments about yourself that will help you build a fearless life of curiosity, resilience, tenacity, determination, creativity, perseverance, improvisation, confidence, courage, audacity, self-love, passion, purpose, self-belief, self-worth, motivation, dreams, goals, accomplishment, connection, time well spent, wellness, gratitude, embracing change, love, intuition, mastery, success and hope.

Life will always be a work in progress but with these learned attributes at your side you'll be ready to take on the world. Even better you will be able to pass your fearlessness on to others because you will know: (*a*) how you got there; (*b*) what you need to keep doing; and (*c*) that it is all possible for anyone to achieve.

So get ready to fly. Like a mother bird I will show you how. Then, after that, you won't need me. You'll have your wings and you'll have the knowledge. You just have to flap and leap.

In the meantime – read the book, mull it over at your leisure, then go back and put in the graft.

....

Three Stages of Courage

1. CURIOSITY – you picked up this book

2. CREATIVITY AND CREATIVE THINKING – this book will help you develop your creativity and creative-thinking skills to help you FEAR LESS

3. COMMITMENT – if you commit to doing the work and creating a daily practice you will become self-caring, resilient and flexible in the face of your fear and life's challenges

....

FEAR LESS not Fearless

I'll be frank. I'm not going to make you totally fearless all of the time. Instead, I'm going to give you the ability to FEAR LESS. Absolute fearlessness is foolhardy and will get you into trouble. You'll drive too fast, jump off cliffs, burn yourself, date idiots, eat uncooked trout, gamble away all the money you don't have and hurt others. No, what I'm talking about is taking fear, and then by using your natural human capacity for creative thinking/problem solving and self-preservation, turn it into something powerful and constructive.

One potential client wrote to me recently saying that life felt pretty scary for her right now and that she looked at me and thought I seem to be happy and doing what makes me fulfilled. I am and do, but I wanted her to know that I had once stood where she is, and felt what she feels. I know fear. But with the tools and techniques I use to help others, I learned to help myself too. I replied:

'I have felt all that you feel, but by using the coaching tools, I manage to keep moving forward in an upright position. We need to keep a very tight ship; we need a vessel to hold us safe to set sail, and be all that we can be. That's what coaching is about; learning the tricks of the trade and then applying them in a daily practice through thick and thin. Creative coaching is tapping into our core creative selves so we may fire on all cylinders. My clients know they have to invest in themselves to handle the darker side of life. It takes courage, it takes a lot of hard work, and it takes perseverance but it, and you, are worth it.'

The very fact that I stand before you now is proof that it works. Fear less and be more.

We have a choice to see FEAR as:

FEAR = death, sweat, palpitations, panic, holding breath and
          racing thoughts.

or

FEAR = your (sometimes overzealous) friend. It shows you where you need to grow.

Here's a quick review of what FEAR LESS can look like:

F Flip your view of the future right here in the present, and the future will take care of itself. Set goals, dream big, let go of control, create a vision that excites you – one that keeps you curious and makes you look forward to the day.

E Engage enthusiastically and energetically with the present. Take little steps, manage your time, self-care, learn not to procrastinate, breathe and be powerfully present.

A Affirm all that is right in your world. Build self-confidence by finding evidence for the good things you've done, what others like about you, for what you like about yourself.

R Relief comes with reassurance. Relief from perfection. It's a roller coaster, but know that the highs will be brighter and that you will ride the lows more easily. Know that everyone finds it hard!

Turn FEAR into FEAR LESS.

L Learn from everything. As they say: 'What doesn't kill you makes you stronger.' The successful believe that you win, or you learn. Think about that before you face your fear.

E Embrace failure. Experiment. Play, get creative, take risks. Failure is the tool of the 'Billionaire Mindset', so get comfortable with it.

S Seize every opportunity no matter how terrifying. Say yes first and think later. Prepare, research then leap. The more you put yourself in front of opportunities the more luck will come to you.

S Soul-search for your core values. This is the foundation upon which you build everything. Your choices will become clearer, and your decisions easier. It will give you meaning and purpose when you have identified what really matters to you.

Fearing Less is . . .

Saying YES to these:	And saying NO to these:
Yes to respect	No to being lied to
Yes to honesty	No to be cheated on
Yes to transparency	No to dishonesty
Yes to autonomy	No to being taken for granted
Yes to choice	No to being used
Yes to freedom	No to having your time hijacked
Yes to equality	No to having always to be nice
Yes to your values	No to being underpaid
Yes to truthfulness	No to being unappreciated
Yes to engagement	No to having to play small
Yes to purpose	No to holding yourself back
Yes to fulfillment	No to being ignored
Yes to self-care	No to being leered at
Yes to possibility	No to being patronised
Yes to potential	No to being hoodwinked
Yes to self-determination	No to being controlled
Yes to challenge	No to being neutered
Yes to connection	No to being humiliated
Yes to laughter	No to being deceived
Yes to creativity	No to being conned
Yes to flow	No to being the butt of others' jokes
Yes to play	No to smoke and mirrors
	No to sneaky behaviour
	No to being terrorised

Section One is an overview of what we can aim for with fearlessness, how fear affects us, and why the use of creative strategies and self-care can help us turn fear into fearing less.

Section Two is the practical self-help coaching programme based on the creative coaching practice I run with my face-to-face clients. The programme is interwoven with real people stories, my own experiences, the multi-layer aspects of fear, and the creative strategies for tackling, overcoming or living better with them. There are coaching tips and core-work exercises to do to embed your personal development as you go. This section is a workbook for life-long learning, and your progression comes from committing to and embracing the process.

Read the whole book through and then come back to do the exercises over a six-week period (depending on your other workloads). Improvise with the various techniques; no one size fits all. I've tried to cover as many ways of dealing with the multitude of fears as I can, but the methods are transferable; use them as you see fit. I'm sorry that I am not with you in person on your transformational journey, but I have tried to write in the same way as I talk when I work with my clients. I hope you find the tone encouraging and supportive, not dry and preachy or too airy-fairy. I try not to get bogged down in the science, but I hope you get enough of the sense of the thirty years of research I have done on the subject; enough I hope for you to start to believe that this stuff works. I hope the stories will inspire you in the choices you make at every stage. I hope you get to laugh a bit along the way and I hope you feel stronger for the fact that you have had the courage to commit to the programme. By the end of the book, I hope you know how to love and care for yourself in all the creative ways that a human being has access to, and that it helps you live life to the fullest.

Fearing less is based on mind and body science, but it is the art of living fearlessly that I offer you in this book.

Section One

1. FEAR LESS

I'm an artist and a life coach, and over the years I've learned a thing or two about fear – both creatively and personally. Both my fear, and other people's. I know how powerful its hold is on us, but I also know that fear is the worry about what hasn't happened yet, when the reality is that we have no way of actually predicting what the future will bring.

In 2015, I found myself facing an 'empty nest' as my daughter finished school and prepared to head out into the world. I was scared. How huge was this loss going to feel? I wouldn't be able to protect her, is she going to be all right? But on the other hand, I did really want her to go out there and be everything she could be.

So, I re-imagined *my* fears for *her* future by conjuring up fearless-ness in the form of the character *Brave New Girl*. She was a stick figure with a triangle dress, no face and sometimes no arms (which was how Ruby used to draw when she was little). *Brave New Girl* can do anything, not like some fantasy Superwoman, but like any of us when we put our imaginations to good use. By imagining her as invincible I quietened my fears; I had re-imagined her future and satisfied my present. And then I created *Brave New Guy* for my son. Or rather – I created him for me. I created them both so that I could let go and worry less about an uncertain world, in the belief that he and my daughter could go out and be their own kind of super-heroes. They have that certainty of youth that all will be well, and if it's not – we'll deal with it then. I have the fear of every mother wanting to protect her young and yet I want them to live life to the full. So I gave them these characters, and that makes me feel better. This book is for you to create a *Brave New You* for the days when you feel a bit wobbly.

Imagination is the key to either a fearless, or a fearful life. Fear is imagining the future will turn out badly. Fearing less is when we imagine being and doing anything we want.

Now, I know that bad things do happen; I've experienced them myself. I once lived on a street in edgy 80s London where people chased each other with machetes and a police van was a permanent fixture on the street corner. One night when I was taking a taxi home, the driver put a knife on the seat next to him. I asked him what he was doing and he said you couldn't be too careful going to the street where I lived. I was mugged outside my home and I was hassled on the tube. The IRA exploded bombs and people died. I was twenty and I saw a darker side of life.

After art college, I decided enough was enough and moved to the wilds of rural south west Scotland thinking I'd be living a stress-free

existence in the middle of nowhere. But on 21 December 1988 a terrorist attack on the flight Pan Am 103 blew the plane out of the sky
and rained down hell on our small town of Lockerbie. One of the
worst things that you could ever imagine had happened. And all 259
people on board and eleven on the ground were killed.

The impact on all our lives was devastating. I hadn't been personally injured or lost anyone in the fireball, but I became constantly
anxious and fearful. I imagined the worst outcome in every situation. That ancient 'fight or flight' mode of my brain was permanently switched on. My imagination was at full throttle. Everything
was a potential horror movie. I could visualise every detail of every
possible disaster at every turn. I held myself back, out of fear.

Eventually, I decided to do something about it and trained as a
life coach. I learned the tools of the trade, got myself sorted and
started helping others. People come to me with **stress** issues but
with a little investigation we usually find that it's some kind of **fear**
that's lurking; their imaginations running riot in subtle, life-sucking,
ways.

But if the imagination is that powerful in a negative way, why not
flip it to conjure up a rose-tinted future that is bright and exciting?
The future hasn't happened yet, so who's to say what is going to
happen, and why ruin the present by dreaming up dismal or disastrous results of us trying to do and be our best selves? Why let a
malign imagination make us fearful and stressed out when we can,
instead, learn to imagine positive visions of the future.

> Re-imagine fear of the future
> As fearlessness in the present

How you use your imagination is the key to a fearless or fearful life.
Fear is fed by your imagination; it paints a picture of tomorrow to
the point where it disrupts today.

Learning to tell the difference between real and perceived danger helps you to let go of what you cannot control, and to work with what you can. We can re-educate our creative brains to quell our animal instincts of *fight or flight* when it's not needed, and to give ourselves the chance to live to our full potential. This book teaches you how to build your creative muscles so that you can **re-imagine** fear of the future as fearlessness for now.

Fearlessness is Dreaming Big

And that is about imagining that anything is possible.

At this point I want to give you an example that illustrates how to get past today's fear and into tomorrow's potential.

I interviewed former magician Jonathan Newman about his path to success as a film director, screenwriter and entrepreneur with a multi-million-pound coconut-based health food business.

For Jonathan, dreaming big means big. It's tempting when we see successful people to think they had it easy or they have something special, or a trust fund, that sets them apart from the rest of us. There is probably a certain amount of luck involved, but there is also, always, hard work, commitment, perseverance with plenty of failure and fear thrown in.

Q: You were born in Britain but raised in LA. When did you know that you wanted to become a writer and director?

A: I knew I wanted to become a writer–director back in high school. I realised very early on that I had a **FEAR** of being a spoke on someone else's wheel. I recognised that I didn't want to work for someone else and fulfil someone else's dream for the rest of my life. That was my earliest internal philosophical debate and it led me to seek out a profession that would allow me to be in **control of my destiny**. I was always into film, I was always making short films when I was young, and I was also into magic and the creative arts. And so this seemed like a great way to access the life that I wanted.

Note to reader: Use fear as a 'call to arms'.

Q: Back then, having established that it was going to be film, what were your dreams and ambitions?

A: I am a firm believer in **dreaming big** and I think that was probably something that was instilled from an early age by my family. It gave me the **confidence to believe**, whether it was self-deluded or not, that I could achieve anything. And it could have been a misplaced confidence but it doesn't matter because what confidence gives you is **drive and determination to take action** instead of believing that you can't do something, which stops you and doesn't allow you to move forward. So I have always dreamt big and I still do now, and I believe in **reaching for the stars**. Only recently I wrote myself a 'cheque' for £100 million, post-dated, so I'm hoping to be able to cash it then!

Q: So then, if you were dreaming big, what was big to you? How big was big?

A: At that point, starting off, you couldn't get any bigger than a director. The director is top of the food chain in the film industry.

Now, I think it was George Clooney who said directing is the best entry-level job in Hollywood today, and it's kind of true because filmmaking is so accessible when given all the jumps in technology with iPhones and filming equipment. Anyone can make a film. All you have to do is jump on Netflix, Amazon or YouTube and see the amount of low budget or small independent films that people have made with very little money, just with enough self-belief and passion. So there is almost no excuse not to be taking action and making movies if that's your chosen profession.

Q: But it wasn't always like that. So, from knowing where you wanted to go from where you were, what were the first steps you took to getting there?

A: After I left film school, having done a Masters in film production, for a while I didn't take any action. Then a friend of mine went and made a low-budget film and I thought, well hang on, what am I doing sitting around not doing anything? And that jump-started me, **changed my frame of mind**. I realised if I was going to do this then I needed a bit of money. Strangely I was leafing through a booklet and I saw British Telecom had attended MIPCOM (TV festival) in Cannes and I though this is odd, they must have some interest in media and there was a picture of a woman and her name and telephone number. And I **called that number** and, bizarrely, I said I want to make a film and could you give me some money and she said yes. The reason she did was because they were testing this new technology at the time called Broadband! And they needed to own some content. So, she gave me £10,000. And, originally, I was going to make a short film and I said: 'you know what, maybe I should just make a feature instead'. So I went and wrote this low budget feature film. I shot it in 21 days with David Tennant (*Dr Who*) and James Dreyfuss (*Gimme, Gimme*) and I'd made a film. And this was 1998. It wasn't a great film but I managed to sell it and then I found myself at Cannes and met sales agents, and we got distribution. And that was the beginning.

Note to reader: Imagine doing everything that it takes to make a film and then thinking it's not a great film. Would you be too scared to ever make another one? Or would you grit your teeth, learn the lessons and do what it takes to make the next one?

Q: Was it plain sailing after that?
A: You kind of get complacent after you do anything creative because I guess you're expecting maybe the world to come to you, or you get a 'golden key', or an easy ride. And what I realised was there is no easy ride. And every film project I make **I suffer the same fear** that I will never work again. And that is a good thing to be honest because what it does is **motivate and inspire me to take action again** rather than remain complacent and sit around on my butt. I remember, after I made *Swinging with the Finkels*, having that fear. So I went and wrote *Foster* and, quite remarkably, before we had locked picture on *Swinging with the Finkels*, we were on set shooting *Foster*, having raised the money again. And that's a really good example of **not resting on your laurels and not remaining complacent**.

Note to reader: Complacency is no friend, but maybe fear can be!

Q: Now you have your big dream, you know what you need to do, and you are very motivated to get going. But then, in the early days, how did you create a structure to your day? What was your work pattern?
A: In the early days I was writing a lot, which was a means to an end. I was a director first and the writing came second because I wanted to generate my own work. And I was really **disciplined** with writing – you have to treat it like a job. Writing doesn't happen by walking

in the park. Writing happens by sitting down in front of a computer and **actually, physically, doing the work**. And the amazing thing is that inspiration comes to you when you're writing. I find that you're channelling something. It's a very odd phenomenon being creative, but it's the act of *doing* which channels it, not the act of *waiting*. So I was very disciplined and I'd sit down and I would knock out maybe a dozen screenplays (half of which were real rubbish) but it allows you to **make mistakes and learn your craft**. It's like a muscle. The more you exercise it, the more it develops. I firmly believe that.

Q: Inevitably there are brick walls and shut doors, although quite often the doors have opened for you. What have been the challenges you've faced?
A: I have a thick file, which I still keep, full of **rejections**. The one thing about being in this industry is that it makes you very thick skinned. But I always say it's not the rejection that kills you, it's the hope, it's the dangling carrot which is always just out of reach. It's one person saying: 'I love it, it's great, I want to make it, I want to be a part of it', and then it fizzles out. That's what really destroys you, and I've had a lot of those. So it's taken a long time. I've had **a lot of doors slammed in my face**. It's only because I am constantly 'buying lottery tickets' that I'm in the game. It's a numbers game. Your number will eventually come up and it's a combination of luck, talent and taking action working in synergy together that creates success. You need to have all three of those things. If you don't have one of those, it doesn't happen. The most important thing is, **your luck is going to be limited if you're not taking action** and seeking out opportunities. Opportunity can take any form, from a chance meeting to a chance phone call, to actually physically writing that script, entering it in a festival, going some place you hadn't intended to go to. But then it needs to be backed up with talent and some form of experience. And therefore, those three things

working together create this chemical reaction of success and you can't get stopped by a no or rejection. That's the most important thing. *Because if you let rejection, fear or any of these internal, mental blockages stop you then you won't progress and so you must push through those things.*

Note to reader: it's worth re-reading that sentence. Very often!

Q: One person's rejection that stops them making that next call, is the next person's call to action. It really is internal, isn't it?
A: You can't let it bruise, or dent, or stop you, because here's the truth: there is no truth. There is no reality; there is no right or wrong, especially in this industry. And there are countless examples of filmmaking history to prove that. I'll give you one example: *The King's Speech* was turned down by the BBC. Or consider *Slumdog Millionaire* – the path to getting that made was tough and difficult. And then it goes on to win Oscars. Nobody knows anything. The difference between a good and a bad script is having Tom Cruise attached. Everyone has an opinion and opinions are just that. There's no reality or truth to an opinion. But if people keep telling you the same thing about a script then you have to be open in order to make it the best possible film or story that you can. There is also the balance between that and trusting your instinct. **Instinct is the thing** that, over the years, over time, is something you must trust. You've got to know when to listen to your own internal voice, while not being arrogant and remaining open. I have really learned to trust my own instinct and that's come from listening to other people's opinions instead of trusting my own and in retrospect realising I should have followed what I felt. It's a powerful thing when you have the confidence to listen to your instinct. Sometimes it's against popular opinion. Some of the most visionary people have trusted

themselves when everyone else is telling them that what they are doing is wrong, or that there is no place for what they are doing in the world. That is how the light bulb got invented and planes fly.

Q: Have you had times when you went against your own instinct and it didn't turn our well?

A: I think in everything I've done, it's a balance between appeasing other people that are involved in the project – whether it's a producer, another creative, or an actor – and **believing in yourself**. I guess it comes down to wanting to be liked and wanting to be open enough to trust someone else's opinion but there comes the point where you have to have the integrity to stay true to your vision of what it is you're creating. If you don't, you'll end up regretting it and blaming someone else, and that's not a fun place to be. You want to be able to make something and take full responsibility. You want to be able to say you made all those choices at the end of the day and if it succeeds, great, you can take the credit, and if it fails, equally you take the blame.

Q: What was the critical turning point in your career, when you felt like things were going to be OK from here on? When you thought 'people are going to keep letting me do this'?

A: I never feel like they are going to keep letting me do this, to be honest! No, the critical point was after I'd made a few short films which all did exceptionally well. And this all happened within the space of a year or two. I'd done the short film *Foster* which won at a dozen festivals, I did another short film called *Finkels*, which was runner up at a big competition in America, and then I did another short film called *Father's Day* which won Grand Prize for the Ford Mustang competition. It was at that point, the critical mass, when it all caught the eye of one producer who I ended up working with on two feature movies (*Foster* and *Swinging with the Finkels*), each on budgets of around £2 million. Then it was after that. It was enough to convince people I can work on a budget with whatever money they've given me. I made the movie *The Adventurer – the Curse of the Midas Touch*. We did that on £25 million, delivered that on time and on budget (although we were severely under-budgeted on that one). But I still don't feel there's any security in the industry and it's probably because you wait so long in between projects. Unless you are James Cameron, or someone who has a career making big blockbusters that are making a lot of money, you are always in this tenuous world of 'when is my next project?' unless you are in the Hollywood system. If you're not in that then you are in the independent system, and that is 'when is this next film getting financed etc.' and **long periods of downtime and insecurity and doubt as to whether you will work again**. And most people in Britain, if you aren't working in television solidly, for example if you are working in film, you're in that place. I even remember going to a screening of *The King's Speech* and afterwards, Tom Hooper, who won the Oscar, said that he thought his Oscar meant he would be handed this 'golden key' to Hollywood. Then he realised there was no golden key and he didn't have a job. You've just won an Oscar! When does that sense of insecurity go away?

Q: In order to survive, to raise a family, and not feel like you are completely down on your luck, every time you find yourself between projects, what have you done?
A: It's perfectly acceptable to have another business to fall back on, especially if it's earning you a living. Fortunately, I made a few films that I have earned a living from but there's always downtime and you can spend money very quickly in this day and age. So, I fell into coconuts! I launched my coconut water business in 2011 and quite to my astonishment it took off and I now find myself running a multi-million pound business selling drinks to thirty countries, and

to 3000 stores in the UK including all the supermarkets. It's been a tremendous ride and learning curve. It has given me the knowledge that I otherwise wouldn't have in running and creating a business and it's been fantastic fun. It's also allowed me to develop my film projects without too much care of how much time goes by in between. And **it gives you some sense of purpose, instead of waiting**, instead of that dangling carrot and the hope that I spoke about before. It gives you something to do on a daily basis when you're not writing or developing a project. It allows breathing space and time for both. But I'm passionate about it. **It was hard work and I had a vision. And I'm also being true to my original philosophy of not being a spoke on someone else's wheel**. It's my own dream, I created a brand from scratch, raised the money, developed it, worked tirelessly for two years with no staff, no wage, and built this business into what it is. Have no illusion; it doesn't fall in your lap, it takes work, and it involves taking massive action. There's no other way to do it.

Q: You've got this fantastic business, that is aligned with all your values, in that it is a healthy product, and I believe you are also now doing good work off the back of it?
A: Yes, we are building wells in India, working with Drop 4 Drop (www.drop4drop.org), and we've committed this year to building six wells in villages that don't have running water. We built our first in November and that's been a really, truly fabulous project, to be able to work on and give back and it's an important part of what we do. I really believe that if you create a business, no matter what your motives, whether they are vanity or a true desire to help people, it's all about the end result. If you can deliver something like that then you should. If you are making money, **it doesn't hurt to give back**.

Q: You are running a multi-million pound company and you have another film project. Tell me about that, and how you do both?

A: Films happen in intense bursts of time. So when I am making a film I am completely focused and immersed in that. Having said that – I do think the way we as humans use time it is not utilised to its full extent. And what I mean by that is that we make excuses for ourselves about time. It always bothers me when someone says: 'I don't have time' because the funny thing is I always have time. I'm really busy, but every day I have time. I have time for something, time to make a phone call. I'm making films and running a business, but I have time to put my children to bed. I have time to go to the gym. **We all have time, it's how we choose to use it**, and what we choose to do with it. If you truly look at your day you'll realise how much time we actually waste, whether that's on social media, socialising or going for coffee for three hours or whatever, or doing nothing, often the only person we're really kidding about time is ourselves.

Q: Do you create white space around all the other stuff you do? Space in your diary just booked out for nothing, to switch off from everything, to mull or meditate?

A: No, I need to find the way to do that because I'm always switched on, and the only way I've found that comes close to that is going to the gym. And I think that's really important, whatever that is for you, to **be able to switch off**. Even at home when I'm done with my business, I'm still switched on and it's terrible. So, the only time for me is in the gym. Physical action allows you mentally to switch off because you're focused on the act of doing something. And that's why I think sports, exercise, walks or whatever are extremely important for anyone who is constantly switched on. You need to find something to help you switch off.

Q: And you manage to get everything done?

A: My philosophy is to **not procrastinate**. At the end of my physical day, I try to have as few things as possible that carry over to the next day. So, any email or problem or issue I get, I deal with there and then. Because of this, my inbox is exceptionally clear, there'll only be ten emails because I've dealt with everything and filed it away, and the only thing I keep in there are the things I'm unable to deal with today, that need following up another day. And that is a very efficient way of working. It really bugs me when people can't return a phone call, or an email, or get back to you, because all it means is that they're leaving something to another day and the likelihood is that they've seen it and are just sitting on it, which is inefficient. So be efficient with your time.

Q: How do you create balance?

A: I've been a real workaholic up until now, but now **I take health very seriously**. I go to the gym five days a week because that's my downtime and I'm taking that exceptionally seriously, like a job. And I diet at the same time. So I'm training hard, I'm working hard, and I'm trying to be present with my family, as much as I can. Every night I'm home to put my children to bed. I'm there in the morning to see them, feed them and take them to school. Then at the weekends I'm there for them 100%.

Q: And is that because that is a decision you've made? It's aligned with your values, with what's important to you, so you make that happen?

A: You make that happen. That's what I choose. I love my children more than anything, and I know that ultimately no amount of material success is more important than children. I know that deep down. Therefore it's a constant reminder when I'm looking at my phone, to put it down and be present for my children. Because that time goes so quickly. And spiritually as well, that's an area I'm always conscious of wanting to work on myself and understand that ultimately you can't take anything with you, and that's why it's really important to **focus on the present**. Not the past and not the future. **And to be present**. So I am always looking at self-improvement and ways I can better myself. You know every Olympic gold-medallist needs a coach, and you shouldn't be afraid to seek out ways of self-improving. When you feel stuck then often it's about 'you don't know what you don't know', and you sometimes need someone to point that out. It's arrogant to think we know everything. **We can learn a lot from other people** if we're open to that experience. It's really about ego and being able to put ego aside. If you read philosophy a lot of great teachings are about putting ego aside. From Kaballah to Buddhism, it's all about how ego gets in the way, how it dominates us, and our need to be right over other people. That's also what stops people from taking instruction – we think we know it all. We think we know everything. But life is about growing and learning, ultimately.

Q: Having achieved what you have in your life, are your dreams the same, have they got bigger, or have they changed?
A: I still dream big, that hasn't gone away. Now that I have run a business I've got the confidence to do it again so I'm launching some other products (a freeze-dried healthy snack range). I feel that with the experience now behind me I can get it off the ground and do it quite easily. Likewise with film, I still **really dream big**, and I'm expecting big things from the next project. It's about growing, it's about everything we've discussed. It's about balance, trying to fulfil your dreams while maintaining a family, and whatever it is that you want in your life that you want to manifest. You can't put all your eggs in one basket, but at the same time, if you want to succeed in film, you must keep buying that lottery ticket. You *can*

do things simultaneously. In fact, you should be doing both because it can be soul destroying sitting around and waiting if you're not taking action or you're feeling stopped. So you shouldn't be afraid to spread your eggs a little bit. One of them will hatch. There are failures, but **every failure makes me more determined to take action to get over it. Every coconut has a silver lining**.

Two Takeaways

1. Lots of people have big dreams but they don't chase them, or they get knocked back by the pitfalls and brick walls they come across. Jonathan has had his fair share of doors slammed in his face but he takes every failure on the chin. He grieves the loss, picks himself up, and then takes action. Fear of not making it is part and parcel of doing what you can in order to make it.

2. He never takes anything for granted, he never leaves for tomorrow what he can do today, and he uses his time efficiently and productively. He has learned to put his ego/fear aside and be prepared to learn from those who can help him improve. He takes every failure as a stepping stone to success, and he always finds a silver lining.

That Could Be You

Jonathan shared his journey of following and achieving his dreams. I believe that if you learn to understand your core values, build your dream on them, use your fears to drive you not hinder you, learn from failure and keep persevering against all odds, then you can achieve anything you set your heart on. Dreaming big doesn't have to mean becoming a multi-millionaire, it can be anything. It can simply be living fearlessly in the way that makes you happy.

I'm lucky to meet people who manage to FEAR LESS against all the odds; they remind me that anything is possible when you set your mind to it, even in the most adverse of situations. Martin Symons is one such person. He thought he'd be dead by now, but he keeps on keeping on. When I was asked to make a documentary film about Martin called *Being Martin*, I went to meet him with his friend, Sandy. Martin was very small, and Sandy was very tall, and together they looked like an amiable, if comedic, coupling. Martin wore a large fedora and, with his disability, he had a bit of a John Wayne swagger about him. He regaled me with a five-minute long catalogue of his disabilities finishing with a flourish, 'Oh, and a club foot.' Well, that was his Klippel Feil Syndrome dealt with. By all accounts his fearless adventures to date were an equally long list; including an attempt on Everest Base Camp, climbing Snowdon and Ben Nevis and canoeing down the Mino river in Spain.

Undaunted by his now weakening body he had decided with the help of Sandy to tackle his 'Final' challenge – a coast-to-coast adventure in an off-road electric wheelchair while being kept alive on a ventilator at night. That's where I came in. I was to direct a film about him doing it. Delighted to, of course, until I, and the cameraman Paul, realised we would have to do the trip too. One hundred miles. Filming on bikes. And camping. In seven days. I managed an hour's practice on my bike the weekend before only to find myself unable to walk the next day. It didn't bode well. I was afraid that I wasn't going to be able to do this. But we were committed, there was no backing out, and, after all, what did we have to moan about? We didn't have a twisted spine, hole in the head, web neck, weak heart and respiratory problems. Oh, and a club foot. At the end of the first day, I did, however, have a sore bum.

There were eight of us accompanying Martin, and there was something about his spirit that pulled us together. A very mixed bag of ages, fitness and abilities, but not once did anyone complain. We were there for Martin, and we were starting to show signs of having caught his rare condition, his lust-for-life syndrome. The classic symptoms were smiling and laughing, encouraging and supporting each other, and not giving up when faced with difficult and scary challenges. By the end of the trip, the whole group was stricken. And the trouble is that, once you have had it, you are very likely to have reoccurring bouts throughout your life. Martin completed the challenge and, dipping his toes in the sea at the end, said, 'If you want to do something, just do it.' We remembered how we thought, back at the beginning of the trip, that this was to be his final challenge. We now laughed loudly at the very idea of it. Not likely. Not being Martin.

Whenever we say 'I couldn't possibly do that', we can look to those who really shouldn't be able to – but do. Use those people as your benchmark. If they can, so can you.

As part of another film, called *First Step*, that we were making for a charity called Pratham (which was set up to help children in India learn to read and write), we went to a refuge. It is a residential school for boys who have been found alone, begging on the streets.

The school is in a mainly Muslim residential area, and we had to get to it through the mosque complex. With stone steps smoothed by bare feet, and arched windows lining the corridor, the building drew us to the top floor. Shafts of light lit our way, a door opened, and we entered the refuge. In a huge room was a circle of small boys sitting cross-legged in the middle of the floor. They were dressed in brown shorts, striped shirts buttoned up to the collar, bare feet and oiled hair pressed down to their scalps. Their brightly coloured satchels were placed neatly in front of them, their exercise books, pencils and rubbers laid out beside them. They listened intently as one boy stood up and read from his book. They were all oblivious to the camera as every eye watched the boy before them, sounding out the new words in his repertoire.

There was little furniture in the room apart from three miniature computer consuls in child-friendly rounded plastic; the primary colours dulled with age. On the walls were brightly painted slogans:

'Every child has a right to life'
'Shhh, be quiet, great minds at work'
'We are the architects of our own success'
'These are our dreams'
'This is our star student'
'Say no to child labour'
'Equal rights for all'

Along the edge of the classroom was a line of trunks, each with a bedroll on top. This was where these boys slept at night after class.

In the office was a decorated box. The teacher explained this was for children who wanted to say something but were too scared to say it out loud. They would write down their concerns and anxieties and post them in the box. One letter read: 'I would very much like to visit my father on Friday, but I would also very much like to come back here afterwards.' He was afraid that if he went home he would not be allowed to return. This place was where he got to learn. This place was his future.

The boys had a place for their fears, and they had a place for their dreams. On a big board, the boys had each pinned little stars covered in glitter. In the centre of each star was a dream. Doctor, lawyer, teacher, musician, IT manager and so on. Before we left, the boys brought out some instruments, played music and danced some routines they'd just learned. Six weeks before this they'd been living and working the streets. Goodness only knows what terrifying experiences they'd had. But now, here they were, with a safe bed and a roof over their heads, learning to read and write, dance and sing, provided with an outlet for their fears, and a springboard for their big dreams.

The door in front of you may be locked shut, but go and bang on all the other doors until you find the one that opens. There is very little in life that we can't do if we put our minds to it, and with the support to get us there. My clients come from every walk of life, at every different stage, with as many different fears and foibles as you can imagine. They've been through the process, done the work, and achieved the impossible in spite of, and because of, their fears. It can be like it for you too when you work through this book.

2. FEAR

Before we learn to FEAR LESS we need to get to grips with what FEAR is, and how it manages to get its talons embedded so deeply into our psyche.

Let's **look fear in the face . . .**

There's the first hurdle. Which fear? There are as many fears as there are people, and just as many perceptions and interpretations of what fear is. So how on earth can we tackle them all? For now, let's brainstorm some popular Top of the Hit Parade fears:

Flying, falling, failing, succeeding, being wrong, standing out, being invisible, being too loud, not being heard, not being valued, being valued only for your money, not being able to pay the bills, letting your family down, being controlled by your partner, never finding a partner, dying, getting ill, losing the race, entering the race, getting off the couch, food, starvation, obesity, failing the diet, starting the diet, getting the job, not getting the job, starting the job, losing the job, letting down your boss, going it alone, following your dreams, never having a dream, war, terrorism, climate change, dogs, snakes, spiders, fear for the welfare of animals, for your own welfare, for those in war-torn countries, that you will never come to much, that it takes too much hard work, that you'll never make it, staying put, moving away, adventure, risk-taking, living a dull life, etc.

How imaginative our fears are! If we can imagine it, we can fear it. How creative we are in our fear-making scenarios. They can be monumental fears or quiet, lonely fears, like this one from one of my clients as she was about to start working with me:

'I don't have children or a partner and I regret and feel sad about not having either. It doesn't really affect me day to day but the sadness/ need is definitely inside me. I wonder about adopting or fostering. How much do I want that? I don't know . . . it's a bit scary.' – Client J

Don't devalue your fear. You feel what you feel. Don't pile on the burden by judging yourself for it. It is what it is, right here, right now. And that's what we have to work with. I used to make sculptures. I couldn't afford marble, so I carved in polystyrene. I made what I could with what I had. I could have been too scared to make anything because it wasn't marble like the 'proper' sculptors used (hear the judgment there?) but I took my fear along with my chisel/ kitchen knife and I used what I could afford. I could practice my carving, and I was able to get better at it. Then I was offered a public art commission for a twenty-foot sculpture alongside the M4. I made a model and decided the only way to make it was out of scrap steel. Could I weld scrap steel? No. So, I had to learn. Fast. Was I scared? Terrified. I had to prove to the Council's engineering department that my ad hoc welding and the overall design of the piece was a) going to stand up on sixteen-foot stilts, and b) still be standing in fifty years' time. I made it on a wing and a prayer, with high octane self-talk, and with a launch to 400 people. And thirty years on I'm *still* scared every time I go past in case it's fallen down . . .

And what about J? She tackled each of her fears and it led her to something better. She trusted the coaching process, she did the work, and she transformed her fears into action:

'My coaching sessions with Lou helped me to:
- Identify what's really important to me in life currently, and I have the tools now to identify what's important in the future
- See that I can do what I want to do in life – achieving those important things
- Take action to bring those things to fruition
- Believe in myself more
- Become more self-aware
- Stop some limiting habits and develop new positive ones that help me to live well on a daily basis, i.e. bringing more structure to my day, drawing every day, eating better and preparing for sleep. I think this was one of the most impactful outcomes because I could start the new habits straight away, and the knock-on positive effect of those new habits made a noticeable difference straight away
- Trust my instincts

The impact that Lou's coaching has had on my life is that . . .
- I am being a more authentic me and I notice when I am not being so
- I like myself and am proud of the things I do and who I am. I think I am OK!
- I understand the concept of 'living well' and am learning to do this'

When were you scared, and when did you *not* let that stop you? Write it down and give yourself a pat on the back. Yay!

Anxiety Emergency Rescue – Five Top Tips

Before we get too heavily into FEAR, I want to give you some quick mind hacks that you can practise. The breathing, power posing and moving are particularly helpful when you suddenly feel a wave of anxiety rising up in you. Do them – they really help calm down your nervous system. Practise, practise, practise!

1. **Scan your body** for tension, tightness or discomfort. **Breathe in** through your nose for 4 seconds, then breathe out for 7 seconds, imagining the breath softening and loosening the tightness and blowing away the stress. Do this three times every night before drifting off to sleep or whenever you feel nervous.

2. **Power Pose** when you get up to tell your mind that you are in charge of the day. Raise your arms in a V above your head and stretch out your body. You can also do this just before going to do something you're anxious about.

3. **Walk for 30–90 minutes** each day, preferably in nature. Pick a colour for the day and look for it wherever you go. It distracts your mind from your concerns and focuses it on the present moment, allowing you to enjoy and engage with your surroundings.

4. Do a **daily brain dump** for 10 minutes every day. Write down on a piece of paper everything that worries you or makes you feel angry. Write without stopping and without judgment. Get it all out. Do not re-read. Tear up the piece of paper and throw it away. It acknowledges your stress but at the same time releases

you from it. This technique, used to help chronic pain, is also excellent for anxiety (to read more, please see *Back in Control* by David Hanscom MD).

5. **Get creative**. It can be anything: doodling, gardening, baking, flower arranging, pottery, poetry or model-making. It can be anything that stimulates your imagination, which will otherwise be hijacked by your fears. Creativity can push back your fears, lower your anxiety levels and make you feel calmer.

Booster Tips:

The gut is known as the second brain. It has its own (enteric) nervous system, has a direct two-way communication with the brain, produces hormones including the feel-good serotonin, and a whole eco-system of microbes which can be boosted to create wellness and wellbeing with a healthy diet and de-stressing techniques. If you feel fear, you often feel it in your belly as a 'gut reaction', butterflies, sick feeling, churning, tightness etc. (To read more, please see *The Mind–Gut Connection* by Dr Emeran Mayer.)

- I use slow, abdominal breathing to soothe these feelings, like an internal massage and that seems to calm my nerves.

- Gluten is also known to cause depression and anxiety so avoiding grain, most carbohydrates and sugar might help you with this. You can find out more in Dr David Perlmutter's book *Grain Brain*.

Real Fear

Let's get real for a moment. What if you live in Syria and bombs are raining down on you and your family? Even the hospitals aren't safe. How on earth, in that heightened state of alert, can anyone survive, or even go about their daily business? But they do. And you do. 'But my fears are nothing in comparison to those people trying to live in a war zone', you might retort. Well, you know what, your brain doesn't know that. Fear is fear. It pulses through you whether the perceived threat is a woolly mammoth, a nuclear missile, an irrational boss or a marathon race time you're scared of not achieving. You can't compare your fear with someone else's. Fear is fear. You feel what you feel. And the tools to help, are the tools that help.

And so, over to the nitty gritty of fear. What doesn't kill you makes you stronger. Let's go there.

Survival

The Beast in You

Before you start trying to mute the sound of thundering hooves of fear trampling through your brain, it's good to first understand why it's there at all. Much as we like to think of ourselves as sophisticated twenty-first-century souls who can launch rockets into space and speed-date on the internet, we still also house our ancient animal brain. It's the beast in you who bares its teeth at the first sign of danger. It is what keeps you alive when the big hairy mammoth in the shape of your boss/traffic warden/psycho comes hurtling towards you.

In ancient times, when a sabre-toothed tiger came after us, we scarpered, or we fought it off (depending on how brave we were feeling), and back we went to our daily grind. Fear switches on survival mode; danger over, fear switches off. Nowadays hyper-anxiety has become a modern phenomenon, we are under constant stress, perpetual alert. Our 'off' button has malfunctioned, and we are left in a permanent state of believing the toothy predator is right around the corner.

Back when threat really did come with giant teeth, you stood there to fight it out, or you took flight as fast as your own hairy legs could carry you. Fear kept you from being food. Once you were out of danger, your body calmed down and you got down to the business of eating your attacker, procreating or sleeping. In modern times you're living on your nerves, and your brain sees savage threats everywhere.

You have to incorporate an off-switch for your bleeping warning light, so that you can keep going to cafés, flying on planes, doing your best work, dyeing your hair pink (if you want to), letting your face wrinkle (if you want to), becoming that rocket scientist, show jumper or United Nations Envoy. Fear is there to make us sit up and question. Is there real danger or are you creating a mountain out of a molehill? I like to think that what your fear is telling you is that no matter the challenge and struggle ahead, the risk of failure, the obstacles placed in your way; moving forward will be worth it. In spite of your fear. It will be hard, but you will grow because of it. Apparently, actor Dame Judi Dench says her fear gets worse as she gets older but she uses its power to energise, not hinder her.

When you have fear lurching round like Quasimodo at the back of your brain, the problem-solving part of your brain can't do its job. So, you take action; you learn what you need to learn and you charge your fearful thoughts with more productive ones. Let's say you have a job interview coming up and you're pretty nervous about it. You can either get lathered up about it, or you can take some little actions. You learn about the company and the job. You decide what you are going to wear. You work out the route to get there and how long it will take. You rehearse what makes you unique and why you think you can fulfil the role. You figure out a couple of great questions to ask your interviewer at the end. You do your deep breathing on your journey there. You practise a power pose in the bathroom before you go into the interview. You give yourself a big smile, tell yourself you can only do your best, and in you go.

To begin making your mind work for you, it's useful to understand in simple terms how your brain works. You have three independent yet interconnected sections in your brain, each with its own allotted purpose:

The Reptilian Section is the instant 'survival mode' fight or flight response section of the brain. It is the oldest in terms of our human evolution. It has been known as the 'old brain' or the 'reptilian brain'. Think road rage or frozen panic at your first public speaking event.

The Limbic Section is the section of the brain that first emerged in mammals. It generates our feelings and emotions in response to our current perceived reality. Someone lays into you verbally at work, you retaliate and then you feel upset about it for the rest of the day, churning over the scenario and keeping the negative emotions alive. Your limbic brain doesn't know that the event is over if you keep re-living the moment in your mind. It cannot discern between what is happening, and what you are imagining is happening. Or what you remember has happened.

The Neocortex Section is the evolved 'conscious' section of your brain, which is most in line with your true unlimited potential. It generates creation, manifestation, imagination, awareness, development, logical thinking, objectivity, empathy and most importantly: consciousness. It is 'The New Brain'. This is the part that you can work with to fulfil your potential and improve your life. I like to think of this as your Creative Brain.

The brain is plastic (to read more about this, please see *The Plastic Mind* by Sharon Begley). It is not set in stone at birth. You can develop and change it through repetition over a period of time (30 days it is suggested, or 90 days to be really safe). When you do this, you fire up new connections between your brain cells (neurons) and mould your brain towards what you focus on most. If you let your old and reptilian brain rule by fear, then you are held hostage to a host of malevolent forces or thoughts, which immediately impact your negative emotions triggered in your limbic section. You can let these emotions run you ragged, or you can switch over to your New Brain. It is only when you get creative with your thinking, take oppositional action and repeatedly build up healthy habits that you can raise your wellbeing out of your cave-dwelling doldrums and emotional cesspit of fears, and into a productive, content and rewarding existence.

⊱═ FEAR QUESTIONS ═⊰

1. What circumstances trigger the animal fight, flight or freeze response in you? (Reptilian Brain)
2. How does this affect you emotionally? Do you brood, ruminate, dwell over the event or incident? (Limbic Section)
3. When have you successfully found ways to 'get over it'? Write a

list of ten methods you have used to get past your worries, guilt, fear, anger, etc.

4. Try this exercise: you get told off at work for something you didn't do and you respond angrily (Reptilian Section). Afterwards you brood over the unfairness of the accusation and beat yourself up for showing your anger. What fears are at play here? Do you fear that your boss might think you aren't up to the job? Maybe you think you aren't up to the job? Your brilliance isn't being recognised? Why are you 'always' treated as everybody's punch bag? Why can't you keep a lid on your emotions? Does everyone think you're a loose cannon now? Will you lose your job because you lost your rag (Limbic Section)?

5. How can you turn the whole incident to your advantage? How can you feel better about what happened? How can you learn from your response? What can you do to flip the situation into one where you take responsibility and make your boss feel better about what happened? Use your imagination. Write down everything you can think of (New Brain).

6. Pat yourself on your back. All three parts of your brain are in good working order. In section two of this book you will learn to be the boss of it, for the most part. There are no absolutes in the art of living.

Fears, Stresses and Strains of Ordinary Life

In many ways life isn't *that* bad; you get through the day, feed yourself, keep a roof over your head, survive numerous sideswipes in the act of getting by. You're probably relatively successful and happy in many ways. **But underneath lurks the negative voice that trips**

you up and holds you back. Fear stops you from being everything you want to be, from living abundantly with passion, freedom and creativity. That niggling doubt scratching away with low level anxiety, dread, hidden fear or outright anger, is one of the biggest causes of stress, which in turn is a major contributor to illness and disease (to read more, see *The Telomere Effect* by Dr Elizabeth Blackburn and Dr Elissa Epel).

Why does it feel like life sucks? Why are you held back by fear? Why do you always feel so stressed out? Stress is caused by fear. Nervous, worried, agitated, anxious, fretful, dread, foreboding, unease, concerned, frightened, fearful . . . **all** these responses trigger stress and have a harmful long-term effect on your body. What if there was an answer, not too far away? Imagine being anything you want to be. What if you could change the fearful story of your future and start really enjoying your present with purpose and passion? **To do that you have to dig down and tackle your fears, whether they are around:**

MONEY – TIME – HEALTH – WORK –
RELATIONSHIPS – SOCIAL – PURPOSE

You have probably run the problems round and round your head and still don't seem to be getting anywhere in solving them (which is why you have found yourself sitting down with this book). It's time to take the feast away from your fears, get out from under the table and build a better future.

Given direction and constructive boundaries your imagination will override your daily fears and keep you excited, motivated and exposed to opportunity and growth.

When you stop focusing on the obstacles and trip-wires, you lift your field of vision to the big stage. Blue-sky thinking doesn't happen in muddy puddles of worry. When you set yourself small daily tasks in the pursuit of a goal, you channel your imagination with regular hits of success; sparking it to unleash its potential in a direction that you dictate. It starts to answer to you, not your anxiety. Your life gets traction with training. Clouds take on the appearance of positive metaphors for happiness, bobbing across your line of sight. Short, sharp bursts of actionable forward thinking, regularly administered with plenty of time to recover in between. If you physically work out non-stop you burnout, and it's the same with the mind. Inner training requires resolve, support, regularity and rest.

One time I was off on a trip to southern Ireland, somewhere I had never been but had always wanted to go. The only trouble was that in order to get there we had to go by plane or by ship. I was scared of flying so we decided to take the boat across the Irish Sea – a stretch not known for its calm waters. As we arrived at the port, the winds were whipping up a storm. Force 6–9 gales to be exact. At 2.45 a.m. we boarded, found a sofa in the boat lounge and fell asleep. Half an hour later I woke with a lurch in my belly and a swell of nausea in my chest. We were tipping, then lifting with a heavy pause, only to crash back down again. I was heaving with fear at every surge and drop. I felt sick. I didn't know if I felt worse lying down or sitting up. But that was nothing to the air-raid sirens going off in my head. We were going to die. I was sure of it. My mind was a cine-projector of the *Titanic* in its final moments; upended and sinking slowly, dragging its passengers into the dark bottomless terror of death by drowning. My partner's calm and rational endeavours to explain that we weren't sinking and that all would be well, fell on deaf ears. My capacity for creating disaster movies is second to none when my reptilian fears are unleashed. But somehow I managed, eventually, to reach up to the clear vision of my New Brain that told me simply to breathe. I heard its message. I slowed my breathing to the rhythm of the sea, gradually my panic subsided, sleep wrapped its blanket over my fears and I slipped into some restful space between unconsciousness and calm. We chugged gently into the port of Rosslare as the soft, damp grey Irish skies lifted the storm and my fears away.

Fear is the pessimistic projection of a story we tell ourselves, with a beginning, a middle and a cataclysmic end, packed full of suspense along the way. We are capable of scaring ourselves like children who quake in their beds at the belief of a bogey man lurking beneath. We interpret and respond to the telling of these mind movies relative to our degrees of confidence, self-esteem, and self-awareness.

When we are on top of our game, we can create a gap between what is imaginary storytelling and what is the reality. You can equally use the coolness of logic to make preparations that allow you to be adaptable if the winds of fortune were to shift. You can devise ways to play out your future by improvising the present under the belief that no matter what, you are at the very least taking charge of the meanderings of your mind. By channelling your thoughts, you are more able to govern your feelings, balance passion with judgment, become more confident, and in turn loosen yourself from the clutches of fear.

⊨ FEAR WORK-OUT ⊨

1. On a big piece of paper jot down everything that comes to mind when you think of the word fear. Be spontaneous; don't think too hard.
2. Draw circles around the words that resonate particularly for you.
3. Now imagine a little girl or boy tells you a story about one of those fears. What is that story? Write it out and then write a reassuring letter to that child.

⊨===⊨

Do you find it easy to imagine your favourite team winning the championship, or your toddler taking its first steps, or you winning the lottery? Great, we will use that skill in the coaching programme but first, let's talk about the downside of this human capability. Unfortunately, as we can see from my fantasy boat disaster, your creative imagination carries the shadow of fear. It sticks to creative thinking and vision building, like a trail of molasses, holding you back from doing and being your best. Unless you keep your creativity sparking, your fear will suck it up and use it for its own ends. And no good comes in those dark woods.

We all feel the fear of failure, but committed and creative thinkers fear failing to try at all. Our biggest regrets are the chances not taken. So yes, you feel fear, but when you harness that fear you change its energy into a creative force. Creativity means having lots of bad ideas, trying them out, discarding them or transforming them into something else. Those who fail the most are the most successful because they are the ones that try the most. Picasso was hugely prolific. He practically vomited art. He thought he could outrun his fear and self-doubt. Except that in his mind he didn't move fast enough. He only signed 10% of his work because he thought the rest was either unfinished or not worth finishing. History has a different take on the value of his work, signed or unsigned, but that's another story.

You have to create a gap between what you are doing with your life and the self-doubt that hot-foots behind you. Fear lurks in every brush-stroke, each word written, every innovation invented. It skulks around start-ups and dance classes. It masks itself in procrastination and people-pleasing, perfectionism and incompletion. When you dare to live your life creatively or curiously (one and the same thing) then fear will be your shadow. It is what will block you or drive you to addiction, or it is what will energise you and keep you curious. It is how you use your fear that leads to a fearful or fearless life.

As a novice runner, I find running is the perfect metaphor for life. When it's going well, you feel on top of the world, when it's not going well, every sinew, every pore, every cell tells you to give up. The day before yesterday I bounced through 10K. I felt like a machine made of springs that could run and run. Yesterday I inched my way through 5K with my legs feeling like wooden posts being pummelled into the ground with a lump hammer, and then being yanked out again in splintering exhaustion with every step. My Inner Spoilt Brat (or my Limbic Liar) silently seethed venom and blame at my trainer for 'making' me do this. But the will to keep going kept me going. I didn't give up. I collapsed through the front door and found I'd done my fastest time yet.

Like life, it may feel like hell. But push through and you'll really feel the accomplishment. Don't let fear win the race. Persistence will help you through.

Fear may well hijack your imagination and perceptions but getting to grips with your creativity can give you an active strategy to regain territory, recalibrate your vision and dampen down the negative emotions. To fight fear, first you must learn to recognise the masks that it hides behind because these are the things that will trip you up and stop you from reaching your goals. Unless you recognise them for what they are, they'll wield their wicked ways with you and you'll be putty in their hands.

In the coaching programme, I will cover fear's Disguises: People Pleasing, Procrastination, Unhealthy Habits, Cult of Comparison, the Imposter Syndrome, Naysayers and Bad Beliefs.

But first I am going to reassure you, because I can bet your bottom dollar you have felt fear and **persisted** in the face of its threat.

PERSISTENCE CHALLENGE

Write a list of fifty times in your life so far that you have persisted in the face of fear e.g. learning to walk, learning to use a potty, walked into the classroom on your very first day at nursery, etc. The first twenty should be straightforward to come up with. But keep going.

Persist! You will start to remember the smaller things, the times you've long forgotten, the things you didn't consider significant. But persistence is very important and it's vital that you have a log of proof, so that in the future when fear makes you want to give up, you will be able to remind yourself that you are a persistent person and that you're going to keep going.

All is Lost

'OK,' you say, 'but bad things do happen.'

And yes, really bad things do happen. We protect ourselves, we do good, we wash our teeth, share our toys, perform random acts of kindness, remember to breathe, eat broccoli, don't eat sugar, live in the sticks and so on.

And still, stuff happens. I was eighteen when I left home to go to art school in London. A big step from a little village. But I loved London, had always hankered to live there, the busyness, the people and the melting pot of culture. I took the rough and tumble of city life pretty much in my stride. I was young. But gradually the energy it took to be a young woman in the city in the mid-eighties started to get tiring. You had to be vigilant, aware, with eyes in the back of your head. It took a lot of nerve, and it definitely took its toll.

By the time I got my degree I was ready to leave, try something new. Escape to the country, real country, the big country. And so, I moved to south west Scotland; a cottage in the wilderness. And with the little town of Lockerbie just up the road, there was civilisation when we wanted it.

At 7.15 p.m. on 21 December 1988, I heard what I thought was thunder. A huge clump outside in the darkness. I ran to the window, but there was nothing. No storm. Strange. Then an explosion. The black sky turned neon orange. We thought it was one of the swarms of jet fighters that buzzed low across the Dumfriesshire landscape. Or Annan power station blowing up. The phone rang, and it was our landlady asking if we were alright. 'Yes,' I replied, 'what's happened?'

'A jumbo jet has just exploded out of the sky above you.'

The sky was lit up over Lockerbie, just 1 mile away, the A74 a gridlock, sirens. BBC journalists came running to our door to use our phone but the lines were now down. I couldn't let my parents or grandmother know we were OK until hours later. We switched on the telly and watched what the world was watching, as it played out in the darkness beyond our window. All night we stayed up staring at the screen, wondering what we would wake up to when daylight came. A plane, with 259 passengers, had come tumbling out of the sky and exploded on the ground in a 1000-foot fireball killing everybody from the flight and 11 people on the ground. Terrorism had reached us in this sleepy little town and shaken us to the core.

In the cold grey morning light, we walked along the road into town, twists of yellow plane metal in every garden. We daren't look up to the trees or the roofs; there was carnage everywhere.

Indescribable horrors. The cockpit landed on the hill behind our house, the fuselage buried in a huge crater where there was once a small cul-de-sac, the rest scattered across the town. The hideousness of what had happened was too massive to sink in, the shock delayed, for years. Many of us had survivor's guilt, post-traumatic stress, slipping over the years into an undercurrent of anxiety and dread. An ever-present ticking time bomb in the back of your head. If it can happen once, it can happen again. In a fracturing world, it *is* happening over and again. I have two children and I fear for them. I fear for my friends, family, for myself. It's no way to live. It ruins the many precious moments that do exist.

We can't hide from life's explosions; in a twist of fate we are on the plane or we miss it. We went to work that day or we stayed home sick.

My great-grandfather was a vicar. In July 1940, there was a knock at the door. Nana answered it. The family heard her cry out. She came in clutching a telegram. My great-uncle Pat had been shot down in his Hurricane plane over the English Channel, defending his country. A life lost too young. A son, a brother, gone.

My great-grandfather read it, and slowly stood up. 'The boy has done his duty,' my granny recalls him saying.

How do you withstand those moments, how do you not collapse? When you have a solid sense of self and something flies at you from the battlefield of life, you confront it as it is. It is the main weapon in your psychological defence. My great-grandfather had it. Maybe because he was a vicar. Maybe because he had lost other sons and learned resilience.

And if something sinister and devastating befalls you or your family? When you have the strong emotional tools already well-rehearsed, you will be better able to sit with grief, loss and despair without damning yourself or others.

But from pathos to bathos. From bombshells to the banalities of everyday worries and concerns. Fear has no shame; it allies itself with both.

Let's say that a new date decides he doesn't want to carry on into a full-blown relationship. If you are emotionally confident you tell yourself: 'OK, his loss'. If your mind is already a porridge of self-doubt, you will add this incident to your running catalogue of why you are so unattractive to every man on the planet. So next time you go for a date, this seething soup of voices telling you you are never going to find the right guy, inevitably reveals itself in your face, your posture, your demeanour. And this date also fizzles to an unremarkable finish. A nicer outfit, higher heels, another diet, brighter lipstick, sexier lingerie is never going to do the trick. Build up your self-esteem and you could go to dinner in your pyjamas and bedhead hair and the guy that's right for you will adore your confidence and easy-going sense of self. He'll see you for who you are. A healthy mind radiates like sunshine.

So how do we prepare our children and ourselves, without scaring them and us half to death? Prepare for all eventualities; the trivial and the tragic.

Something for your Life Survival Kit

If you do nothing else: keep a journal. Every morning write down your woes and worries. Hold nothing back. Don't re-read it, just release the feelings and move on in a stream of consciousness. When the big bolt hits you, you will be practiced in baring your soul and there will be comfort in that. You will always have your journal, think of it as an unfailing friend. Use it to pour out your frustrations, your loneliness, your boredom, your thrills and spills. Write three pages, no holding back, surrender to the flow of your pen, then shut the pages without a backwards glance and you'll realise you feel a little bit better, and you can get back to the day ahead.

I hazard against re-reading the darker pages. They are for the moment they arise and then best left in the past. Writing them down releases them. Re-reading them keeps them alive. Let go of the demons. Live for now and the creation of new adventures, experiences and loves. Don't lean back, stand for now and look forward to less fearful futures.

Aftermath: Dark Night of the Soul

So you prepare for disaster and you live through the experience. But what about afterwards? When the smoke settles, the impact does not disappear. You continue to be haunted by the horror, and you experience terror of what else may befall you or the people you love. You survived the crisis or atrocity. Maybe you were physically maimed and altered, and you had to relearn everything that you once took for granted. But something else much more insidious happens and you don't need to have lost a limb or a loved one to be affected by it. Fear sinks into the crevices and snarls away from the back of the cave. It permeates everything; subtly like the ghost of the black dog. You ruminate and relive the experience, you keep it alive, you think you're going mad. What you are experiencing, however, is a perfectly 'normal reaction to an abnormal situation'. It's called Post-Traumatic Stress Disorder, or PTSD.

What helped me get over the trauma of Lockerbie was learning about PTSD, its effects and its treatment. As a filmmaker, I used my creativity to understand what it was, and to share it with others in the hope that it would help them too. In 2004, I made a documentary called *A Brutal Peace* that looked at PTSD in soldiers. It was used by the scientists at the World Congress for Traumatic Stress in Argentina to help people understand how it effects people's lives well beyond the battlefield.

In the years since, trauma has increasingly dug its claws into the wider population as the borders of war play out in our cities between terrorists and civilians. Baghdad, Bangladesh, Brussels, Istanbul, Cairo, London, New York, Paris and Damascus have all become battlefields. An airport, a plane, a café, a rock concert, a market place, a memorial service – nowhere is safe from the suicide bomber set on destroying civilisation and peace. Those who witness a bombing feel the shockwaves, those who lose loved ones, or are themselves maimed, are all direct victims of the fallout. The insidious shock and fear creeps into all our minds as we contemplate each horror, each aftermath, and feel the ripple effect of trauma in our society. We start to feel numb to the news events (yet another bombing, another decimation of life), and our minds start to shut down. But the heavy-weight deadening effect belies the fact that we continue to be affected whether we realise it or not. You don't have to deal with it alone. Get help and support.

Post-Traumatic Help

As ever, the way out is found with creative approaches:

1. Writing your experiences down.
2. Forming or joining support groups to talk and share.
3. Distractions such as listening to uplifting music.
4. Taking long walks in nature.
5. Breathing through the panic.
6. Turning down the nightmarish imagery through a special creative technique called EMDR.
7. If you have PTSD you will also benefit from psychotherapeutic support.

Our film *A Brutal Peace* explores the issues and treatments from the soldier's perspective. Somehow trauma is easier to look at when we see it through 'other's' eyes, so let's explore PTSD from their angle and find out how you can not only survive what you have gone through, but also learn to thrive.

Combat Trauma or PTSD is the reaction to an extreme event in battle, or a build-up of events over time. If the signs and symptoms persist for over 28 days after a traumatic event, then we talk about PTSD being a possible diagnosis. Those soldiers who don't receive help often can't get work, they can develop alcohol and drug problems, and can end up in prison. A quarter of rough sleepers on the streets are ex-service personnel.

War is grotesque, whether it's on a battlefield or on a city street. And it takes extraordinary courage to try and find peace in the aftermath. Whole families are traumatised, having witnessed unbelievable horrors, lost close family members, their homes, their livelihoods, their sense of safety. If the psychological damage is left neglected and untreated, the hurt, pain, suffering will continue as the symptoms take over.

One Falklands veteran, Dave Brown, described to me what it's like:

It's literally like watching a television screen and seeing yourself in the picture of whatever's happening. It's so real you can hear the people talk about you, you can smell everything, you can hear the sounds. They come from nowhere, you know, you can get them in broad day-light sometimes. A lot of people say you only get flashbacks at night. But certain sounds, certain smells, can set people off.

Nothing can prepare you for the sight of people being killed. And so, in the aftermath, what can be done to help repair the damage to your mind, when you have witnessed or experienced catastrophic carnage? One Second World War veteran, David Holbrook, wrote about his experiences in his book *Flesh Wounds*. He told me that one day, years later, he found himself finally finding a way to unburden his mind:

It must have been in my mind because when I started I wrote 10,000 words in one day you know, about D-Day, so it was all boiling up. I mean you know it was in my mind and I suppose I wanted to put it out there.

Writing the book got the trauma out of his system. It helped him finally to find peace. In an extract from his book he describes:

There are moments, short moments from which we never recover and these few minutes up the beach was one of those for Paul, as it was for hundreds of thousands of men besides . . . this first minute's baptism of fire changed Paul's sensibility forever, forever to be a little deadened.

For those who can't find a way of dealing with their emotional wounds, they become unable to cope. Dave Brown says:

The key to the whole problem is when nothing's being done and it's been left to rot inside you for so many years, it's in your brain – it's deep inside you. And because you've not been able to confront it, deal with it, it's terrible, like it's actually inside you, and it eats you alive – it's like a cancer . . . you feel like you're climbing a mountain. To get over this you've got no one to help you at all. You're on your own; you're climbing up this mountain. And every time you think you've just got to the top of that mountain you either fall off or someone pushes you off that mountain so you end up at the bottom again.

Dave Brown now helps many veterans and their families through the South Atlantic Medal Association 1982 (SAMA). It was set up to represent the health, welfare and interests of anyone involved in the Falklands War. He tells me:

I found that the work I was doing with the veterans and the welfare, organising social events, everything was my therapy. I was doing something positive. I was helping other people. The lads knew they could contact me and that was my way of coping and dealing with the issues that had caused me so many problems for so long.

Dave Brown has worked out how to live his life in a way that is not controlled by his PTSD. When he and the others meet up they have a few beers, and they're able to go around and sit and talk with each other about how things are going:

[A]nd sometimes lads will pick up something that someone else has said. And they say, you know, what's up? You OK? You know. The contact and the support that these lads have. They just have to come and knock on the door or phone us and we will put it in place for them.

He says he tries to tell the lads three things:

Always remember RAC. Recognition, admission and control. Recognise you've got a problem, admit you've got a problem and control the problem. If you feel yourself in a vulnerable situation, get yourself out of it. You recognise circumstances. You recognise situations. So you try to avoid situations like that that can trigger events off and can aggravate the condition. . . . . You haven't gone mad. You're not a mental case. You've got a debilitating illness that can from time to time cause little hiccups in your life. But it's not the end of the world when this happens. It's a perfect normal reaction.

We went with Dave Brown and a group of ex-paras to Arnhem in Holland for the annual commemoration of soldiers who had died in the battle there. Alcohol cloaked many of the ex-service personnel, like a heavy blanket to numb their own memories, but still their pain was palpable. As they stood stiffly with respect in their battalion berets, shoulder to shoulder with their comrades, their hollow eyes hunted for peace. Dave Brown stood strong amongst these men. He had beaten alcohol and drugs, and the nightmares that left men feeling like they'd been skinned alive, such was their fear and vulnerability. He had turned a corner and his mission was to turn around the lives of his desperate friends. He'd seen too many lose the will to live, lose their wives, their families, their self-respect. He understood their torment but could see a way through. His was a simple act. He put himself at the end of a phone and he was there when they needed him, there when they stood at the edge of the abyss longing to jump off. He helps them to imagine a future where they can hold their heads high, where they can sleep peacefully at night, where they can turn a corner of a street and not fear the blast of a suicide bomber. He leads them with baby steps, gentle and soothing towards a place where they can dream freely and live safely.

There is a treatment for PTSD, which has been used in America for many years. After an initial scepticism, it has recently started to be used in the UK too. It is called Eye Movement Desensitisation and Reprocessing (EMDR). It's a way of scaling down the impact of the images that run over and over in your mind like news footage. It is your imagination and memory in full IMAX surround sound technicolour. Every time you relive the event your brain thinks it's actually happening and goes into emergency mode. Over time this reaction becomes increasingly debilitating. But EMDR shrinks the screen replaying the images in your head until they become as small as a pin prick in your mind. A gap is created and you are not triggered in the same dramatic way.

I interviewed the trauma consultant, Mark Collins, at the Priory. He finds time and again that EMDR is an incredibly powerful way of addressing trauma. It allows a resolution of symptoms in a way that is much swifter, and more permanent, than anything that he tried before, and he has increasingly been using it in his clinical practice.

A patient is asked to picture the traumatic event and to be aware of how that makes them feel. The doctor moves his finger from left to right in rapid succession. The patient describes how they feel again. After repeating this several times, the picture seems to zoom away in the patient's mind, getting smaller and no longer triggering the traumatic feelings.

As Mark Collins explains:

In my experience it is rather like doing the ironing – when you've removed a crease from a shirt it's gone, that crease won't come back.

I waited too long after Lockerbie to get myself sorted out. But Dave Brown inspired me to do just that. I urge you to get the help and support available. Allow others to help you tap into the creative and healing side of your mind, tell your story, not just the facts but the story that tells your truth; the effect the trauma has had on you and those around you, how you get through, day by day, night by night. Share the chinks of light and the moments of humour that inevitably sneak past the locked-down barriers. Be a storyteller so that you can re-emerge from your experiences to rewrite the rest of your life with hope and not fear.

3. CREATIVITY

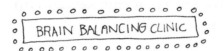

Next, in this section, you will learn about:

1. Your creative brain, how it works and why it's useful.
2. How to build a daily practice of self-care through creative core-work.

Even if you don't think you have a creative cell in your body, you do have the ability to think creatively. It is hardwired into your brain as a human being.[1] But it is also like a muscle. Children are encouraged to use it a lot, and so it packs a big punch. That's why they develop at such a phenomenal rate in a short space of time. Gradually, however, the academic system forces you to concentrate on using the analytical, logical, systematic part of your brain. Which helps with exams, but is not much good when it comes to tackling the problems that life throws at you.

Traditionally, scientists have talked about the left side of your brain being the logical, intellectual and linear thinking side, and the right side of your brain being the creative, lateral thinking, intuitive and instinctive part. Now they recognise that it is more complex than that and each of us toggle between the different processes in our own unique ways. But for the sake of this book and to keep the process simple and straightforward I will use the right/creative and left/logical as a visual metaphor for the complexities of the brain systems.

Your Creative Brain

If creativity is your best friend in **counteracting fear**, it makes sense to read the manual and understand a little more about its key features. How do these moments of creativity happen?

Survival and the evolution of humanity fundamentally depends on innovative imagination. Our ability to think in novel and useful ways is one of the defining features of the human species. It uses fear; you imagine being mauled to death by a sabre-toothed tiger, and then you imagine what you can do to protect yourself. For example, you imagine digging a hole and covering it with branches and leaves to hide the hole. You dance on the other side of the hole to attract the predator, who runs towards you and falls in the hole. You are saved – and as an added bonus – you have dinner (as opposed to being dinner). Your imagination dreams up a fearful outcome, then it imagines a positive alternative that requires specific action. So, the better your creative muscle, the more options you have for successful survival.

Creativity is not the ability to paint the *Mona Lisa*. As a human being, you are built to be creative in order to evolve.

The Science Bit

(for which I had a some help from the BBC)

Previously, studies on creativity have been done through psychology and observation from the outside. Now, with the tools of neuroscience you can see what is happening on the inside when creativity occurs and inspiration strikes.

According to the BBC programme *The Creative Brain*[2], it seems you are thinking differently when you have a creative moment. In a flash of insight, the left lobe (positioned just above the ear) doesn't really react, but the area above the ear in the right hemisphere, does. They are actually wired slightly differently too. The left lobe (logical) has short wires for pulling in information from nearby, while the right lobe's (creative) wires branch out more broadly, gathering sources of information by reaching out and connecting to distant, unrelated ideas. It is here that new concepts and solutions get made.

However, just before the spike of awareness occurs in your mind, there is a burst of activity at the back of the head on the right side as it momentarily shuts down part of your visual cortex, like closing your eyes to block off any distractions; just enough to allow the new idea to bubble up as insight. When someone asks you a difficult question, you might look away, or down, anywhere but at the distracting face in front of you. You look inwards, and your brain works out the answer.

So, if you want to have more creative sparks, you need to shut off your mind from the outside world on a regular basis. Like standing in the shower. It is relaxing, you can't look at your phone, you can zone out and your mind can fire up. Many people have solved problems in the shower. Or on the toilet, or walking in the woods, or window-shopping (or actual shopping).

Insight is only part of creativity. Divergent thinking also plays a big part. One of the ways scientists test for creative divergence is to score people on the most creative different uses they can think of for a simple object. For example, a 'brick' could become a building block, a paper weight or a work of art in the Tate Modern. This measurement is different from the traditional IQ test which tests for intelligence. There is overlap between intelligence and creativity but they are different from each other. In the brain, the neural pathways thin out in the creative areas of the brain, like long winding roads that allow new thinking to emerge.

I understand it like this. When we go from driving on Birmingham's busy Spaghetti Junction and head for the hills, we feel ourselves relax, our minds slow down, and space clears in our heads for creative thinking to gestate. Intelligence is about speed, the quickest route from A to B. Creativity is slow and meandering. That's why, throughout the book, I will bang on about self-care, because it creates a space for creativity to happen. And the more you use creativity as a force for your own good, the less fear can get a word in edgeways.

As I said, the ideal state to increase your creative agility is by doing something mundane, that occupies you on a basic level, but gives room for the creative mind to wander, pause, question, fire up, and bring solutions, associations and new ideas to the surface. Fishing, washing up, ironing, doodling, polishing the car, digging the garden, flipping burgers, bean counting or taking a shower. When I took a temporary job working in a clothes shop I became known as the 'Queen of Steam'. Not because I loved ironing clothes for hours, which I certainly didn't, but because the mechanical act let my imagination get to work. I was writing a screenplay, and most of the legwork got done when I was steaming.

Creativity is stimulated by boredom, by mundane tasks, or by trying different and new experiences. Just performing an activity that isn't normal to you boosts your creativity levels. Our lives benefit from having insight into our problems and fears, and by being able to think our way out of a fix, but moreover, by boosting our creativity, our experiences become richer, more vibrant and colourful, and less fearful.

Creative Challenge

- Slow down
- Empty out a part of your day to let your mind drift
- Practice thinking of different ways to do the same thing
- Improvise more by ditching your routine
- Put yourself in front of new and unexpected experiences, often
- Take risks
- Try doing something that scares you every day
- Alternate your problem-solving work with mundane physical activities

Creativity as a Fear Buster

Developing and using your creative brain is an act of self-care – using the compassion and kindness you show others on yourself is the path to leading a less stressful and more fearless life. This book and its coaching programme aims to help you develop that creative part of your brain, use it to instil a daily practice of self-care, learn to re-imagine your fears as a powerful energy for action, and slowly build a resilience to whatever the world throws at you.

It starts with the usual life-coaching techniques:

1. Scoring all areas of your life and seeing which ones you feel need improving.
2. Dreaming big. Envisioning with a vision board the life of your wildest dreams.
3. Creating goals and making a solid, specific, time related, and real-isable action plan.
4. Addressing the key areas that trip us up even with the best intentions.

But self-care requires self-love. And to do this requires tapping into and developing the creative aspect of the brain.

My self-styled creative coaching builds on life coaching by developing the creative mind, the use of the 'right' brain. Mainly by the repetition of what I have called our essential creative core-work (sometimes used in some forms of therapy but not generally in coaching). Just as to be a strong runner you must develop your core muscles, to live life with less fear you must develop a dialogue with that deepest and most essential part of you. The bit that is your pure potential creative energy.

By doing our core-work we can use creative thinking to love ourselves first. We can feel happier, more content, less fearful and exploit our full potential. It also means that, although I am not with you as your coach to act as your personal nurturer and supporter, you have a mechanism at hand to be your own championing coach.

What is Creative Core-Work?

As an artist, and as a coach, I was inspired by Lucia Capacchione's *Recovery of your Inner Child.*[3] She developed the process of using your non-dominant hand and dominant hand while journaling, to tap into your subconscious needs and desires. I found it very helpful in my coaching work as a way for my clients to get past their Inner Critic, past their fears, and into a place where they can learn to nurture and support themselves through all the tough times. I have developed it further for the purposes of this book. It will help you unearth the issues that are really troubling you, then help you find a way to deal with them and create an action plan for moving forward. I call it creative core-work.

Doing your core-work is how you tap into your creativity, and your creativity is how you transform fear into fearlessness.

Before you start the coaching programme properly, I want you to be well rehearsed in understanding core-work. I am going to use fear, love and self-love as a way of exploring it. I will also give you examples of how I use it myself, and how my clients have used it.

Have a notebook beside you and, if you have the urge to start the dual-hand dialogue, please do follow your instincts. Practise, practise, and practise until it is second nature. Hopefully it will become a lifelong practice of support and guidance.

⊨ CORE-WORK ⊨

FOR FEARING LESS

We can only ignore our fears for so long before they gather strength, the clouds thickening and blackening above our thin skin of self-protection. They will come to get us eventually – one way or another. In the dead of night or in the throes of success. Fear will not be pushed aside. We must address it daily. Question it, give it space, then kill it with kindness.

1. Get yourself a notebook and on the first few pages draw two columns. Title the left column 'Nurturer' and title the right column 'Little Me/Core Self'

   In your dominant hand (for right-handed people this is your right hand) under 'Nurturer' write the series of questions below. Then with your non-dominant hand (if you are right-handed this is your left hand) write your answers in the right-hand column. Don't think, just write and keep writing until Little You has said everything he/she needs to say for each answer. Don't hold back.

   Ask the question, then answer it before going on to the next question:

   - How are you feeling today?
   - How can I help you feel better?
   - What daily habits can I do to help you feel nurtured and loved?
   - What little treats do you like doing that I can make sure I provide regularly?
   - When do you feel really good about yourself?

- How can I help you feel better about yourself?
- What makes you feel safe?
- What makes you laugh?
- What are your three favourite things?
- How can I help you keep fit and healthy?
- How can I make you feel happier?
- When are your favourite quiet times?
- What do you need to have in place so that you can work to your best ability?
- What hurts you?
- What can I do to help you heal?
- How can I help you grow as a person?
- How can I show you compassion?
- Tell me your fifty top achievements
- Tell me fifty things you like about yourself
- Describe a place (real or imaginary) that makes you feel happy and safe
- Tell me what makes you a really kind, caring friend
- Am I doing that for you? If not, what can I do to be more kind and caring and loving?

Declaration: I promise I will do all these things for you and check in regularly with you to make sure I am helping you to feel loved, nurtured and safe.

2. Now it is your Nurturer's job to check in every day:

- How are you?
- How can I help you?
- What could make you feel less fearful?
- How real is that fear?
- Do you have evidence?

- How would it feel if you gave me the problem and you got on with your day?
- How are you feeling now?
- Are you ready to give yourself a challenge?
- What could you do to help you feel less fearful?
- How do you feel now?
- Have a great day

Once you have got into the swing of the different versions of 'you', you can do away with the columns and, still using dominant and non-dominant hands, write the questions and answers flowing one after the other down the page.

NURTURER: *How are you?*
LITTLE YOU: *I feel terrible.*
NURTURER: *What can I do to help?*
Etc.

You don't need to title them once you have 'got' how it works. Then you can let it run like a conversation. I don't stop until Little Lou is ready to say 'Thank You!' with a big smiley face. Then I know we've cracked the fear of the day.

Big Fears

Sometimes you get overwhelmed or something big happens that feels too vast for you. Relying totally on others for support doesn't help you when you are on your own with your thoughts and your demons and your rampant imagination. This is when you need your inner coach. And this is where your core-work is invaluable.

Continue your daily check-ins, but also come to your core-work when you feel fear bubbling up. Let Little You tell you its darkest secrets through your non-dominant hand. Keep questioning, and keep answering and when you feel ready, take little actions. What one thing can you do right now, or today, that can give you control of your day, or life, your fears, your slippery road. You need traction and that comes through doing. It is harder to feel fear when you are baking power balls, or riding on your bike, or painting, or playing the piano, or digging weeds, or making a list of things you need to make your stay in hospital more comfortable. When your Nurturer makes a decision to take an action agreed by you, and follows through, Little You feels comforted and secure. Core-work is a meditation that provides expression of inner torment, a release from turmoil, it gives a sense of peace, safety and security and provides an actionable way forward. It is always with you, to be dipped in and out of whenever you need it.

You will be using this technique throughout the book to address the various topics, coaching sessions, personal developments and issues that are raised around your own individual fears along the way.

This is the core tool for addressing fear that I use with my clients; it is powerful, effective and fast. It works in collaboration with your inner coach no matter what fears comes tumbling down from the sky at you day or night.

You will see extracts from my own core-work diary, some from my clients (either named or anonymously according to their wishes) and some from imaginary scenarios, to give you an idea of how it works and how useful it is.

The Dual-Dialogue Method

Developed originally as a therapy tool by Dr Lucia Capacchione, the method's simplicity belies the speed and depth of its success in resolving issues, healing psychological wounds and having a constant, reliable source of access to what you need at a deep core level, and how you can obtain it. You need to keep the channels open. It is not enough to ask yourself for help only when you are in dire straits. It should be a daily dialogue. Dr Lucia Capacchione herself used this method to heal herself of a physically devastating and debilitating disease. She found out what she needed on an emotional and physical level using the two-handed dialogue technique and she was able to cure herself. Her many clients over the years have also found release and healing with the same method.

I have developed a way to use it in coaching to tap into your innate creative self. When you find, take responsibility for, and heal your Little You, you release yourself to be a whole adult, capable of being spontaneous, free-spirited, ingenious, creative, inventive, fun, joyful, unburdened, confident, fearless, trusting, and above all, loving, lovable and fearing less.

The dual dialogue is about acknowledging and coming to terms with your unmet needs, your sorrows, your grief, or maybe even of the loss something you never had. Your starting point is the here and now and two parts of yourself: the one that is in conflict (your inner child) and the one who has the tools to heal you (your Nurturer). Your inner child is the little vulnerable, angry, bitter, tormented or anxious you, and your Nurturer is the big compassionate you who has decided enough is enough and is prepared to do whatever it takes to get 'little you' feeling cared for, nurtured, and listened to. The 'big you' has to be patient, measured and consistent because your wounded inner child with its critical counterpart is a force to be reckoned with until its needs are met.

Client S Case Study

One client's mother was very domineering, highly critical, masculine, and tough. She 'wore the trousers' in their household. Her father was an island; emotionally distant and weak. My client consequently believed that to be a woman you had to be strong, hard and independent. She had a long relationship with a man who always said to her that he felt she didn't need anyone. She, like her father, was an island. He wanted her to be more 'feminine' and softer. She railed against heels and make-up as symbols of weakness. He criticised her appearance a lot over those years. In retrospect, she realises that what he was asking her for (and she heard it as criticism or her own Critical Parent) was for her to open up to him.

Her unmet need was for a nurturing parent, but who she chose was a Critical Parent (or someone she thought was playing that role) and she kept him in a critical place by playing out the tough, domineering role of her mother. She saw his requests for her to release her femininity as an accusation that she wasn't good enough just as she was. She said she felt happy in her 'natural' state and wasn't going to change for anyone. But her tough-nut exterior wasn't her; it was the embodiment of her hardnosed mother.

Of course, the only one who can heal the unmet childhood needs are ourselves. We can't change the past, but in coaching we can change the present. When we did the two-handed dialogue I asked her what a nurturing parent would look like. Her petulant Inner Child responded with her non-dominant hand, 'how should I know, I never had one'. So, I asked her to imagine someone who was the complete opposite of what her mother looked like and to describe that. What poured out were words like soft, caring, kind eyes, vulnerable, playful, resilient, curious, flexible, funny, compassionate, intuitive, instinctive, gentle, open, feminine. I asked her to spend the next week writing a further fifty words that summed up 'femininity' for her, to look around and observe men, women, nature, her surroundings, textures etc. and find the feminine in the world that wasn't the armour-plated shell she had grown up believing it should be.

You can't love from a place of rigidity and iron-will because that is the carcass of fear and over self-protection. Love cannot thrive in arid conditions. Love needs a soft fertile ground in which seeds can be planted, nurtured and given the conditions to mature. It requires vulnerability and a willingness to be open. Through dialogue work, S saw past her fear and into new possibilities for herself. She could try on different ways of being and not be fearful of what others, or her own Inner Critic, had to say on the matter. The fortress of fear she build around her heart dismantled as the kind words of her Nurturer started to heal her Little S.

This is how to meet your own unmet needs. Not by searching for someone else who can be your saviour, but by being your own self-caring champion. Not by finding someone who replicates the worst traits in your parents, but by recognising and living up to the best traits in yourself. When you are emanating your true, authentic and unmasked self, the scar tissue of your past will soften and fade.

4. SELF-CARE

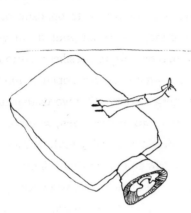

We all want to feel loved and cared for. We may even hunt out a mate who we believe is going to do this job for us. All the while we bombard our minds and bodies with everything we possibly can to cause eventual self-destruction (through pesticides, herbicides, environmental pollution, processed foods, sugar, alcohol, fags, pharmaceuticals, emotional stress etc.). Our lovers can't be our caretakers, and why do we expect it? Only we can take on the mantle of loving self-care and ensure we give ourselves the best chance of wellbeing, longevity, happiness and contentment.

We all have cancer cells floating about in our bodies, and it's only when the environment in our body becomes inflamed and acidic that they start to proliferate.[4] So the good news is, you have the opportunity to reverse this. For example, you can create an alkaline environment in your body by getting rid of any of those things that cancer cells thrive on and stop the inflammation. In the same way we can create a healthy approach that zaps away those rogue fears that haunt the corridors of our minds.

Understanding that we set the stage, and that we can also reset it, empowers us to reverse the story and retell it as one of healing and wellbeing. Our minds and bodies are intricately interlinked so we would do well to tend to both, as we would a garden. Think of weeds as our fears gone rampant.

We can control what we eat and learn to love food that is good for creating a healthy environment in our bodies. We can take responsibility for our greenhouse emissions by reducing our carbon footprint, using less water, recycling more, leaning towards a more plant-based diet and by showing love for ourselves and our children through caring for our planet. We can exercise regularly to keep our bodies fit. We can do our daily core-work to keep our inner selves nurtured and tuned.

Good intentions are all well and good, but even the most motivated people find it a challenge to keep on loving themselves in all these ways. It's hard work and extremely easy to fall off the wagon. The outcomes of disease, divorce, and a destroyed planet seem a long way off when faced with a juicy steak, a glass of Prosecco, a flight to Barbados, and a good dose of tossing blame in your lover's direction when your own toxic thoughts get too much to bear.

So how can we stick to our path of self-care and thus ensure a healthy relationship with ourselves, our lovers and our environment? Well, let's take toxic stress as an example. A certain amount of stress is good for us. It motivates us and helps us grow. But when we can't switch it off and it goes into overdrive, it starts to do physical damage to our bodies; our telomeres, our immune system, our ability to fight off disease. Much of this stress is entirely in our heads. But equally we can also use our heads to de-stress.

Client T Case Study

Client T has had a series of unsuccessful relationships. She's been hurt, disappointed and downright pissed off. But now she's met someone that, after six weeks, she really cares about. She thinks she's falling in love. She thinks he is too. They share similar interests, enjoy each other's company and the chemistry is there. She's heading into the crazy-in-love part of the movie. But last weekend she freaked. He'd been on holiday that week with some friends, including two women, and on returning, T noticed a few texts coming in from one of these women. Normally she would have jumped to conclusions, thrown a fit, maybe thrown objects, certainly accusations and blame, and then withdrawn to seethe in a hurt that has no foundation other than her own imagination.

However, in the past that behaviour has got her nothing other than the back of a lover as he walks out the door. She cares too much about this guy to risk that, so she reassesses her thinking. She tells him she is feeling insecure and scared because she has been hurt before. She doesn't want to be hurt again but she does want to let go and enjoy the potential relationship fully. He asks why she's suddenly feeling insecure and she explains about the texts and her subsequent imaginings. Because she talks about it while owning the feelings as her own, and because she doesn't make false accusations, he doesn't become defensive. He listens and then he is able to reassure her. She feels better and their relationship becomes a little more surefooted.

It took a huge amount of emotional effort and courage for T to keep ownership of her feelings and to turn it around into open communication. She's learned to do this because *not* doing it in the past has left her deserted and depressed. It has caused her pain and anxiety. The perceived threat mounted by her imagination causes her to behave irrationally. This time, she visualised the scenario as it would play out if she let rip, pissed off her date and dug an early grave for her relationship. She gave herself the time needed before

'reacting' so that she could recognise her feelings (Little T), listen to them
and understand what they are masking (Nurturer), and then take positive
action based on what she really wanted (to form a strong loving relationship
with this man). This is the process that I describe as the dual-hand dialoguing
creative core-work, and I encourage you to use it through this book.

Let's imagine doing the core-work exercise around this scenario:

NURTURER: *What's up?*

LITTLE T: *He's getting texts from a woman he went on holiday
with. Perhaps they had a fling. He's going to dump me now.
I'm going to be alone forever. What a bastard.*

NURTURER: *What is this making you feel?*

LT: *Scared. I've been hurt before. I don't want to be hurt again.*

NURTURER: *So, you are feeling threatened. But you don't have
any hard evidence that he is cheating on you?*

LT: *No.*

NURTURER: *And your imagination is making you feel as if he has
already cheated on you?*

LT: *Yes.*

NURTURER: *OK, so we've established these feelings are yours
but not based on fact. Let's try to formulate an action plan.
Let's agree you're going to sit down with him and tell him
what you're feeling. Tell him it's because you are insecure
due to past experiences. You don't want to be with a man
that cheats, so before you go any further you would like some
reassurance that you are both on the same page with the
same values of integrity and trust.*

LT: *Hmmm.*

NURTURER: *How does that sound?*

LT: *Scary.*

NURTURER: *How about you stand right behind me and I'll do the
talking. Would that feel more possible?*

LT: *Yes, that feels better.*

NURTURER: *Great let's do it!*

LT: *Thank you* ☺

And, in essence, that's what she did. Her boyfriend responded well and they could move forward, a little stronger for it. T turned potential toxic stress into a challenge. Ultimately that relationship didn't work out, but through her self-soothing practice she is able to feel nurtured, loved and supported by her own inner bonding. It makes her a strong contender for a great future partnership with someone.

Love yourself with:

- Exercise
- Plenty of water
- Organic, whole foods
- No sugars or sweeteners
- Minimum of pharmaceuticals
- Use natural remedies where possible
- Spend time in natural environments as often as possible
- Eat lots of plant-based foods
- Breathe properly
- Focus on one thing at a time
- Find your purpose in life
- Do what you love
- Live by your values
- Surround yourself with people who love, and not diminish, you
- Take time out just for you
- Keep your creative core-work journal going
- Learn to quieten the destructive Inner Critic

Love

A good relationship is not perfect. You may well be chalk and cheese. You may enjoy different hobbies, have different friends, hate each other's jokes. You may be an extrovert and want to spend the weekends partying, whereas they may want nothing more than to snuggle up on the sofa with a good book and a bit of introspective navel gazing. You may love late-night drunken sex, but they may prefer sweaty early morning, messy hair, stinky breath, messy sheet sex. You may have grown up in a council house and attended the local comprehensive, whereas they may have catapulted between their family stately home and an exclusive boarding school. None of the differences matter if you share the same fundamental values and if, in the moments when you are both being your best selves, unencumbered by tantrummy inner demons, you get on like a house on fire.

The problem comes when you have unresolved issues, and you allow them to wreak havoc on your relationships.

Are you stalking their phone, listening out for any hint of betrayal or drop in love declaration? Do you analyse every text, do you criticise every false move? The flowering of love is fertile ground for FEAR in all its myriad of forms. And who wants this stuff to rise to the surface? The best option for some, therefore, is to dip out of the race. For those guys amongst you that stick around for the next extra date or two and get into bed with your potential beloved, this is the point, so to speak, where you find that maybe you can't get it up. Nothing. A few limp-wristed attempts and the humiliation is full-scale crucifying. Your fears have corralled at the erection gates and the result is a no-show. So, you go all Free Willy and head for the hills. You are not alone. This is happening a lot. And girls, it's not you. Guys, it's your inner kid freaking out. Have you seen the video of the baby elephant swinging his trunk this way and that and round and round, just because he's loving being an elephant and owning a trunk? That's what we need to aim for in self-love.

Every hurt, trauma, disappointment, sadness and pain inflicted on you as a child is harboured as scar tissue on your psyche. Whenever you're feeling depressed, anxious, fearful, suffering from eating issues, over-shopping/drinking/working, catastrophising, having intimacy problems, a history of failed relationships – it could be your inner child at work, trying to self-soothe, tantrum, or hide. Little You can't fix you, however. It's not a kid's job because it doesn't have the tools, the knowledge or the experience. But Big You can. You can't remove the original source of the wounding, but you can do some psychic plastic surgery. Starting from here, whatever your baggage, you can move forward. You can protect Little You, give yourself a hug, listen, take time, appreciate, give acceptance, be kind and be loving. Big You can be the loving, attentive parent that Little You missed out on. (Every parent makes mistakes, and every child, even subconsciously, weaves those mistakes into the micro-biome of their gut and therefore psyche.[5])

The exercises below will help you connect to that wounded child and find out what it needs at different times, and in different situations.

⊨ EXERCISE ⊨

1. Creative Child Scrapbook

   Include:
   - A letter of apology to Little You, for not protecting and nur-turing. Promise to have more fun
   - Pictures from a weekly date where Little You chooses where to go
   - Reconnect with a weekly activity that you loved as a child
   - Collect images of the long-lost big dreams you had as a kid
   - Create a special place for Little You to play and feel safe (even if it's just a little shelf or a chair)
   - Go to a toy shop and buy Little You a present. What appeals, what makes you smile? Indulge yourself
   - Create a gift-box of things that have a special meaning for you
   - Start a collection of things that remind of you of times you enjoyed as a child
   - Draw a picture of Little You and surround yourself with images that make you feel good
   - Take yourself to an art gallery, music concert, the ballet, theatre or football match
   - Have a party and surround yourself with people who love you and appreciate you

2. Practice the dual-dialogue hand exercise between Little You and Nurturing You with these questions:

   Nurturer's questions:
   - Who are you?
   - What's your favourite colour?

- What does it make you think about?
- How does that make you feel?
- Picture your favourite place and describe it
- Think about someone you admire. What are the characteristics that appeal to you?
- How can you find more of these qualities in your life?
- What do you need from me?
- What would you tell your Little You from the perspective of an adult?

Love Yourself Without Narcissism

Throughout this book I am banging the drum for loving yourself first so that you can welcome in love from others. Loving yourself first, means you enter the muddy waters of potential love, with a wholesome openness, curiosity and loving acceptance that your values are aligned – even if your characteristics and personalities may be wildly different. You want to be loved, so you are loving and self-loving, and not governed by FEAR.

What you don't do when you learn to love yourself first is don the bitter cloak of narcissistic self-obsession. When clients first tiptoe onto the ice of self-love they are terrified of appearing narcissistic. Indeed, as children we are told not to boast, not to push ourselves forward ahead of others, not to sing our own praises or stand centre stage. And so, to allay fears of slipping down the slope into narcissism, you need to know what to avoid doing when you are setting out on project 'Love You'. Non-narcissism is cultivating empathy over selfishness. Self-compassion over self-absorption. Confidence over inflated ego/fear. Self-perception over blaming

others. It's about turning, 'it's all about me' into, 'it's all about loving myself first so that I can love you, and you can love me back in
a symbiotic and healthy, balanced way'.

Self-reflection can only happen when the narcissistic self has its
ear to the ground. Only then will it hear and acknowledge the difference between, 'LOVE ME ME ME' and, 'I Love Me, and therefore I can love others.' The narcissist cannot take criticism. And in
a relationship of two equals, each should be able to learn and grow
around each other in the act of mutual respect and honouring of
values. Get over yourself by listening carefully, and taking on the
fact that there is always room for growth.

Narcissism is not a healthy self-love. It is FEAR and EGO in
action.

Self-love is:

- Empathy
- Protection
- Trust
- Honouring
- Listening
- Support
- Encouragement
- Connection
- Kindness
- Compassion
- Humour
- Freedom
- Relaxation
- Creativity

Too Scared to Love

What if he/she turns out to be the wrong one? What if they hurt me? What if they die? Well, they might. But are you going to do without, for the 'just in case'?

Client Sa Case Study

Client Sa had broken up with her partner because she felt they had a lot of issues they couldn't get past. When they split up she came to see me. It turned out there were many more issues that she had going on in her head, and all of them were hers, not his. She had been a people-pleaser all her life. When her sibling died as a young adult her parents had fallen apart, gone bankrupt and divorced, her people pleasing kicked in with full force.

But she had no boundaries, and everyone else was very happy to take advantage of her caring and generous nature. She was running on empty. So, she came to me to refuel. And she came because she was in her mid-thirties and all her friends were settling down and having kids, and she desperately wanted to join them. But she'd broken up with the man she thought she would marry and spend the rest of her life with. She was scared she would be alone forever.

The problem was that in all her experience of putting everyone else's needs before her own, she'd lost sight of what her own were. Through the coaching process she tapped back into her core values, re-established some healthy boundaries with her family and work, gave herself personal time to develop and grow, and created good habits for a more balanced life. She learned to say 'no' when she needed to and stopped being so afraid of the consequences that no opened with other people. Having a clearer idea of what she was after in a partner, she even started dating again, braving the online dating world, dipping her toe in with an open mind and heart.

However, a couple of months down the line, she'd let some of the critical areas for herself slip. Her work was taking over again, she'd stopped making time for herself and she was disillusioned by the dating. In addition to that, her ex-partner had been in contact and was wanting to get back together. She still loved him but her head was telling her all the reasons why she shouldn't be with him. She was feeling confused and dispirited. So, I decided to do the dual-dialogue core-work with her. First, we established a connection with her Nurturer and Her Little Self. Then I introduced her to her Critical Self. With her dominant hand, she wrote down all the accusations her Inner Critic had to say to her Little Self. They flowed from her pen: 'Why don't you do this?', 'why haven't you done that?', etc. There was a long list. I asked her to write with her non-dominant hand in the Little Self column about how those accusations made her feel. Of course, they made her feel terrible about herself.

She took stock. Suddenly she had a different perspective. The Critic was ruling the roost and telling her that life 'should' be a certain way, that she 'should' be trying to find a man who matched all her core values. I got her Nurturer (dominant hand) to ask this question: 'If I were to provide you with all the things that matter most to you, i.e. passion, bohemian approach, curious outlook, family values etc., what one thing would you ask for from someone else in your life?' The immediate response from her Little Self (non-dominant) was 'love'. We continued:

> NURTURER: *So if I meet all your needs and values, the one thing that you'd want from someone else is love.*
> LITTLE SELF: *Yes.*
> NURTURER: *And do you believe that I can meet all your other needs and values, through the work we have already done.*
> LITTLE SELF: *Yes.*
> NURTURER: *And when you think of your ex-partner and how you feel about him, what do you know?*
> LITTLE SELF: *I love him.*

NURTURER: *And what do you need to tell your Inner Critic?*

LITTLE SELF: *To back right off.*

NURTURER: *So if I ensure you maintain your healthy boundaries and everything that really matters to you, do you feel clearer about what you want?*

LITTLE SELF: *I want to be with him.*

NURTURER: *How does that make you feel?*

LITTLE SELF: *Scared.*

NURTURER: *Love can be scary. Not having love can be scary too. Which would you prefer?*

LITTLE SELF: *Love.*

By doing this exercise, my client became so much clearer about what she deeply wanted at her core, and she was freed from her Inner Critic or Over-Protector. She learned she needed to love herself first before she could build something strong and loving with someone else. Over the ensuing months she kept up the dual-dialogue and eventually realised that he wasn't right for her and, in the end, met someone who shared her vision for the future.

Learning No as an Act of Self Love

You would think it would be easy to say no to violence in a relationship. No to coming home drunk and shouting and hitting me. No to beating the children. No to laying a single finger on any one of us. No to the emotional manipulation. No to the blackmail. No to the coercion. No to the controlling. No to the mean words. No to the constant picking of fights. No to the constant stream of criticism. No to the endless taunts. No to the put-downs. No to the threats.

But whether it's full on battering or a subtle knife-twist of words, you can go for years just taking it. Justifying it. Ignoring it. Covering it up. Making excuses for it. Denying it's even happening. You let the first few times go, thinking it's an aberration. You think they'll change. You make false promises to yourself; 'when', 'if', 'just until'. Slowly your brain normalises their behaviour. You make more effort because, as they tell you, it's your fault anyway. Everyone puts up with stuff, right?

Your resistance becomes weaker; your boundaries are broken. Of course you get angry and upset, but you turn it inwards. Why are you so weak? Why do you put up with this shit? Now the abuse isn't just external. *You* are ladling it on too. You try to appease and please your partner. You become 'good', 'sweet' and a 'perfectionist'.

Know this: it doesn't have to be like that.

Client J Case Study

One client cleans the entire house until it's sparkling, puts on sexy clothes and reapplies make-up before her partner comes home. She does this every evening. Because even after 30 years of marriage he demands spotless cupboards and party-time in the bedroom. Sometimes he'll wake her up shouting at her for her collection of shoes under the bed, or for a cluttered untidy fridge. He'll re-organise her knicker drawer.

She is a bright, strong woman and yet she's decided life is easier if she doesn't say no to his behaviour too often. She throws out the shoes and clears the fridge of half-used jars, only to replace them by re-buying them at the shops when she needs to cook him a meal later that night. Occasionally she'll raise merry hell when he has pushed her patience too far and he'll back off on his manipulations and over-controlling behaviour. But ultimately, she just takes it and does 'what she needs to do'. She loves him and she wants to stay. Nothing *really* bad happens. In general they have a 'good life'. Whatever happens she doesn't want to end up like her childhood, when she was raised in desperate poverty.

FEAR of living with nothing is as real for her today as it was as a little girl. So she'll do anything to keep her home and her family whole. Her values of safety, security and family outweigh his obsessiveness. But sometimes her boundaries are weak and fear stops her strengthening them, and that's what we worked on together.

Connect with your core self, your values, needs and boundaries. It's about loving yourself first. As you start to feel better about yourself, your boundaries become stronger. People with unhealed Inner Childs take advantage of slack boundaries just as a toddler does with a harried parent. They push and push just to see where those boundaries are. If the parent caves in, the toddler pushes to the next level. Adults do the same if they can. It is up to us to be the person that is clear about what is acceptable, and what isn't.

Imagine your partner's unacceptable behaviour as coming from their inner toddler. They want to know they are loved and safe but they test the conditions of your love. If they are mean to you and you take it, they will up the levels of abuse. They are acting out their own fears of conditional love, of abandonment. They are playing out their insecurities and low self-esteem. But you can't fix that by giving in. They must heal themselves, and the most generous offering you can give them is to lead by example. Show yourself kindness, respect and compassion. Honour yourself. Love yourself first.

⊨ EXERCISE ⊨

Write a love letter from your Nurturing Self to your Little Self. Here is an example.

Dear Little You,
  I am so sorry that I have been more prepared to please others than to take care of you and your feelings. You have

*been so patient and quiet in there, but I want the sun to shine
on you. You deserve to bask in its warm light. You are so sweet
and gentle and generous to others, and I want you to be on
the receiving end of such selfless kindness. I love you and I
want you to know that from now on I am going to put you
first. Before I do anything else I will check in with you and see
if you are OK with it. If it doesn't settle well with you, then I
will not do it. I will become more aware, I will take time out
before acting in order to ask you how you feel. I will honour
and respect you because you are worth the world to me.
Your happiness is my happiness. I will put those boundaries
in place to protect you from your fears. I will say no when it
means your safety is at stake. I will say yes to opportunities
that allow you to flourish and grow. I will nourish you because
you are like a flower. I will breathe calmness through your
veins. I will let you play freely. I will seek creative pursuits
for you to explore. I will listen to your quiet intuition. I will
be guided by your wisdom and instinct. I will trust you. I will
understand when you are enraged and I will empathise with
your frustrations. I will not stand in judgment over you. I will
give you room to express what you need to express, and I
will help you find a way to feel better. I will ensure that you
may sit still when you need to and take the right action when
required. I will have a conversation with you every day so that
I may always know how you feel and what you need from me.
I will not abandon you. You are safe now. You may lay your
trust at my feet, put your dreams in my hands, and together
we will walk towards the full potential of life.*

   Your Loving Nurturer

The Die-Hard Critic

It might not be your partner who is wreaking emotional carnage. If you are in the habit of conducting a continuous dialogue of negative internal chatter then you are acting as the Critical Parent and Little You will be reduced to a quivering victim in a dark corner of your insides. Walking into a room of strangers will be a nightmare for you. Presenting your project will feel like sitting in the executioner's chair. Painting a picture, choosing an outfit, starting a diet, learning to run, beginning a new job, asking for a raise; indeed most things will come under the hawk eye and scrutiny of the Critical Parent in you.

'What do you think you're doing? Who are you to think you'll be any good? If it's not perfect, it's not worth doing. You are a waste of space. You're always so vague and lost in a dream you'll never get anywhere, you are never going to earn any money doing that, you won't succeed, you don't deserve it, you're rubbish, your sibling will never have that so you'd better not either, no one likes a show-off, you're fat, you'll never lose weight, don't go running, people will laugh at your ass.'

And so on. It is a running dialogue that keeps you small. It judges you and paralyses you.

Client V Case Study

I asked a client to do the dual-hand dialogue core-work exercise. The left-hand column, written with her dominant hand, represented her inner Critical Parent. She wrote a list of accusatory finger-pointing, blaming and defaming. It flowed from her: 'You, you, you . . . jab, jab, jab . . .' I then asked her to imagine me as a little girl and then say those things to me. Looking me in the eye between each statement. She couldn't do it. She burst into tears. She couldn't say one single critical thing to me and yet she allowed herself to damn herself in a torrent of abuse all day long, every day for as long as she can remember.

She told me her parents were always criticising her and always had, her mother hen-pecking, and her father doling out unhelpful advice, money and doom-laden diatribes, telling her that without him she would be powerless. Her expectations to please them were monumental. And in her eyes she always falls below par. She internalised their critique and created a monster in her head. It is not her parents' fault. They have their own demons and there is not a parent on the planet who has 100% perfect parenting skills. And, as a consequence, many people carry the mantle of internal abuse. With her non-dominant hand in the right-hand column, I asked my client to write as her Little Self to her Critical Parent. In slow, wobbly writing out flooded the sadness, fear, frustration, anger, bitterness, resentment and bewilderment. Out came the built-in layers of acrid silt that had covered all the years of her life. The expulsion and expression of her hurt released the pain. I then got her to scribble in brightly coloured crayons over The Critical Parent's list of accusations. Relief flushed across her face and her shoulders relaxed.

Self-criticism corrupts self-love. If the negative chatter is turned up full volume we can't love ourselves at all. And we turn the criticism not only on ourselves but outwards to our loved ones, our partners and our children. And so the cycle continues. But we can change how we do things now. We can silence our Inner Critic, or at the very least give it less airtime. I asked my client to write a letter of apology to her Little Self:

> I apologise for all the cruel things I say to you. I am sorry for being so unsupportive, so mean, so judgmental. I am sorry for criticising you all day long. I am sorry for hurting your feelings. I am sorry for abusing your trust in me. I am sorry for never protecting you or making you feel safe. I am sorry for not believing in you.

With a fresh piece of paper, I asked my client to draw two columns once again. This time the left column was titled Nurturing Parent and the right column Little Self. I asked her to imagine someone in her life or in the public sphere who represents a truly nurturing personality. She pictured her deceased grandmother. I then asked her to write a thank you letter in her non-dominant hand in the right column as Little Self to her Grandmother for all her nurturing ways:

> Thank you for loving me unconditionally, for protecting me, nourishing me, keeping me safe. Thank you for spending time painting and flower pressing with me. Thank you for teaching me to embroider. Thank you for hugging me every time I came into the kitchen. Thank you for always giving me food I like when I come to stay. Thank you for always smiling at me. Thank you for never judging me or criticising me. Thank you for not putting unrealistic expectations on me. Thank you acknowledging my achievements. Thank you for your grace and tranquillity. Thank you for your relaxed presence. Thank you for your consistency. Thank you for not frightening me with random outbursts. Thank you for always being the same. Thank you for your loving acceptance. Thank you for being there.

In the Nurturing Parent column I asked my client to write this question with her dominant hand: 'Is this how you would like me to be with you?' And, of course, the reply in the Little Self column with the non-dominant hand, was: 'Yes please. I would like that very much. Thank you.' Then I asked the Nurturing Parent to write a Letter of Promise:

> I promise that from this moment on, I will love and nurture you. I will support, protect and keep you safe. I will do everything in my power to help you to be all that you can be. I will be your inner coach. I will cherish and honour you. I will respect you and listen to you. I will endeavour to hear your messages and understand them in the spirit they are sent. I will not judge you or criticise you. I will heal you and help you. I will be your rock. I will stand up for you. I will always be here for you. I will not let you down. I will check in with you every day to find out how you are feeling and how I can help you. I will be your number one champion. I will watch your back. I will be there for you 100%.

Then I got my client to draw in her non-dominant hand with some chubby kids crayons, a big circle. And in the circle a picture of her Little Self being held and protected by her Nurturing Self. This is to be her protective bubble that nothing can penetrate. I asked her to put the drawing up somewhere prominent to always remind her of her promise to her herself and as a daily reminder to check in and listen.

Six months later, my client wrote about her reflections on her coaching experience:

> It helped me to see things with perspective, not to be hard on myself and set goals to achieve one step at a time and celebrate each small accomplishment that little by little makes things happen with grace and fulfilment. To recognise myself and that I'm in charge of my life.

To be brave and creative and have fun in the process. I felt cared for and looked after by you and very inspired.

>== EXERCISE ==<

Write a letter of apology from your Inner Critic to your Little Self.

>===<

In the Heart of Fear (as it happened . . .)

In this section I will demonstrate how I used creative core-work and self-care to work through fear.

I have something wrong and daren't say its name. It's not been diagnosed yet but the optician looked and referred me instantly. She didn't even charge me for the emergency examination she did when I came in off the street concerned about what I saw in the mirror. Her kindness was like a hammer nailing in the fact that something was definitely wrong. And now I am hanging in that slippery time between suspicion and being presented with a diagnosis. Fear and imagination join hands like lovers as they paint vivid pictures of worst-case scenarios.

And yet, despite myself, I find ways to be hopeful. I cycle to the gym along the river and swim in the outside pool on a frosty February day. I notice the warm water holding my body to the surface, letting me glide through it at my own pace. I look up at the clear blue sky; watery winter pale but soft in its hue. A bird sails across the canvas swooping and soaring. I can't help but smile; drink up the day. Everything seems heightened. I feel so very alive. Like when you first fall in love. Like falling in love with life. How could I have taken so much for granted? I cling to each moment.

But of course, as sleep beckons beguilingly, try as I might, the fear grips me tight by the throat, wakes me for a dose of the midnight blues and wide-awake terrors. I toss and turn as nightmarish scenes play out on the technicolour IMAX screen of my imagination. In the night I cannot erase them. But dawn comes with renewed vigour in my veins. I can fight the fear by performing my self-loving rituals. My early morning writing, my power stretches, a breakfast that packs enough punch that will surely perforate the poisons and proliferate healing in my cells, mundane admin and emails, then off to the gym before getting back down to work.

I understand that in loving myself I am opening up to the opposing tides of woe and joy. That to weather this storm that has struck my personal planet, I must release myself to both and in so doing create a balance; where grief for my health and love for the world around me are both given a hearing. I am not illness, but energy for change. My deepest demons tried to rise from the pit of my psyche but until my body presented them as disease I did not listen. But I am listening now and I am taking action. I ask my Little Self what is wrong and she tells me. All the stuff I didn't want to hear. There it is, bold as brass, right in my eye. Literally. Physically and metaphorically.

I must let myself love. That's the message. And do it through my sense of purpose. To use creativity to inspire others and help them create happier lives. Whatever my experience turns out to be from the moment the consultant opens his mouth, it will be for that end. And that is what will get me through and beyond. Maybe it will be a long torturous road, maybe a disfiguring one, maybe a life-battling-death one, maybe just a hiccup in the bigger scheme of things. But I am armed with all that I need.

NURTURER: *How are you feeling today?*
LITTLE SELF: *Scared.*
NURTURER:: *How can I help?*
LITTLE SELF: *Just hold me.*
NURTURER: *OK.*
LITTLE SELF: *Thank you, that's nice.*

Day by day by day, my Nurturer checked in and Little Me responded. Often not well. But the dialogue helped me through, and eventually I got the all clear from the doctor. I know now that I have a method to hold me through the scariest of times. I know that, tough as circumstances might be, I have my Nurturing Self to prop up my Little Self and, if that's all I have – that's just about enough.

Round up

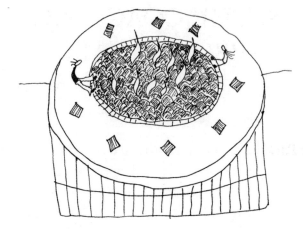

So now you know

1. What fearing less can actually look like in its full, technicolour, life-enhancing and powerfully mind-expanding capacity.
2. That fear is something we all experience, but we can use its force for our greater good.
3. That the key to fear-transformation is in our ability to develop our creative brains.
4. We do that through the regular practice of core-work in self-care, love, listening and understanding.
5. The process has worked for others, and it can, with trust and commitment, work for you too.

5. THE COACHING PROGRAMME

Welcome Pack

In Section Two you will have the opportunity to work through a version of the coaching programme that I normally do as one-to-one sessions with individual clients. The programme is divided into six sessions, which you can do weekly or bi-weekly. I wouldn't leave it longer than two weeks between each session, because you want to be able to keep up the momentum. If you like, read the whole book first to get an overview, then return to Section Two and do the programme.

Your Questions

How does coaching work?

Coaching is not therapy. Therapy looks back to uncover where past pains might be unearthed and healed. Coaching takes you from where you are right now, baggage and all, to where you want to be, ditching the baggage along the way. We get you excited by helping you to imagine a big, wonderful vision of the future for yourself, and then set short-, medium- and long-term goals that allow you to move towards it. You start to feel the victories in the everyday (not just the Oscar wins and marathons runs.) We'll look at what holds you back and we'll crack those bad habits, limiting beliefs and self-sabotaging, confidence-knocking tricks of yours.

How long will it take?

Take it at the pace that feels right for you. You may want to skim it all and then go back and work through slowly. Try not to skip the steps. The process is designed to work this way. Find a buddy to do it with, or to bounce off your progress and achievements.

What do I get from doing it?

My aim is for you to feel inspired, supported, transformed and motivated by the full range of expertise that I am sharing with you. It is a tried and tested process that works. I give you everything a life coach does, but I also give you the creative coaching methods I have developed or adapted for the programme. You can use the tools, tips and techniques to support those you care about and work with. If you commit to it, you'll win in your pitch against fear.

What am I committing to?

You are committing to a life-changing experience. There are no guarantees in life, of course, but by working through this coaching process you are giving yourself the best chance of beating back your underlying stresses and strains. You will become more resilient and flexible. You are committing to a life of creativity, self-love, fearing less and being more.

....

Your Contract

Please do this. The act of signing this promise registers in your brain as a commitment to yourself.

I ....
hereby commit to working through the creative coaching pro-gramme, to trusting the process, to doing the work and to cre-ating a daily practice of helpful strategies.

I commit myself to creating a life in which I fear less, and live and love more.

Signed   Date

....
....

Before you begin

It is important to establish where you are right now, before doing the programme. Then, when you have completed it, you can look back and see how far you have come. Take your time with this, really think about it and be deeply truthful in your answers. The more you reveal, the more helpful you will find it. If you are struggling to open up, use your non-dominant hand to answer the questions.

What are your top five achievements that you are most proud of?

....

....

....

....

....

What are the five biggest disappointments in your life?

....

....

....

....

....

What are your five top skills and abilities?

....

....

....

....

....

Think of three short-term goals you would like to work on during the next six weeks:

....

....

....

What do you think has held you back in the past?

....

....

....

....

....

....

Brainstorm all the fears you have in your life:

....

....

....

....

....

....

Which fears do you feel are the most destructive to you?

....

....

....

....

....

....

What would you most like to achieve through this coaching process?
Let yourself imagine the best-case scenario:

....
....
....
....
....
....

What are you putting up with in your life?

....
....
....
....
....
....

What are three of your own emotions that increase your fears?

....
....
....

How are your current fears impacting on your life at present?

....
....
....
....
....
....

What inspires you?

....
....
....
....
....
....

What makes you laugh?

....
....
....
....
....
....

What makes you happy?

....
....
....
....
....
....

What are your top five simplest of pleasures?

....
....
....
....
....

How do you rate your health and fitness? What, if anything, would you like to improve?

....

....

....

....

....

Filling in this questionnaire gives you the opportunity to get used to taking time out for you, and to reflect and work on your personal development. Before you begin this coaching programme, make sure you have established a specific time and place, each day, to commit to the process.

Sending you good wishes, grease to your elbow and wind in your sails.

LET THE ADVENTURE BEGIN!

Section Two

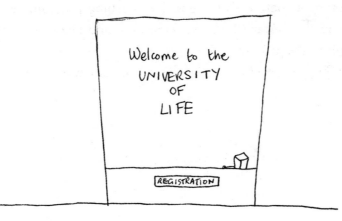

The Coaching Programme

To FEAR LESS is not to remove FEAR but to know that even WITH FEAR you can survive and thrive through your self-care initiatives and learned creative strategies.

This is the part of the book where I give you the tools, the seeds, the compost, water, sun and air, and you put on your wellies and gardening gloves. Then together we can start the process of planting, watering, weeding, nourishing and enjoying the garden of your mind.

Ten tips for making the most of your coaching programme

- Be patient. Personal development takes time to nurture. You'll need to keep going back and practising repeatedly until your new way of being becomes second nature

- The process is not magic. It's practical and powerfully effective when you commit to it and trust it. The results can be astonishing, life affirming, enhancing and changing

- It's not a one size fits all. Think pick 'n' mix. Read it all and then return to work through the programme, focusing on the areas that really resonate with you at the time

- When you are doing the core-work exercises and using your non-dominant hand – don't think, just write. Don't judge, just write. Don't hold back, just write. Be open and truthful. You'll gain much more that way

- It's time to stop living small. Listen to the nurturing part of yourself and use the tools to turn down the volume on all the negative chatter

- When you feel resistant and irritated with the process, then look inwards and dig deep. What's *really* going on? It's not the process; it's something in you resisting the process. Do the core-work and release that knotty bit

- Get yourself a journal with a cover that inspires you. Keep notes and updates on your progress. Write your core-work, your gratitudes and your achievements in it. Use separate bits of jotter paper for the daily brain dump of toxic mind waste that builds up in your head

- At the end of each week summarise what you have learned. The act of doing this is an acknowledgement to your brain that you appreciate your hard work and commitment and that you are indeed making progress

- Get out of your comfort zone, take risks, push yourself a little further. Show your fear who's boss

- Nourish your gut flora. Cutting-edge science says that when you feed your gut with nourishing, mainly plant-based, diverse nutrients, it sends messages of wellbeing to your brain and reduces the 'gut feelings' of anxiety, depression and stress[6]

What we will cover over the six weeks

1. **Envisioning the Future:** Fear Wheel, Dreaming Big, Day Dreaming, Values and Goal Setting.

2. **What's Holding you back:** Needs, Beliefs, Habits, Imposter syndrome, Procrastination, Self-sabotage, People Pleasing, Compare and Despair, No to Naysayers.

3. **What Really Matters:** Self-Love, Purpose, Gratitude, Flexibility.

4. **Hazards and Hiccups:** Failing, Resistance, Rejection, Imperfection and Courage.

5. **Creative Healing:** New Mindset, Intuition, Curiosity, Humour and Hope.

6. **Optimising your Creative Muscle:** Doodling, Looking, Connecting, Improvising, Finding your creative compass, Creative Leadership, Helping Others.

Week One

ENVISIONING THE FUTURE

- WHERE ARE YOU NOW: Fear Wheel
- WHERE DO YOU WANT TO BE: Big Dreams, Day Dreaming, On the Shoulders of Giants
- HOW CAN YOU GET THERE: Goal Setting, Values, Rewards

Where Are You Now?

To get from here to where you want to be, we need to know where you are right now. You will have a good idea from your preparatory 'Who You Are' form, but now it's time to score each area of your life in terms of the fear you are experiencing, so that you know what you might like to focus on improving. You will envision an exciting future and you will create a structure for making it happen.

Fear Wheel

Fear can furrow beneath the surface of one area of your life and spread its tentacles into the other areas if it isn't identified, isolated and chiselled out. We look at the whole picture; where you are now across all areas of your life, see where there is 'inflammation' or fear, and work to both calm those fears and build emotional resilience so that the fear can't get a foothold again.

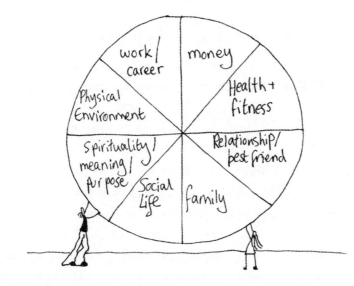

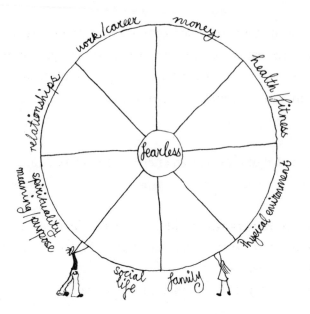

The centre of the pie chart scores '0 = No Fear' and the outside of the circle scores '10 = Big Fear' in how you are feeling about some aspect of that area of your life.

For instance, in the physical environment section, you may have a great place of work, and love your home, but if you have to walk a long dark alley from work to home and it fills you with dread every night, then you might score that section a Fear Factor of 8 or 9. Look at each area and score it in terms of fearfulness. Be honest with yourself. Make notes on the chart about what exactly is scaring you, making you worried, fearful, anxious, full of dread, despair or depression. It might be a niggle or full-on panic attack. Score as it affects you right now.

What would it look like not to be fearful?

On the outside of the circle, next to each section, jot down anything you can imagine existing that would change those fears into a more comfortable, secure feeling. For example, instead of walking home on your own down a dark path from work, you could arrange to walk back with someone. Or you could get a guard dog to protect you as you walk. Or you could not buy a cappuccino every day, save the money and use it for an Uber or taxi to take you home safely. Don't judge your ideas, just let them pop up and make a note of them. Brainstorm the flipside of your fears.

Example:

- Scared of flying, which you have to do for work

Flip to:

- I use hypnotherapy to reduce my fear of flying
- I use my core-work to help me overcome my fear of flying
- I turn my fear of flying into love of flying
- I change my job so I never have to fly again

Explore all options. Keep it in the present so your brain sees it as real, and not speculative. Let your creative brain bounce around, make connections, chuck in absurd or impractical ideas. Don't hold back. Let your brain start to feel what it's like to be fearless in that area of your life.

Client A's Fear Wheel

I first met client A when she came to my talk 'How to be Fearless' at The School of Life in London. Afterwards, she told me how it had helped her to realise she didn't have to feel the way she was feeling, that she liked the sound of a more creative approach to beating back her fears and that she would like to do the coaching programme.

When she'd completed the Fear Wheel she decided to look at the 'physical environment' section as an area to improve. She had moved to London a year prior to me working with her and was really struggling with anxiety around her job, where she lived and the impact her worries were having on her relationship ('Relationship' section on the Fear Wheel) and mental wellbeing. She felt lost and without direction ('Meaning and Purpose' section on Fear Wheel):

> Moving to London has been a bigger struggle than I want to admit and I feel weak that it's been that way. Not only have I missed my family/friends/familiarity, but it feels like I have faced one obstacle after another and I do not always have the time to recharge. I have had the most amazing times and I will never regret it, but it has taken its toll on my happiness and mental stability. The constant looming decision/pressure of moving or not moving has its weight and makes me fear my future. I let my fears of moving away from my partner and the complexity of our relationship affect the present and impact my happiness. I just feel really tired. Not really physically, but this mental fatigue that makes everything seem so much harder to deal with. I don't feel as hopeful for my future and am worried I will not be successful. At times it feels like I am on pause and I am not sure which way is right.

At this early stage you may, like my client, feel totally helpless and overwhelmed by your fears. Or you may just have a residual, underlying feeling that life could be better – but you don't know how to get there. It's good to remember that by going through this process, your fearfulness will transform into fear-lessness; you will feel more in charge and less controlled by external circumstances. The internal battering by your Fear Bully will only be audible when you really are in danger and when it needs to protect you from being run over by a bus or to remind you to revise for your exams.

Here are the reflections that client A wrote on completing her coaching programme:

Where was I?
- I think of who I was when we had our first session in Soho and I barely recognise her. I feel like a completely different person. It is incredible

What have I learned?

- Kindness towards myself
- That my ego was taking over my life and when left unrestrained, has the power to distort my world and make me unhappy
- That I have achieved a lot and can be proud
- That I am living the life I want, even if at times I couldn't see that
- That I have a tendency to project my ego onto others, making me more judgmental and less understanding
- That self-love makes everything better
- I need to be my biggest champion, not my constant adversary!
- That I am growing, I can acknowledge who I was . . . the diagram with the bus and my parents and Critical Parent. If I keep up the hard work, I can cruise along the path of life, with my parents around me enjoying it. Critical me is out of the picture. That is what I always work toward, I think I am getting there

---

⊱═ REMEMBER YOUR CORE-WORK! ═⊰

In running, if you don't do your core-work and build your psoas muscle (the one that joins the top of you to the bottom of you and holds you all together) you can pick up injuries that seem totally unconnected. The same with your emotional core-work. Keep your inner self supported, cared for, listened to and appreciated.

Choose an area of your Fear Wheel that you would like to look at, then respond to your Nurturer using your Little You, non-dominant hand:

NURTURER: *How does it feel when you think about that fear?*

LITTLE YOU: ....

NURTURER: *Tell me more about your fear?*

LITTLE YOU: ....

NURTURER: *If I could wave a magic wand, how could I best quieten your fear?*

LITTLE YOU: ....

NURTURER: *If I were to tell you that no matter what I would be there for you, how would that feel?*

LITTLE YOU: ....

NURTURER: *Describe what your life would look like without that fear dominating or holding you back.*

LITTLE YOU: ....

Do this core-work on the three highest scoring areas of your Fear Wheel.

Where Do You Want To Be?

Big Dreams

Thinking small is only going to keep you where you are. It won't propel you forward past fear into a future worthy of your full potential. You have to dream big. And that takes a leap of imagination. Logic and reality belongs to Goal Setting, which we will come to later, Creativity belongs to the process of punching through that glass ceiling of fearful living. Rocket launching into fantasy will get you out of a mindset that is hounded by 'can't', 'should' and 'mustn't'. Let's free up your brain so you can see exciting horizons and infinite possibilities. Let's have you let go, let rip and live it large. Your imagination is like a huge hound yanking on a short leash. It wants to run across acres of landscape, not go to the corner lamppost for a wee and back. If you do that to a dog it becomes neurotic and unstable. If you do it to your imagination it feeds on fear, and it will leap at your throat with teeth bared, intent on slamming you to the ground in a battle of wills. Get your imagination off the leash and let it run for the hills.

Envisioning Big Dreams

When you're trudging to work on a Monday morning in drizzle, traffic or overcrowded tube/metro/subway it's hard not to see the freedom of the weekend slipping away into the fug of oncoming doom, anxiety and an over-laden desktop.

'Dreams are for the mildly insane,' you think. 'Who has time to fritter away idle precious seconds dreaming of wild adventures?'

You tell yourself, as you neck back that treble-strength espresso and launch into the Monday mayhem of demands, deadlines and office squabbles: 'Such thinking is for the likes of Richard Branson and J. K. Rowling.'

J. K. Rowling is a woman who once had nothing but the dress on her back and a bunch of dreams that she had the courage to weave into the wild and wonderful adventures of Harry Potter. Her path was paved with failure upon failure and she got used to picking up the pieces of shattered hopes until, with perseverance and determination, she cracked the code and her dreams took flight.

Dreaming is imagining. It is creating images in your mind where you envision yourself doing better, being better and making a difference. Manifesting a dream is about building confidence, fighting off fears, risk taking and thinking outside the box. You must be willing to take risks, collect your failures along the way and manage your own destiny. Dreams come in all shapes and sizes, and when you find one that niggles away at you, keeps you awake at night, gives you goose bumps and shivers of excitement when you allow yourself to think about it, consider the option of diving in and making it happen. Life is too short not to.

When I was filming the *Death* series for Channel 4, we were meant to be filming for six months. That was the prognosis for most of our contributors, who each had a terminal illness. However, things didn't go according to plan. Most people didn't die in that time-frame. We spoke to a neuropsychoimmunologist who explained that when someone with a terminal illness has something specific to look forward to they are often able to live longer. In this case, people were enjoying being filmed and felt it important to tell their stories of dying. We ended up filming over three years and the series increased to five parts, one of which was solely dedicated to what helped people live longer. When someone has a specific event like a big birthday, a wedding or a birth that they want to live to see, they are imagining it in their minds. They are picturing what the day will be like and seeing themselves being there. They can feel what it will be like and it feels good. That sends positive signals to the brain, which gives a boost to their immune system and to their sense of wellbeing. In this way they greatly increase their chance of seeing that day really happen. Many more people die after big events in their lives. There is an increase in deaths after New Year's Day.

But let's not wait until we are dying to make use of our ability to imagine the future and then make it happen. We've seen what happens when people have big dreams: Steve Jobs created Apple, Bill Gates created Microsoft, Richard Branson created Virgin, Arianna Huffington created the *Huffington Post* and J. K. Rowling created Harry Potter.

If a dream is to capture your imagination, or that of others, it must affect you in a way that rises above the struggle to manifest it. You feel lit up, engaged and propelled by it. Can your big dream change your attitudes and beliefs, can it open up new ways of seeing and thinking? Is it a game changer? Does it transform your experience in some way? Does it define all that you can be? Is your dream simple, intuitive and clear? When you tell people about it do they 'get it'? Do you really want it?

The Facebook phenomenon is a testament to the global impact of a simple idea. It started as a social network on a platform that has become extensively integrated not only with the world, but our lives, and has 2 billion active monthly users. And Mark Zuckerberg wants to extend it to billions more, by enabling everyone worldwide to have access to the internet. He has inspired others to create online tech businesses and helped people that need each other, connect. For example: non-medical care and products to cancer patients, ad-hoc jobs for people who have to be based at home, supply teachers who can be contacted at the drop of a hat and so on. You name it, there's an app for it.

My son Sol always wanted to be an architect, got into UCL and realised in the first two terms that it wasn't for him. He didn't love it enough to put in the graft. So he got a place at another university to do business. He loved that so much he couldn't wait to finish his degree and get cracking. So he left. He spotted a gap in the market and took the leap. He and a mate decided to create an app bringing estate agents, landlords and students together on a social media platform. Suddenly Sol had found 'his thing'. They gathered a team around them, they raised investment, they worked like the devil and they remained focused. A lot of the time, they admit now, they hadn't a clue what they were doing, but being bold allowed them to bounce back from their fears and failures. They continue to learn, grow and move towards their dream.

Big ideas and dreams are contagious; they have the power to change our lives for the better. You don't have to be a CEO of a multi-national company, you can dream big as an individual, or you can join up with other like-minded souls and create a revolution. You can improve your own lot and you can affect the empowerment, evolution and transformation of others. You just have to start with the dream and ignite your spark.

Create a Vision Board or Scrapbook

1. Return to your Fear Wheel. Look at the three areas where your fear hangs out most. Choose the area you'd like to work on first. Imagine life going as well as you could possibly dream of. Go big. Really big. Like your fairy godmother granted you any wish you wanted. This is the time for creative adventures of the mind. No holds barred.

2. Collect up magazines and start cutting out images and phrases that inspire you. Don't think about it, if something leaps out at you, grab it. When you have collected a good stack of images, spread them out in front of you. Order them into groups that seem to form a theme. Then stick them down in these themes on a large piece of cardboard or in a scrapbook.

3. If you are artistically inclined you can create an art journal,
   drawing your dreams, sketching images and phrases that
   catch your eye and spark your imagination. Draw every
   day in your art journal to plot your progress and keep the
   dream alive.

It becomes your book of the future. Your life is a blank canvas,
fill it with colour, thrills and spills, adventure, calm, dance and
daring-do. Whatever rocks your boat. Don't hold back, this is
your springboard to success. Enjoy!

Day Dreaming

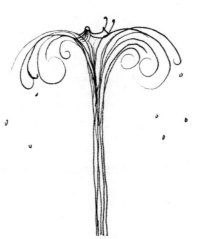

Take Your Time!

Dreaming big takes time; like a chick growing in the egg before it
hatches. You don't just grab the first idea and run with it. Test the
vision in your mind, try it out for size. Incubate. How tantalising is

it? Could you imagine spending every day for the rest of your life working towards it? Would you wake in the middle of the night because you excitedly have another idea to add to it? Before you make the leap and start committing your dream to action, enjoy this period. Don't let fear rush you into making hasty goals and long-term plans. This is the time to really tap into your internal mindscape – and you do that through daydreaming.

Daydreaming is an underestimated skill, condemned as divergent from more important things like paying attention in class or earning a living. But children, writers, artists and scientists know the importance of zoning out and drifting into an unregulated place where anything is possible and magic does happen. This is the fertile ground in which you sow the seeds of your vision.

When reading non-fiction, every few pages I stop, put the book down and stare into space. My mind peruses the information I have read, then floats off to explore its own references, connections and imaginings. It mulls over what I have learned, turns it over, sniffs it for new ideas, chews the essence of it before digesting and absorbing. My eyes refocus and return to the page, ready to read more. Without the interference of daydreaming, the information becomes facts learned by rote, it doesn't promote intelligent understanding or creative consideration, it misses out on the benefit of the imagination to build architecture from bricks of words. It deepens the experience, but it does take longer to get through a book!

Equally, when you perform mundane tasks your daydreaming capabilities are unleashed, freed to wander away from the practical and into the cerebral. More than fifty years ago, pioneering research led by Yale's Jerome L. Singer established that daydreaming is widespread and a normal aspect of human experience. Singer found that most people are 'happy daydreamers' not only enjoying vivid imagery and fantasies of the future, but using the experience for planning and relieving boredom.[7]

Singer called this 'positive-constructive daydreaming'. This constructive internal reflection helps you to learn from past experiences, come up with creative ideas and solutions, consolidate, and make sense of memories and life events. Mental time travel enhances your ability to dig into your deep desires, opens you up to your intuition and helps you find your purpose. It is associated with openness to experience and reflects a drive to explore ideas, imagination, feelings and sensations. It promotes emotional wellbeing and positivity.

However, we do have to be mindful of the nature of our daydreaming. Those who allow themselves to ruminate over destructive feelings, affronts, imagined negative scenarios, blame, self-criticism and regret, only succeed in developing and manifesting their neuroses. People with depression often talk about not being able to focus, being restless at night, unable to sleep, torturing themselves with negative thoughts which then perpetuate further feelings of worthlessness and misery. Their daydreams resemble dystopian nightmares, full of worry, anxiety and sadness. When their brains aren't working overtime on a rehash of *Blade Runner* and *Mad Max*, they are spaced out and numb.

Learning the art of mindfulness aids your capability to retune your brain circuits.[8] It helps you modulate and harness your wild imaginings back into the direction of optimal learning, creativity and wellbeing. It's like steering your boat from the tumultuous, crashing waves of the Bay of Biscay and sailing into the calm waters of the Mediterranean. Modulating between positive mind-wandering[9] and mindful focus is how your imagination creates a landscape ripe with ideas and hopeful images of yourself living a life you can cherish.

You can choose to let your mind be inspired by meanderings over future triumphs, or you can chain your brain to external realities, fears and mundanities – as in the old myth of the three stonemasons, which I've re-imagined:

....

*Many moons ago a traveller was trekking across the plains when he
came to a group of workers alongside a flowing river. He'd been alone
for days and was grateful for the chance of a chat. He approached one
worker and asked what he was doing. The labourer was abrupt and
grumpy in his response as he pointed out the obvious. 'Cutting stones,'
he said. The traveller sensed he was in the way and moved on to the
next stonecutter. 'Good stonecutting,' he said, 'what are you building?'
The stonecutter replied curtly. 'A wall.' The traveller could see it was a
wall and wanted to know more but realised he wasn't getting anything
else from this worker, who'd turned his back to munch on a pie. The
traveller stopped by a third stonecutter who was absorbed and whist-
ling a tune to himself. The traveller stood and watched, reluctant to
interrupt. But the stonecutter noticed him, straightened his back and
smiled. 'Do you like our wall?' The traveller nodded. 'It's a very nice
wall.' The stonecutter looked up to the sky. For a while he said nothing, just stared and stared, as if awestruck. 'Not just any old wall.
We're building a cathedral.' The traveller looked up at the empty sky
and saw what the stonecutter saw. A dream coming true. The traveller
got excited, 'When will it be finished?' The stonecutter got back to
work. 'Not in my lifetime. Maybe not in my son's lifetime. But one day,
hundreds of years from now, there will be a spire 400 feet tall. It will be
the tallest in the country.' He cracked his lump hammer on the splitting
head of his chisel, sweating with the backbreaking work in the swelter-
ing sun. The ringing of metal on stone echoed across the plains as the
traveller went on his way, lighter in step as he headed towards his own
new horizons.*

....

Daydreaming helps you to consolidate memories, synthesise plans,
form a sense of identity, self-belief, discipline and personal meaning,
and therefore create a more positive outlook. You need whiteout

time in your diary to let your mind wander, reflect and contemplate. Life can be what you dream it to be when you don't let fear get in the way.

....

White space in your Diary

1. Daydreaming should be an important part of your day and week. If necessary, blank out a space in your diary where you let your brain bunk off.

2. Find a favourite spot, where you feel warm, comfortable, safe. Have a cup of herbal tea or lemon water with you if you like. Do not have your phone anywhere to hand! Let people know that for the next ten minutes or so you are unavailable.

3. Sit upright but comfortably. Breathe deeply three times, loosen your shoulders and neck, then release a big sigh. Smile and then relax your jaw muscles. Relax the muscles around your eyes. Look around you. Notice the colours, the textures, the shapes. When your brain tries to wrench you back to the worries of the day, sigh again and release. Watch the internal workings of your mind. Breathe slowly.

4. Pick up a pencil and paper, and start to walk a line around the page. Let it meander and curve and curl. Don't take the pencil off the paper. Keep it moving, at whatever pace feels right. When you have filled the page with a wiggly line, add dots, lines, circles, triangles, whatever takes your fancy. Let your mind drift and wander, let it do its daydreaming thing.

5. When you're done, put away your paper and pen, breathe three times, roll your shoulders and your neck. Straighten into a power pose and release a big sigh. Now you are re-charged and ready to go again.

....

On the Shoulders of Giants

Help yourself to dream big by being inspired by others who have created big dreams and made them come true.

Stepping out into a cold, empty landscape with no shelter, no food and no companions is a daunting prospect. Our early forebears must have quaked in their moccasins as they set off to inhabit new parts of the world. But they discovered the secret of fire, invented tools and weapons, and they learned to build shelters, spear food and raise children against all the odds. They used their creativity to get ahead and transformed their fears into fuel. From those first footsteps of human habitation, others have followed, building on the boulders of previous invention, inspiration and innovation.

Nothing's new; it's just a twist or development on something that's come before. We don't reinvent the wheel; we find different uses for the wheel. Being unique is putting your own stamp on an old idea. We rehash, recycle, disassemble and rebuild. We ride on the shoulders of the giants who rode out before us. When you're feeling scared, remind yourself of all that you have already achieved. Remember who has trodden these paths before you, and turn the fear into a tool for creating something new. When you are constantly searching for ways to do things better, you take your attention away from the anxiety attached to it. Look at how someone else has done something similar. Take inspiration from them and make one small step.

When all hell is breaking loose in the office because profits are nose-diving, when the boss is having a nervous breakdown, and when the coffee machine's exploded, it's time to do something differently. As the adage goes, 'do the same thing, you get the same results', so how about following Bill Gates' example and upping your 'corporate IQ', as he calls it. He gets people to swap roles and departments, and bring their own perspective to bear on traditional ways of doing things. I once saw the (former) boss of WH Smiths working the till in a high street store on a Saturday. All staff through the 'ranks' were encouraged to take their turn. When the executives feel the pain of their employees, they are likely to make changes for the better.

When I directed a documentary on Indian classical music (a 3000-year-old tradition passed down generation to generation), I learned about the value of giants inspiring learners. Nothing is written down. The disciple learns from his or her guru – it is a harsh, grinding daily practice for decades before they are ready to perform and build their own interpretation of what they have learned. Then they take the role of teacher and pass on the tradition. The essence remains unchanged but the vessel through which it passes is different. It grows and deepens through the passage of time. One significant change is that it used to be chamber music, performed in small spaces to a handful of guests. Now it is more accessible to all ages, genders, classes, ethnicities and localities. It is broadcast with large venues, microphones and electronic recordings. Western jazz musicians learn the music in India then take it home and reinterpret it into their own style. Yet another incarnation. It doesn't take away from the original but it does create something new from it. There is security in building on what's gone before, but also in the opportunity to learn, progress, be curious and make new connections inspired by old ones.

Ridley Scott pitched his film *Alien* to the film studios and, apparently, simply said: 'It's *Jaws* in a spaceship.' They got it. *Jaws* was a sensational success; but how much scarier is putting something like *Jaws* in an alien form, and then enclosing it within a vessel in space? Scott's pitch was successful because he built on an idea that had already worked but added his own twist. The film studios always have a fear of films failing. Climbing up on a successful formula is what keeps them commercial.

So we learn something and build on that learning by creating something else. Adaptability is a natural phenomenon in human nature. We make a for Plan A, build in a Plan B, and when circumstances preclude either option we intuitively conjure up a Plan C. And how do we do that? We 'remember' how similar things were done and we adapt our knowledge to the current problem. That is creativity at work. Building on what came before. It breaks the back of fear, which wants to muscle in and prevent anything new or unknown from taking place. You trick fear by saying: 'Hey, it's only slightly different from what that other gal did; it's OK fear, go back to sleep.'

The metaphor of standing on the shoulders of giants (which in Latin is: *'nanos gigantum humeris insidentes'*) expresses the meaning of 'discovering truth by building on previous discoveries'. Don't we look to our heroes and heroines to inspire us in our own endeavours? In his book *On the Shoulders of Giants*, Stephen Hawking brings together the greatest works of Copernicus, Galileo, Kepler, Newton and Einstein, showing how their pioneering discoveries changed the way we see the world.[10] Each scientist built on the theories of their predecessors to answer the questions that had long mystified humanity. This knowledge inspired Hawking's own trajectory of investigation and connection that would, in turn, lead to his theory of relativity, giving us all a slightly better understanding of the universe and our place in it.

....

'If I have seen further, it is by standing on the shoulders of giants.'
                                    – Isaac Newton, in a letter dated 1676

....

Stitch together ideas for your big dream from the achievements of those who inspire you.

Build on what you know

1. **Who are the giants in your world? Who inspires you?** What can you borrow from them, copy, emulate, translate, recreate, and adapt.

2. **Get creative, be adaptable, embrace change, build on what you know.** Make your future an exciting laboratory of pre-loved ideas transformed into extraordinary new inventions.

3. Draw a large circle. This is a round table. **Around the table sit ten people you admire or look up to, from history or present times.** People you've met, read about or seen on TV. Write their names around the table. Find pictures of them if you wish and stick them on the paper. Next to their pictures list their attributes, achievements, inventions and values. Put the picture up somewhere visible. Whenever you have a fear or dilemma, approach your 'Board of Mentors' and ask them each in turn what they would do in your place. Listen carefully as you imagine their response. You will be astonished at the answers and solutions that you come up with through this process.

⊨ CORE-WORK ⊨

- In a dual-handed dialogue between Nurturer and Little You, allow the Nurturer to encourage Little You to reveal fifty achievements you have made in your life so far

- When you have done that, list fifty more! This makes you dig deeper than school grades, your first job, promotion or winning the egg and spoon race. This process takes you to the smaller, more meaningful achievements. It might be that you helped an

old lady across the road, or said 'hello' to the bus driver this
morning, or thanked your best friend for being there

- Let your Nurturer nourish your Little You by reminding you of all
those little moments that give your life meaning. Fear slips and
slides on a bedrock of life's little powerhouses of achievements.
These are the foundation stones for a fearless future. You've
done it before; you can do it again. One step at a time you can
conquer a mountain

Now go back to your vision board or your art journal – can you see
your big dream taking shape? Can you add more images and inspirational captions? Keep this creative practice going and take notes of
the ideas that they conjure up in your mind. Let your possibilities
have a field day.

Let your non-dominant hand fill in the gaps:

My big dream No. 1 is ....
My big dream No. 2 is ....
My big dream No. 3 is ....

How Can You Get There?

Goal Setting

Go for Goals

So you've created your imaginary vision for the future fuelled by
your daydreams. Now you mark out your goals. Fear quivers and
its grip loosens when your creative energies are harnessed to a goal.
This is the accepted wisdom among worldly wizened self-development gurus. And yet before we look at how to create your goals and

define the steps you will take towards them, it's important to look at when goal-setting *doesn't* work.

Most of us achieve things by working out what we want. Say you decide you want to buy a house. You might decide all the required steps: look at house-selling websites, pick some out, go see them, bid for one, get the money to buy it, and then move in. Job done. Goal ticked off the list.

But, it can be argued, when you lay your cards out with an A–Z logic, your destination is a given, and you lose out on all the opportunities that letting your imagination run wild gives you. The 'I want to buy a house' goal may focus you on houses for sale in the vicinity you want to live in and preclude dreaming up other possibilities. For instance, the off-chance of someone approaching you with an alternative offer: 'I have a castle in the South of France and need a house-sitter for the next ten years. Fancy it? There's heated outdoor pool and as much wine as you want'. Imagine you'd just hoiked yourself up to a mammoth mortgage on the house in Croydon!

Could goals even be harmful?[11]

Well, in some cases the pressure to set and hit challenging goals distorts people's behaviour with seriously harmful effects on others. Look at the banking system; it is full of over-strivers who are over-stretching to achieve high-end targets. The system promoted unethical behaviour, and caused cataclysmic disaster for the world economy. The problem seems to be the narrow, myopic focus on specific short-term goals. It stops the mind becoming open to wider long-term possibilities and, indeed, consequences.

Creative coaching encourages people to set goals differently. It identifies your core values first, e.g. be adventurous, loving, compassionate, playful, trustworthy, peace-loving, a team player, funny, creative, thoughtful, courageous or a daredevil. That is the starting point for everything. The goals aren't narrow, myopic or incentivised. They are clear, but they are also open, have wide horizons and encourage you to be adaptable.

Ask yourself 'why' you want something. Take my son Sol, for instance. In the flush of youth and exuberance his initial answer to 'why' he wants to create a business is that he wants to work for himself. But 'why' does he want to do that? Because he values freedom and autonomy. But 'why' does he want that? Because he wants to create his own destiny; one where he can give talks about being a successful young entrepreneur. One where he can help inspire others to take their futures into their own hands. When you are creating a goal keep asking yourself 'why' until you drill down into the core values and meaning of what you are setting out to do. It helps you understand why that goal really matters to you, and it will keep you motivated as you work towards it.

Even powered by your meaningful motivation, there will be times when the going gets tough and it feels like a slog. Have someone you can feedback to on your progress on a regular basis. It keeps you feeling inspired. Stops you falling off the wagon.

And remember that failure is almost inevitable, and therefore we must prepare for it. Just as you use your creative mind to dream up the goal, you can also use your imagination to anticipate the pit-falls. You can plan for them. If you are trying to get healthy and you know that you are going to be out and about and might be tempted to pick up a chocolate bar or packet of crisps to keep you going, prepare a light, healthy snack to bring with you. Psychologists call this an if/then contingency plan, or 'if this happens, then I'll do that'.[12] When you take ownership of your goal it becomes part of your identity. You are more able to put in place strategies that allow you to be on the lookout for hazards and potential face-plants. Identify the blockers. They might be ones you create yourself, or they might be the well-meant suggestions from a loved one, or they might be the pre-emptive strikes from competitors. You know they're likely to happen so map out your defensive strategy for the path ahead.

Imagine goal-setting as a game of chess, use your creative mind to inspire you, prepare you and champion you. Any help you can get along the way makes all the difference. You will have to be nim-ble on your feet, be adaptable and agile. It will be a rough ride, but with persistence, tenacity and vision you will be well on the road to creating the life you want to live.

But before you set your goals, we're going to look at values.

Values

To create goals that have meaning for you and keep you motivated and on track you need to understand and identify what your core values are. Often your belly knows before your brain. Use your gut as a guide and you won't be far off your values.

Client Sa describes what she has learned from coaching around her values:

- My biggest lessons have been to stick up for myself and not be afraid to say no to things I don't want to do, but to say so with kindness and love
- I have built a barbed-wire fence between myself and others when it comes to protecting the inner child in me. This image helps me to stick up for myself and get what falls in line with my values
- I have learned that I can't control others, just myself and my emotional, spiritual state. Taking responsibility for my own success and happiness is a great feeling
- I feel stronger as a person and able to look at my wheel and feel comfortable that I am taking baby steps to accomplish my life goals in work, home, relationships, money, spirituality, health etc. Every day, I work towards them and one day I will reach them and I'll enjoy myself along the way
- I have learned to think about my values and what is really important to me. I find similar minded people to collaborate with at work, in partnerships and friendships
- I have learned to stay positive, turn negatives into positives, embed them into my brain by repetition (reading them time and time again), letting go of the negative thoughts and anger by writing them down and tearing up the piece of paper
- I have learned that if you are glowing, the world will glow back at you . . . so no matter how hard it is to glow sometimes, I have the tools I need to help me do that
- Three values and a sentence that encapsulates how I feel: I use my **knowledge, wisdom and passion** for storytelling to tell stories that represent humankind and our ability to triumph over adversity

When we think of our big dreams, and the goals we decide to set around them, our values help us keep on track. We are steered and driven by them. When you face dilemmas in your life, you can refer to your values and they will point to the way ahead. They influence your mission and purpose in life. They underscore everything. They help you overcome fear.

So what are your core values?

Abundance	Creativity	Frivolity
Acceptance	Colourful	Family
Accomplishment	Certainty	Fearlessness
Achievement	Comfort	Friendship
Acknowledgement	Change	Generosity
Adaptability	Cheerfulness	Genuine
Adventure	Continuity	Growth
Affection	Commitment	Gratitude
Ambition	Communication	Happiness
Approval	Competency	Health
Artistic	Competitiveness	Heritage
Aesthetic	Comradeship	Honesty
Awesomeness	Confidence	Helpfulness
Balance	Contribution	Heartfelt
Beauty	Decisiveness	Humanity
Being admired	Desire	Human rights
Being alone	Dexterity	Humour
Being honourable	Duty	Independence
Being different	Determination	Integrity
Being the Best	Elegance	Intelligence
Being with others	Enthusiasm	Intellect
Bravery	Excitement	Intuition
Boldness	Energy	Investment
Belonging	Equality	Intimacy
Calm	Faithfulness	Imagination
Curiosity	Focused	Inspire
Courage	Fun	Justice
Compassion	Freedom	Kindness

Kinship	Opportunistic	Sensuality
Leadership	Order	Sexual
Learning	Optimism	Space
Legacy	Positivity	Spontaneity
Love	Passion	Supportive
Loving	Purposeful	Stability
Mastery	Preciousness	Status
Making	Power	Success
Mystery	Productivity	Tranquility
Magic	Protection	Tenacity
Making a difference	Peace	Transparency
Meeting of minds	Risk-taking	Travel
Meeting challenges	Reliability	Time
Morality	Respect	Unconditional
Nature	Rebelliousness	Warmth
Natural	Romance	Wellness
Niceness	Role model	Wellbeing
Openness	Security	Welfare (animal/
Outstanding	Safety	human)
Organised	Self-awareness	

This is not an exhaustive list. Can you think of any other values that are important to you?

- Circle your top fifteen
- Then your top three
- Then create a mission statement using those three values
- This is your **purpose**, and it gives **meaning** to everything you are aiming to achieve

*(Mine is: Use **creativity** to help bring **positive** change and **wellbeing** in the world)*

Here are some other examples, but let your Little You play with different values and mission statements. It's harder than you might think, so take your time and try out lots of combinations until it feels like you have the right fit for your life right now. When you feel a warm glow, a surge of energy, a spark of excitement, a gooey feeling in your gut – then you have probably nailed it.

- Have a **simple** life surrounded by **family** and **friends**
- Be **loving, compassionate** and **kind** to all
- Bring **justice** with **respect** to the law and **human rights**
- Look out for **magnificence, elegance** and **creativity** in every corner of life
- **Take risks** so that you may **grow** and build **confidence**

When you are at a crossroads, or feeling scared and uncertain, look at your mission statement. Let it guide you. It is your foundation stone. Let its force be with you. Let it motivate you as you work to achieve your goals and big dreams.

⊨ CORE-WORK ⊨

So let's get you on that path by taking your three top fears and creating some GOALS that will elevate fear into fabulousness.

Here is a core-work example to get you started on exploring what your goals might be for your fears:

NURTURER: ***What*** *is your fear?*

LITTLE YOU: *Flying.*

NURTURER: ***Why*** *do you want to overcome it? What are your* ***values?***

LITTLE YOU: *My big dream for transforming my fear into a magical life is to travel the world so that I can help other people fear less.*

NURTURER: *So **how** can you turn that into a concrete goal?*

LITTLE YOU: *To be able to fly and not feel so scared, even during bad turbulence.*

Nurturer: *OK, good goal. Now let's break that down into manageable steps. When would you like to achieve this by?*

LITTLE YOU: *I am flying to America in May. I have three flights to do, 6 hours, 5 hours and 11 hours. That's pretty scary for me.*

NURTURER: *Remind me why you are putting yourself through that?*

LITTLE YOU: *Because I am going to be promoting my book and doing workshops on fearlessness.*

NURTURER: *Name three of your values that this goal will meet.*

LITTLE YOU: *Creativity, helping people, travelling.*

NURTURER: *So that really fits in with your big dream? You really have a gut feeling for wanting to do this?*

LITTLE YOU: *More than anything.*

NURTURER: *Great, then they are true values, which you need to know – because without that, your fear may take over and stop you achieving your goal. Next we are going to create a Golden Staircase for you of five smaller steps because otherwise the challenge will seem huge and insurmountable.*

The Fifth Step is the Ultimate Goal: In May, take three flights and not feel so scared even if there is bad turbulence. Arrive in America ready to change lives.

The four steps leading to that are:

1st Step: Buy the tickets.

2nd Step: Create a vision board of what flying gives you in your life and how it can transform the lives of others.

3rd Step: Practise your calming strategies in different situations that make you nervous. Deep breathing, tummy massage (with your fingertips gently press, squeeze and release), power pose, doodling or listening to a meditation CD before going to sleep.

4th Step: As the plane takes off, start counting from zero to sixty. Repeat ten times. After this time has elapsed you should be up in the air and through the bumpy take-off. Next, do something that occupies you, uses movement, and puts you in the 'flow' (perhaps doodling). Once you are through your take-off procedure you can relax and enjoy the flight, watch movies, read or sleep. If it gets bumpy, implement your calming strategies once again. Repeat as necessary until you have completed the flight.

NURTURER: *How does that feel?*

LITTLE YOU: *I feel like I can manage each step, and then it's not such a big leap when I get to the final big step.*

NURTURER: *Great! This week go and do that first step and book the tickets.*

LITTLE YOU: *OK, I will. Thank you.*

NURTURER: *That's what I'm here for* ☺

LITTLE YOU: ☺

Build your Goal Golden Staircase

1. Read the section on values. Choose corresponding values for each of your three key goals.
2. For each goal (choose these from your Big Vision) draw a set of five steps.
3. Place the goal and values at the top of the staircase.

4. On each step, working upwards, write down a broad milestone you need to achieve to get you to your goal.
5. Break each milestone into smaller tasks.
6. Now that you've put your Big Vision out there, you need to work slowly on each step and task that will help you achieve your goals. Have a five-year plan, a one-year plan, a monthly plan, a weekly plan and a daily list of tasks. None of these should be too big or heinous. They must be manageable, time-dependent, achievable and specific.
7. Remember to acknowledge and reward your achievements as you tick off your tasks and milestones. It's vital to enjoy the ride!

Rewards

At every step – give yourself a reward. It may link to your other goals too.

For example, one of my other goals was to get past my fears around my repeated knee injuries, and to run further and faster in wonderful locations and landscapes around the world.

Because I managed to get past my fear of flying, I got to San Francisco and my reward was to run along the coastal road in Carmel. It was a dream come true! What's more, I got to run across the Golden Gate Bridge. A dream I hadn't even thought of.

I put the same strategies in place when my partner suggested we go on a whale watching expedition out at sea in the marine sanctuary at Monterey. My fear of boats, open water, sharks, and drowning came out in full force; my mind re-running the movies *Open Water* and *Jaws* in full technicolour and gory detail. (As you will see through the book I have a whole plethora of fears, so I'm really glad these coaching tools work).

So I set up a short term goal:

- What: Go see whales
- Why: Because I want to fill life with adventure (one of my values)
- How: Go on a boat trip
- Step 1. Say yes (and worry about it later)
- Step 2. Buy tickets (and worry about it later)
- Step 3. Prepare for the trip with warm things and by practising calming techniques
- Step 4. Watch the horizon, stay on deck, breathe slowly and visualise success
- Step 5. Watch the whales and enjoy the experience

I did all this and my reward was to see fifteen killer whales being charged by a humpback whale, and then later a blue whale (the biggest mammal ever known to have lived) who came to say 'hello'. If I had let my fears rule, I would have missed this incredible experience. In setting this goal, I knew I could overcome my fear and that I would enjoy becoming a person who is brave enough to go out to sea to watch whales in their own habitat. When you think of your big dream and set the goals to get there, you will know it is aligned with your values when the **process** of working towards your goals makes you feel good about who you are becoming.

End of Week One

⊨ CORE-WORK ⊨

Answer these Nurturer questions with your non-dominant hand:

- What tools have you learned this week?
- What action steps have you taken?
- How are you feeling about your fears right now?
- How can I support you this week?

Give yourself a big well-done for: creating your FEAR wheel, day-dreaming and dreaming big with your vision board, creating goals that reflect your values, identifying the action steps you will need to take to make your goals happen and ultimately make your big dreams come true.

⊨

Week Two

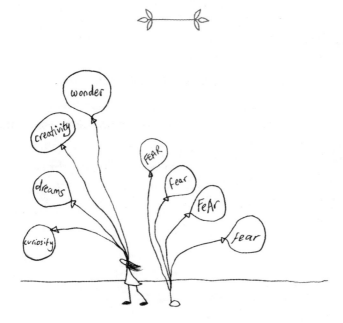

WHAT'S HOLDING YOU BACK

- YOUR OWN WORST ENEMY: Meeting your Needs, Breaking Bad Beliefs, Unhealthy Habits
- WHAT'S HOLDING YOU BACK: Imposter Syndrome, Procrastination, Self-sabotage
- STICK TO YOUR OWN LANE: People Pleasing, Compare and Despair, No to Naysayers

So you're all excited about your big dreams and you're progressing through the mini-steps to your goals. But then, inevitably, life gets in the way. So let's look at all the ways you or others will try to put the kibosh on your plans, and how you can learn to tilt them back into a helpful forwardly direction.

Let's imagine a ship's rudder. It's huge. To turn it on its own would take impossible force. Instead, built into the giant rudder are smaller ones. When the captain of the ship turns these small 'trim tabs', the tiny movements are enough to shift the oppositional force of the water. This allows the huge metal mass of the enormous rudder to move, and the ship changes course. When we turn bad beliefs, needs and habits into healthy ones, they act as the trim tabs for transforming our big fears. It was architect, inventor and philosopher Buckminster Fuller (1895–1983) who first articulated the metaphorical power of the trim tab concept for transforming our lives and making a positive difference in the lives of others.[13]

In week two you are building trim tabs into your overall goals and visions. In this section your Nurturing Self is going to be working overtime in your core-work through this! Not everything here will be relevant to you right now but read it all and do the core-work exercise for the areas that ring some bells for you.

Your Own Worst Enemy

- Meeting your Needs
- Breaking Bad Beliefs
- Unhealthy Habits

Meeting your Needs

There are people who come for coaching who seem to have everything; money, career, family, children, beautiful homes, fast cars, exotic holidays, fat pensions and all the 'stuff' you can fill your life with. But, they say that something's missing; they feel like they are searching and not finding that 'thing' that will make them happy. They are filled with unnamed dread and anxiety; an emptiness that no amount of worldly possessions and 'success' can make up for.

Of course, I also get people coming to me whose lower-level needs aren't being met either: money, relationship strife and struggling to meet basic needs.

We can divide needs into three areas:

Body: Physiological, safety, security, and certainty
Mind: Love and connection, variety, significance or esteem, and growth
Spiritual: Meaning, purpose and contribution

Our needs also fall on the 'two sides' of our brain. It's not quite as simplistic as this, but it's a useful metaphorical aid:

Left: Logical, analytical, intellectual, linguistic, methodical,
linear, sequential and concerned with detailed thinking

Right: Creative, intuitive, instinctive, holistic, non-linguistic,
emotional and concerned with abstract thinking

We bounce between the two when we are problem-solving
and fear-busting. To meet our needs, we need to answer the call
from our minds, bodies and souls, but we also need to develop
both the capacities of our left and right mindsets as a collaborating
force.

For example, when I write first thing in the morning it feels like
the words come from someplace else, like I'm not in charge of what
I write; that something beyond me has taken control. It feels effort-
less, spontaneous and intuitive. Like it taps into deeper reserves
that I am not conscious of. Many artists of all disciplines report this
phenomenon. But everyone has a time of day when they are most
productive. Are you an early bird or a night owl? When do you feel
most energised? When do you feel your work flow out of you? To
get into this state, and tap into its resources, you need to know what
enhances the effect. Do you love to work in the rough and tumble
of an office, or at the back of a café? Do you have your best ideas
after a pint or in the shower? For me it's the early morning, when it's
dark and silent, with no distractions, with a sense of solitude; almost
monastic in atmosphere. It bypasses my fear of being able to create.
I know I *need* that atmosphere to write.

But then, when I come to edit my morning writings, I use my
conscious, rational, intellectual brain to reflect and check the work
is making sense, informed, directional etc. I *need* this 'left' mind
process to work with my 'right' creative brain system to ensure my
work is original and ordered. Interestingly, I can tap into my 'left'
brain process any time of the day and almost anywhere, although I
still need a relatively quiet place to work. Knowing what I need to

work reduces the possibility of writer's block (which is essentially fear and ego in a pact to prevent progress). The simple act of showing up, in the right place at the right time, greases the wheels and off we go.

We must learn to balance all of our needs. Too much certainty and order and we get bored. Too much variety and spontaneity and we feel overwhelmed. Become too successful (Significance) and we may become isolated. Too much growth and we leave behind friends and family. Too much contribution to others and we may forget about ourselves. If we live too much in our creative heads we might dream big but not get things done. If we live life as number crunchers we may feel we are missing a sense of spontaneity and magic.

Fear arises when we suspect our needs may not be met. It arises when silent needs take on new degrees of significance at different points in our lives.

For example, if you don't have a partner then your needs for intimacy, touch and a loving connection may become an issue. You may fear that you will never find 'The One'. Those unmet needs start to scratch away at the back of your head. You notice every 'happy' couple in the street, you always feel like the spare rib at a dinner party. You may panic and dive into the wrong relationship, where a whole other set of needs may not be met. Instead, try to look holistically at the situation. How can you balance out the needs? Can all your needs really be met by one other person? Can you spread the load a bit? Can you stop turning your expectation of others to meet your needs, back onto yourself?

List your top ten needs in order of importance to you at
this time:

1. ....

2. ....

3. ....

4. ....

5. ....

6. ....

7. ....

8. ....

9. ....

10. ....

**Now write down your fears around those needs not
being met.**

Draw Little You in a circle. Fill the circle with your needs.
How can you get them met/meet them? Use your core-work
to ask your Nurturer to help you meet your needs.

⊨ CORE-WORK ⊨

NURTURER: *Tell me the needs that you feel aren't being met.*

LITTLE YOU: ....

NURTURER: *If I could meet those needs for you, how would you
feel?*

LITTLE YOU: ....

NURTURER: *Let's imagine that there is only me and you who have
the powers to meet those needs. Let's work through them one*

by one and create a plan of action on how we can meet those needs and help you to feel soothed.

Continue the dialogue until you feel like you have found a way forward in combating your fears around those important needs in your life. Be creative, try out ideas, think left field, think of something and then try out the opposite, ask others. Or simply take time out, empty your mind for twenty minutes, listen to the sounds in the room, then with three deep, abdominal breaths come back to your dialogue writing.

Breaking Bad Beliefs

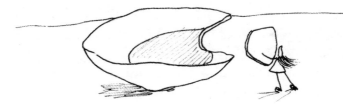

You've got your goals, you've worked out your strategy to achieve them, you're on an adrenalin rush as you start the climb. You've worked out how to meet your unmet needs. You think you've cracked this Hairy Scary Fear Thing. This is it, you think, the world is your oyster and you're coming to get it. And then you get a stone in your shoe, you get tired and thirsty, you wonder whether the climb is worth the end view, your brain starts nit-picking and your well-intentioned belief system starts to unravel. Because when the going gets tough, from the deepest, darkest part of your mind, the Queen of Anxiety unleashes her sharp-toothed bad beliefs and they leap out like cantankerous trolls to snap at your heels. Boy, does fear get into the cracks.

You create a tapestry of beliefs in your life, some that help and some that hinder. You build them on the back of childhood experiences, learned behaviours, difficult setbacks, and proven successes. However, it turns out, you have much more control over what you believe than you give yourself credit for. And when you do pull rank on your cranky, fear-inducing belief systems, you find that you can create a much happier way of living. Imagine living in a mud hut with a wooden bed, a straw mattress, a few tin pots and pans, a couple of chickens and some vegetables growing on a small plot out back. To some this would be a meagre existence.

To the son of my friend this is heaven. He moved to Cambodia from Chiswick and chose to live in a small village and work for a charity helping local kids. He's a musician, and so, living on his wits and a vegan diet, he helped revamp a recording studio and taught the kids to play music or to produce sound. Through his beliefs, and his actions, he enforces the power of music to lift youngsters beyond basic existence into something more meaningful. Those kids now believe in themselves and their ability to sing, play and make music. His own physical needs are just about met, but beyond that his beliefs are his currency; the idea that music can make a positive difference. He took his skills, his imagination, his emotional empathy and belief system and became an inspirer and role model to others. He sees that mud hut as a means to an end.

'There is nothing either good or bad but thinking makes it so.'

– William Shakespeare

....

Coaching Challenge

1. Test your beliefs for truth. If you think you can't do something, then think about when you have achieved something against all the odds.

2. Take a bad belief and set about disproving it for thirty days of alternative action. Turn 'I can't draw' into doodling for ten minutes every day for thirty days. Make a note of what shifts for you as you settle into the task and keep going through the challenge. How has your belief changed? How has your concept of what 'drawing' is, altered?

3. Where else in your life can you break down bad beliefs and start rebuilding them as positive perceptions?

4. You are what you believe yourself to be. Want that goal to happen? Then make sure your building block beliefs are in place for solid foundations, leaving no room for the bashing ball of fear to tear it all down.

5. List fifty Positive Beliefs you have about yourself. Start small if you need to. I can breathe unaided. I can walk to the shops without stopping. I can pay my mortgage. I am a good friend. I am kind to animals. I eat five fruit and veg a day so I am getting healthier.

....

⊱═ CORE-WORK ═⊰

Draw three columns. In the right column, with your non-dominant hand write down all the bad beliefs you have about yourself, as your Inner Critic. In the left column, flip those beliefs to the opposite, as the Nurturer, then repeat as Little You in middle column:

INNER CRITIC: *I am rubbish at completing tasks.*
NURTURER: *You complete tasks when you choose to.*
LITTLE YOU: *I complete tasks when I choose to.*

⊨———⊏

Unhealthy Habits

Having bad beliefs is an unhealthy habit that you can learn to break by working through the previous exercises. You can equally transform all unhealthy habits into ones that serve you better.

Fear holds you hostage behind your unhealthy habits. Your ability to forge ahead becomes gridlocked in a mire of comfort blankets that you use to smother the flames of your fears. Sugar, carbs, alcohol, fags, lateness, forgetfulness, food, late nights, avoiding fitness, over-working are all ingredients for your self-medicating broth of avoiding what scares you. You know that if you take away your cover-up, you might actually succeed at work, with relationships, with getting fit, and that scares the bejeezus out of you. Because how can you possibly keep up 'success'?

Fear fuels your unhealthy habits – unless you get creative and learn to trick your brain. Even if, let's say, your fears have arisen because of a scary health diagnosis. You have a choice: turn your face to the wall and put your body entirely in the hands of the doctors. Or create some habits that will help you emotionally, and physically, direct your health journey upwards. Do you choose **fear** of pain or dying, or do you **focus** on living well? By putting yourself in control with healthy habits you can control your fears.

The good news is that it only takes thirty days to form or break a habit. Coaching is based on the fact that the brain is plastic and malleable (for the science read *The Plastic Mind* by Sharon Begley[14]). You are not stuck with rigid regimes and diehard habits. If you want to add something to your life (like running, going vegan or learning to draw) you need to commit to doing it for thirty days so that your brain will have neatly formed this into a habit. You no longer have to force yourself to do it, because you've built yourself an auto-pilot. The same is true if you want to rid your life of something. If you want to give up sugar, lower the amount of refined carbs you eat, stop procrastinating, or drink less alcohol, you must commit for thirty days and after that it becomes easy. It becomes part of the rhythm of your day.

As humans we are programmed to seek pleasure (such as seeking food and sex), avoid pain and conserve energy.[15] Our habits are formed around, and motivated by, behaviours that stick to one or another of these. Feelings arise from thoughts, which then compel behaviour. So when we are trying to change our behaviour or habits – we have genes, instincts, thoughts and feelings to coral into the mix! No wonder it's so hard to quit smoking, eating chocolate or start making art if you grew up being told to be a lawyer. But you create a vision of this Brave New You – a happy, healthy, living-the-dream vision, and you launch into your thirty-day challenge.

I woke up on 1 January and decided I'd had enough of migraines (pain avoidance) so I gave up alcohol in the hope that that was the trigger. It wasn't the wine that was hard to give up (even after living a Mediterranean lifestyle of drinking a couple of glasses every night), it was the idea of myself, sitting with mates, drinking, having a fun night out that was hard to let go of. How could drinking not be part of having a good time? I needed to change that picture. I had to create an image of me feeling great all the time, not just for an hour or so after downing a Shiraz or two. I had to paint a picture of a happy me who could get-off on life, not just on alcohol, and also be (hopefully) migraine-free. I had to enjoy the process of becoming this Brave New Me by evoking life-affirming self-talk and self-nurturing.

Not easy. But the dual-handed, dialoguing core-work came into full effect! Luckily for me, 5 million other people in the UK were doing Dry January, so I felt like I wasn't on my own with this challenge.

When you start a new habit, you get a sense of euphoria and excitement. You can visualise the big dream, it feels tantalisingly within reach, your adrenalin is pumping. This lasts a little while, until your brain gets used to the sensation. You calm down a bit. And you get down to work. And that's when the next phase kicks in. You get the realisation that it's going to take a lot of hard work, for a long time, to get to your dream. And then you get the dip. For me it was something along the lines of this:

LITTLE LOU: *I'm still having migraines, I haven't lost an ounce of weight, I don't have any more energy. What the hell am I doing this for?*

NURTURER: *Have you had any hangovers on top of your migraines?*

LITTLE LOU: *(whiney voice) No.*

NURTURER: *So if I suggested you started drinking again, how would that be to have hangovers and migraines again.*

LITTLE LOU: *Pretty crap.*

NURTURER: *So shall we keep going with the No Alcohol for a while, until we find the real cause of your migraines? Then we can cure those and you can go back to just having hangovers? How does that sound?*

LITTLE LOU: *I like the sound of that.*

NURTURER: *Good. Well you keep off the booze and I'll get on with that migraine research. Deal?*

LITTLE LOU: *Deal.*

NURTURER: *And in the meantime, as a reward with every non-alcoholic drink you choose to have I'll give you a big self-loved up hug.*

LITTLE LOU: *Thank you!* ☺

You will need to harness willpower, and to do that you will need to pre-empt obstacles by deciding how you are going to react to them. For example, let's say you know that you need to exercise but you really can't be bothered. So you have to trick your brain with a reward. Start by putting out a 'trigger', such as placing your trainers by your bed so they are the first things you see when you wake up. Then promise yourself a reward (perhaps a crumpet). Your brain pleasure spikes when you get the crumpet, so seeing the trainers also spikes your brain because it remembers 'trainers = crumpet'. You start to form the habit of running when you see your trainers and gradually your brain starts to twig that the best reward happens before the crumpet; running triggers a rise in endorphins, so the pleasure feeling is met and the crumpet is dropped. And you have successfully created a healthy habit with built-in willpower.

My partner used this technique when he first started running a year ago. To inspire him to get up and do the 10K route near us he would promise himself a crumpet at the end of it. It became known as the Crumpet Run. Eventually the crumpets were replaced with healthy smoothies and a year later he completed the London Marathon in 4 hours 15 minutes, having raised £3500 for Amnesty International.

If you attach a good habit to another good habit in what we call a Habit Tower, you are even more likely to succeed. Think of it as that stonecutter discussed earlier in the book would. Every stone helps build the cathedral; and every healthy habit helps build a less fearful you. You always do your teeth, so add your run to your teeth cleaning routine and follow it with a healthy breakfast. Add to that reading ten pages of a self-development book, followed by your daily brain dump. You are beginning to sculpt your day into all the habits that make you feel good, creative and in control. Your willpower becomes stronger the more you build up a framework of chosen activities. You lose control as your willpower slips and slides across your life when you have no structure. When I return from holiday, I always feel a sense of anxiety; my routine is shot to pieces and fear has muscled in. As soon as I get back to my daily structure (left brain) of healthy habits, my fears subside and I can enjoy being home again and getting back to work and being creative (right brain).

How then do you change a bad habit? By imagining your triggers/cue, activities and rewards.[16] You imagine in advance that at 6 p.m. instead of ordering a glass of wine with your friends you are going to order a non-alcoholic beer (be specific in your alternative trigger picture). Then, as an imagined reward for having a non-alcoholic beer instead of wine, you promise yourself something that will stimulate a pleasure feeling (such as not having a hangover and enjoying more energy). You imagine or create in your mind a positive outcome or reward.

Trying to lose weight, but fear no diet is ever going to work? Build in the six key healthy habits:

- Eat healthy, whole (unprocessed) and mainly plant-based food
- Avoid all sugars. Reduce carbs, but don't replace with high levels of protein. Do have lots of healthy fats
- Exercise five times a week, minimum
- Don't smoke, and drink only in moderation
- Avoid unnecessary stresses. Build in anti-stress strategies as outlined in this book
- Notice and appreciate the good times

A trigger or cue could be when you go to the shops and see the fruit and veg section. You imagine ahead of time that you are going to buy only healthy, whole, unprocessed and plant-based food. Then imagine that when you get home and put those items in the cupboard or fridge that you reward yourself by writing all the good feelings you have felt in honouring yourself and your body. Next, you go do it all for real. The rehearsal in your mind will help your willpower when you go to the shops. Every time you do something good for your body, acknowledge that action in your core-work journal.

> NURTURER: *You bought some great food today, how does that make you feel?*
> LITTLE YOU: *It makes me feel that I am being nice to myself.*
> NURTURER: *How did you reward yourself for that good work?*
> LITTLE YOU: *I made myself some healthy power balls to have after my run.*
> NURTURER: *Fantastic. I am very proud of you.*
> LITTLE YOU: *Thank you* ☺

According to Buddhist practitioner, Matthew Riccard, happiness is a sense of wellbeing; a deep-centred feeling of serenity and fulfilment, even when times are tough. It is like the ocean, where storms may beat the surface, but below, at the sea bed, the battering waves cause not even a ripple. You can choose to feel good by taking affirmative action in building healthy habits. Or you can choose to suffer by holding onto your unhealthy habits. The choice is yours. Knowing it is a choice is enough to create a gap between your feelings, thoughts and subsequent behaviour. It takes time to unfold new habitual thinking but the brain is plastic, not fixed, and so with repetition of a new mindset, the ability to lessen the feeling of suffering, and increase the sensations of wellbeing, becomes increasingly possible.

You can fill your well-spring with daily healthy habits so that you can determine the utmost quality of your life.

....

Re-configure your habits into healthy ones.

1. Start with one simple habit: teeth cleaning. Attach another slightly trickier habit to it, e.g. a morning walk. Build up your Habit Tower.

2. Use the replicable process of willpower, which is trigger, activity and reward. Keep your healthy habits more interesting and rewarding than your unhealthy ones.

....

⊨ CORE-WORK ⊨

Take a healthy habit you would like to form.

NURTURER: *What is the **trigger**?*
LITTLE YOU: ....
NURTURER: *What is the **activity**?*
LITTLE YOU: ....
NURTURER: *What is the **reward**?*
LITTLE YOU: ....
NURTURER: *How will you feel when you have succeeded in creating this new healthy habit?*
LITTLE YOU: ....
NURTURER: *What will it mean for you life to have this healthy habit in action?*
LITTLE YOU: ....
NURTURER: *What do you need from me to help you keep building this habit over the next thirty days?*
LITTLE YOU: ....
NURTURER: *Shall we check in every day after you have achieved the daily habit?*
LITTLE YOU: ....
NURTURER: *I promise to keep you accountable, to support you and reward you for every day that you keep up the healthy habit.*
LITTLE YOU: ....

⊨⊨

What's Holding You Back?

- Imposter Syndrome
- Procrastination
- Self-sabotage

Best laid plans and all that . . . but fear can be a cunning devil. It has some wicked little helpers to ensure that, try as you might with your big dreams – taking the steps towards your goals, meeting your own needs, creating positive beliefs and building healthy habits – you will encounter some spike-sided, crocodile infested traps to stop you fearing less in your endeavours. Without rigour and directed action, dreams can turn to nightmares.

Let's look at the possible culprits. You may recognise just a few elements, or you might recognise them all. When you understand how and why they exert their force on you (from within), you can start to peel back the fingers of their grip around your thoughts and actions (or lack of). Do your core-work around what resonates for you. Your Nurturer will have to be really nurturing, but may also have to do a bit of gentle pushing, nudging, chipping. You don't get to the fleshy, tasty part of the coconut without cracking the shell . . .

Imposter Syndrome

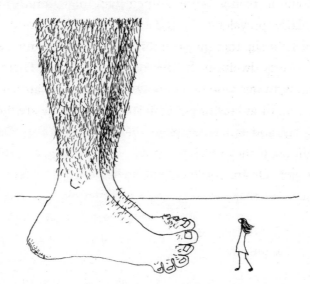

Stress on hyper-drive, modern life is like speeding down the fast lane with no brakes. You are driving towards the cliff of perfection in a helpless attempt to sate the lurking demon within. The devil voice that whispers 'You are not good enough'. You think that everyone will realise that, while it seems that you know what you're doing, you don't. You may pull off the end of month accounts, but in reality you are a number dyslexic with not a maths qualification to your name. You may look like you can string a sentence together, and have several novels under your belt, but soon enough your readers will catch on and they'll never buy another book by you again. Apparently even Meryl Streep believes that after every job she'll never get offered another part. Meryl Streep! The Imposter Syndrome is alive and kicking and it is fear of being found out that keeps you small inside. You've managed to con everyone so far but you believe that it won't be long before you are ousted as a fraudster.[17]

Many of us suffer from feeling like a fraud, no matter how well we are doing in reality. More women than men admit to it and it is particularly prevalent in high-achievers and minority groups. Extraverts let it slip that they feel this way and so get more support, while introverts dwell on the demon in their head. There are the bright young things who don't apply themselves because it's better to be thought of as lazy rather than stupid, and there are those who procrastinate and don't complete things because they think that they might fail if they reach the end.

Is that you? Or are you hell-bent on achieving success but reject compliments or make excuses and explain away your success; you just got lucky this time. You are unable to celebrate your achievements. It's more likely to feel like a relief that, once again, you have just about pulled off the masquerade. There is always a residing feeling that it will be the next test that catches you out and pulls away the mask to reveal the despicable fraud you really are. You ride on the wave of anxiety as you beat your way to the door of each challenge – putting in blood, sweat and tears to ensure you nail it. The overriding fear is that you won't, and you'll get thrown to the wolves for all the charade. The pattern repeats over and over with the sound of the snapping and howling of wild dogs always just within earshot.

If you are an imposterite, you recoil in horror at the idea of getting found out for being a failure, and so you find ways to self-sabotage in creative and resourceful ways. You show up late for important meetings, you don't ask for the pay level you know you are worth, you downsize your job to a role that is well below your capabilities, you bail out of a relationship before you've given it a chance. Critically, you don't ask questions, you don't volunteer ideas, you push your creative capabilities into the background. You are constantly on the lookout for external validation and, when you don't get it, you beat yourself up and see it as proof that you are the world's biggest loser. You feel shame and you feel alone, but you're not. It's normal, but it's not necessary.

The problem is that the world shows you the shiny happy, super rich, super bright and super successful, as the way life should permanently be. Facebook friends share their holiday snaps in exotic places, selfies on a good day, their latest triumphs and woohoo moments. It makes you feel inadequate and miserable. But the truth is that life's not a year-round holiday, party, bright-skin, swingy-hair, wrinkle-free experience. There is no point at staring at your Facebook friends' profiles and crumpling behind the pretence of your own projected perfection. Yes, capture and share the good moments. But let's not harbour the belief that it's meant to be like that all the time. It's not for you, me or for anybody else.

The lack of ability to recognise or internalise one's own abilities and achievements is shared by some of the most brilliant and successful people. Albert Einstein said of himself towards the end of his life: 'The exaggerated esteem in which my lifework is held makes me very ill at ease. I feel compelled to think of myself as an involuntary swindler.'

Feeling fraudulent, undeserving and guilty fuels fear of getting found out.

The key to pulling the rug out from under the Imposter, is being open to failure, growth and learning. Confidence increases when you embrace failure as part of your development, acknowledging that there will always be ups and downs on the learning curve.

When you use your creative mind, you can always find ways to pick yourself up and carry on. You can imagine success and take the leap. You can be resourceful and find solutions to the problems that arise without taking them personally or beating yourself up about them. You can creatively reframe failure and concentrate your effort on growth. You can give yourself realistic and achievable expectations, and you can normalise your fearful imposter feelings and self-doubt. You need to know that you can be vulnerable and no matter how scary it is, just keep keeping on.

Challenge your Imposter

Create a 'This is Your Wonderful Life' scrapbook. In this book you write down everything you have ever achieved. Not just the awards and trophies but the small things you have done that have made a difference to your life or the lives of others. Include the praise and congratulations that people have sent you when you have completed something. Include emails where friends or loved ones tell you how much you mean to them. Be a researcher, collect all the evidence you can to prove to yourself that the good news is true, you really are a terrific person who has achieved lots, often against the odds. Include photos, cards, children's thank-you drawings. Anything and everything. This is your wonderful life in which you do your best and, often, it works out well. When it doesn't you've done things to survive and kept going. That deserves celebrating too.

⊨ CORE-WORK ⊨

One the participants in my Fear Less workshop in California told the group that she had been successful in corporate life and had left that world to become a painter. She loved it but when she had an exhibition and very little sold she decided she was simply a rubbish painter. Her Imposter told her she should get out of the art world; she had no right being there. Of course, her Imposter is wrong. She has every right to be there. She loves painting, it makes her happy; she just has to keep searching for the people who will appreciate and want to/be able to buy her work. And she has to keep painting. Self-doubt and fear comes with the territory of creating original work, but that is no reason to stop. It is a reason to bring out the Nurturer who will encourage you through the ups and downs, support you and drive you forward.

Let's imagine what the Nurturer might say to our pretend Meryl Streep's Inner Imposter

NURTURER: *What are you scared about Little Meryl?*

LITTLE MERYL: *I'm scared every time I finish a job that I won't get another one.*

NURTURER: *Has that been the case in the past?*

LITTLE MERYL: *No.*

NURTURER: *So every time you have finished a job, another job has come up at some point?*

LITTLE MERYL: *At some point, yes.*

NURTURER: *So the evidence shows a continuing pattern of work. And you have been critically acclaimed at the highest level for that work. And, even as an older actor, you still manage to keep getting interesting roles that challenge you. So what is scaring you?*

LITTLE MERYL: *That I'm not good enough.*

NURTURER: *How many Oscars, how many job offers, how much*

applause do you need before you 'get' that you are entirely enough?

LITTLE MERYL: *I don't know. I think I will always be scared of not being good enough.*

NURTURER: *It's nothing to do with the work, is it? No amount of external praise and plaudits and offers will convince you that you are good enough. How would it feel if I told you are good enough, even without all that showbiz and razzmatazz awards?*

LITTLE MERYL: *I wouldn't believe you.*

NURTURER: *Then that's what we need to work on. You feeling enough, without the say-so of outside people. Will you dialogue with me every day until you feel that?*

LITTLE MERYL: *That sounds like a lot of hard work.*

NURTURER: *It is. But here's the choice: always feel you are going to get found out for being a fraud, no matter how much the work comes rolling in. Or, always feel that you are good enough even if the work stops tomorrow.*

LITTLE MERYL: *The second one, I guess.*

NURTURER: *So, will you dialogue with me until you believe me that you are good enough?*

LITTLE MERYL: *OK, yes.*

NURTURER: *Good, see you here tomorrow, same time, same place. Hollywood can wait.*

Now respond to your Nurturer using your Little You's non-dominant hand. Keep the dialogue going until you come to a satisfactory conclusion. I'll start you off:

NURTURER: *What are you scared of getting caught out for, Little You?*

LITTLE YOU: ....

Continue . . .

Procrastination

What if our imaginary Meryl agreed on doing the dialogue daily practice with her Nurturer, but each day kept finding excuses not to do it? She knows dialoguing will silence her fears, improve her life and her self-esteem, but somehow she just can't knuckle down to it. Maybe she's scared that even if she does the dialogue work, she still won't feel good enough. Or worse, that she will uncover more bad feelings about herself. That's called procrastination. Fear of following through.

'Keeping going' is not as straightforward as it sounds. How many times have you put off doing what you need to do, promised that you will, soon, 'honest guv'. But the job slips and slides under your dilly-dallying; a tiny thing becomes a looming presence, dominating your horizon. And yet, you just can't knuckle down. And what is stopping you? Yes – it's the Big, Bad Wolf that is lurking in the woods again, wearing his favourite black leather jacket with F. E. A. R. studded across the back.

We all procrastinate, but is your Procrastometer sliding into the red and stopping you moving forward?

If ever there was proof that everyone is creative, we just have to look at the ways we manage to avoid doing things we don't want to do. We suddenly have a fascination for hoovering dust bunnies, or we create myriad reasons to justify putting off going to the gym we pay for every month. We jump hoops to leap out of the way of a looming deadline. It sometimes takes more energy to avoid something than it does to complete it. So what's going on?

People have struggled with procrastination or habitual hesitation since the time of the ancient civilisations. The Greek poet Hesiod, (I can quote him because he's been dead for ages) writing around 800 BC, cautioned not to 'put your work off till tomorrow and the day after'.

But if you get good results from getting on with things why do you procrastinate? Laziness, fear, perfectionism? Imagine that all your actions are regulated by your internal Chief Executive Officer, your brain boss who ensures you get stuff done. When you hear yourself say, 'life got in the way, the dog ate my homework, I work well in a last-minute panic', you know your inner CEO has taken a lunch break. And you fail to self-regulate when your CEO is not around.

You are the Procrastination Clerk in your CEO's absence. Which basically means you can't resist distractions and avoidance tactics, even if it means missing deadlines, dates or doctors' appointments. You don't persist in the face of difficulty, boredom or FEAR. You let your myopic desire to feel good in the short term override your long-term satisfaction. Your emotions get the better of you, you drown in clutter and you skitter through your days like a duck on ice. Fear is the only winner.

So the picture is not looking too rosy, but what to do about it?

You want an easy life, and beating procrastination takes hard work. Which is a problem. Easy versus hard. We know the likely outcome on that. So you have to nudge yourself toward doing something in simple easy steps. There is the famous nudge theory tactic (a behavioural science concept describing a non-forceful way of influencing people's behaviour), which was implemented in the men's urinals in Amsterdam airport. Men were encouraged to aim into the urinal (as opposed to everywhere else!) by an image of a housefly etched at the back of it. Without any written instructions, men starting to direct their flow to the fly and the men's toilets became much cleaner places. We need to get creative, we need to make the completion of tasks more fun, simpler and automatic than the tantalising distractions we are seduced by.

But here's the thing. There's a caveat to the evils of procrastination.

Original thinkers do things differently. They have crazy ideas and they stand up for them and speak out about them. But behind the scenes something interesting happens. They allow an idea to incubate while doing something for a period of time, something mindless like washing up or playing video games. Then when they feel the idea is bursting out of them, they take action. I recognise this principle. When I am painting I am quick to start, throwing brightly coloured acrylics all over the canvas. Then I slow right down when I come to painting the oils on top. Oil takes longer to dry so I am forced to wait, mull and marinade. I take my time and the painting slowly reveals itself. Likewise with writing; you get an idea, you write down notes, do an outline, start on the painting and splurge out the first draft. And then you slow right down. You allow the work to incubate. You go off and get fit, do chores, work on other projects. And behind the scenes you are percolating the idea, allowing it to grow, evolve, develop and mature. Original thinkers and creatives know that the work is not good as it goes through its incarnations. They understand that it takes time, effort, patience, trial and error.

'A journey of a thousand steps is taken one step at a time.'

– Buddhist proverb

The art is in recognising when you are doing some creative incubating, and when you are just putting something off because a whole host of fears is stopping you in your tracks. If it's the latter then employ simple manageable steps, dotted through the tougher milestones. Know when to let something stew and when to give it a good stir.

So back to our pretend Meryl Streep and her Nurturer. To ensure that Little Meryl shows up every day to dialogue with Mama Nurturer, it needs to be easy, it needs to be in her face, it needs to be quick and rewarding. Her dialogue journal needs to be in a visible place, near where she sits for a cup of coffee. A pen must be attached to it. Let's give it a shot:

NURTURER: *How are you today?*

LITTLE MERYL: *Waiting to hear about a job. Nervous.*

NURTURER: *What one thing have you done since you woke up that makes you feel good enough about yourself?*

LITTLE MERYL: *I dunno. Fed the dog?*

NURTURER: *Great, so your dog won't die today, that's good news. And what a good owner you are – feeding your dog and keeping it alive. Not everyone does that.*

LITTLE MERYL: *Really? They don't feed their dog?*

NURTURER: *Nope. Dogs die from starvation or lack of care. You care for your dog. Lucky dog.*

LITTLE MERYL: *I hadn't thought about it like that. I just feed the dog.*

NURTURER: *Just naturally a nice person.*

LITTLE MERYL: *Haha, yes, I guess I am. Thanks.*

NURTURER: *That's my job. See you tomorrow?*

LITTLE MERYL: *Yes you will!*

Self-soothing and kind words, said every day, go a long way to encouraging us to get past fear, self-doubt and a lack of confidence. It helps us get on with the tasks that will help us be fearless and fabulous.

....

Thoughts for Procrastination

1. Nudge theory – nudge yourself along towards the task you have to achieve. Give yourself little rewards along the way. Put up simple images on post-it notes around your home or desk to spur you on.
2. Accountability – even world-class athletes have coaches. Get a buddy to jolly you along.
3. Manage intrusive negative thoughts by using strategies such as non-negotiation self-talk (Liz Gilbert[18]), power poses (Ann Cuddy[19]) and other practical aversion and re-framing tactics such as deep breathing and 30-second meditation moments.
4. Remember self-appraisal methods and keep a reward system. Keep up your 'It's a Wonderful Life' book in which you record any achievement, feedback or praise. It reminds you that you can make things happen, that you have done so in the past and that you can right now. Fill it with gold star stickers.

....

⊨ CORE-WORK ⊨

Respond to your Nurturer using your Little You's non-dominant hand:

NURTURER: *How are you today?*

LITTLE YOU: ....

NURTURER: *What one thing have you done since you woke up that makes you feel good enough about yourself?*

LITTLE YOU: ....

Continue . . .

Self-sabotage

OK, so Nurturer cheered up our Little Meryl for today, then the phone rings and she's offered the role of Princess Leia in the next *Star Wars* movie (we're imagining this scenario for legal purposes). She's thrilled to bits, but replies to her agent: 'But I could never replace Carrie Fisher. She's Princess Leia. *Star Wars* fans will go ballistic if they see me attempt to walk in her shoes. It'll be a disaster. I'll never work again.'

Instead of leaping at the challenge, she self-sabotages. She gives everyone reasons why they shouldn't employ her for this role, even though she really wants it and she knows she could make it her own.

Self-sabotage is fear writ large. Sibling to procrastination and the imposter syndrome. You'll fail, so why bother? They'll fire you so you won't take the job. You're late so you can slip in the back and not be noticed; even though it's your birthday, etc. It pulls in bad habits and negative self-beliefs. But it can play its hand in the subtlest of ways . . .

Life's great, the sun's shining, your hair did what it's meant to this morning, you're pumped with caffeine and you're on top of your game. Then you trip over a paving stone, leave your cash flapping in the bank cash dispenser, forgot your sandwiches for lunch, accepted dinner tonight with someone who drives you nuts and you're late for a deadline that your job is hanging on the line for.

You curse the gods, blame the bank, the paving stone, your friend and your boss for ruining your day and your life. But somewhere deep in your psyche there's a kernel of doubt. There does appear to be a common element to all these events. You. Could you be in the least responsible? Trying to fit too much in, always running late, surrounding yourself with people who make you feel bad, doing a job you hate. Maybe there is some self-sabotage going on here.

Why on earth would you deliberately set out to shoot yourself in the foot when otherwise everything might turn out pretty well? Of course, you don't do it consciously, but somewhere a little voice is telling you to mess up. As it turns out there are lots of payoffs from self-sabotage:

- Not having to fail
- Not having to succeed
- Not having to be visible
- Not having to be present
- Not having to risk
- Not having to take responsibility
- Not having to commit
- Not having to compete
- Not having to lose
- Not having to let others down
- Not having to show others up
- Not having to be accountable

What's going on? Well, maybe you're protecting yourself from some horrible imagined outcome. Or perhaps you've been told too many times you're no good, that you don't deserve success, that 'people like you' aren't meant to have money. Who are you to have what you want? Fear drives sabotage. It hides bombs and tripwires ready to explode should you even so much as dare to step towards a life that makes you happy. You surround yourself with destructive people because they can prove for you that you are a waste of space. You put their needs before your own. You over-eat, over-drink, and work too hard because you're acting out your inner doubts.

Next time you are in a rush, slow down. Say yes to success. Say no to negativity. Commit to what will serve you, and let go of everything that is trashing you. Give yourself time and space to plan and make the right choices for you and your core values. Be your own best friend. Practice positive self-talk. Find a friend who will encourage you to be your best and to have everything that you want for your life.

⊨ CORE-WORK ⊨

Self-sabotage is not the saviour from pain; it magnifies it. It's time to stop. Identify those curve balls and catch yourself in the act of throwing them.

Nurturer questions:
- How is it helping you?
- What is it costing you?
- Who is gaining most from this?
- What are the pay-offs?
- What could a more beneficial outcome be?
- How can you do it differently?
- What encouraging message/mantra could you give yourself?

- How can you start to notice when you are doing it?
- How can you flip the belief around the self-sabotage?
- What values can you hold onto to avoid self-sabotage?

Continue the dialogue with any of these questions that particularly push your buttons . . .

Stick To Your Own Lane

- People Pleasing
- Compare and Despair
- No to Naysayers

It is too easy to live through other people's eyes, trying to please them, comparing yourself with their successes, playing small when other people's negativity forces you to back down. You are always looking over your shoulder, or over the line at the greener grass, the faster track. But in the end the race is only with yourself; it's your big dream that matters, your goals, your values, you meeting your own needs, you reaching, growing and contributing. Are you sticking in your lane or are you veering off? See what resonates for you, and do your core-work to get back on your own track.

People Pleasing

A kid that brings an apple to teacher has a mission. Get teacher to like her and mark her grades higher. The manipulation is obvious and we scorn such tactics. And yet as we grow older many of us adopt such people-pleasing poses.

People pleasing is so subtle and deeply entrenched that we often don't even realise we are doing it. We are creatures of comfort and we prefer the path of least resistance. Is that you? Do you allow others to take advantage for an easy life and bury yourself under the mound of apples you have ready to curry favour.

Looking to others for affirmation, acceptance and approval, rather than looking to yourself for these validations, undermines your integrity and your sense of self-reliance and self-worth. You believe you are second wicket to everyone else; that they deserve your yes more than you do. Giving away yes when you'd rather say no causes cracks and fissures in your self-esteem. You're telling the world (and your own brain) that your life is servile, that you exist to trail behind in the dust of other people's chariots. Did you say yes to the first salary you were offered, instead of negotiating? Do you go against your core values, instead of standing up for what you believe in? Do you back down in an argument, instead of holding your ground, just to keep the peace? Do you get your underpants in a twist trying to please Peter at the same time as trying to please Paul? Are you pulled every which way but the one you want to go?

Do you apologise for offering your opinion or your insight? Do you sit hunched, arms crossed, legs crossed, ankles crossed instead of pulling back your shoulders and lifting your chin? Why is it so hard to say no, or own your space in the room? Fear of losing love, or of being disapproved of or alienated from the group, or rejected by friends, makes people shut up or bow to the consensus. Sometimes yes is simply easier to say than no. But all this is a short-term strategy, which plays out badly in the long-term. You are living a lie, no matter how silently. You find yourself living behind smoke and mirrors, you become as slippery as an eel, trying to remember one lie against another. Truth slides further and further out of your grasp and your life becomes a tinderbox ready to catch fire the second you get caught out. This is no way to live. It's a smokescreen against your integrity.

You must take responsibility for your thoughts, decisions and actions, and know that you are not going to please everyone all the time.

So you decide 'enough is enough'. You get your coaching and you start to take a stand. You start to say no. When people are used to you being the sweet shrinking violet and suddenly you grow teeth and talons, they react angrily and defensively. They remove love, friendship, approval. The cat is out of the bag and there is no way it's going back in. You have to take the flak and trust your integrity. You have to step away from compliance and out into the limelight to reclaim your territory.

SpaceX and Tesla founder Elon Musk was never the popular kid.[20] He didn't follow the linear route through Silicon Valley's first flush of dotcom mania. He went up against the military and designed rockets, which he uses to send supplies to the International Space Station. He took on the car industry and designed an all-electric car. Yes, expensive to buy but then free to fuel, and cheap to fix, undermining the car maintenance and fuel supply industry. He took on energy and built a SolarCity factory. He wasn't flouting the status quo for the sake of it, but he wasn't kow-towing to Big Brother either. Elon Musk has a bigger mission; he's going to save us earthlings from self or natural annihilation by giving us an escape route to other planets that he will make habitable. The guy's got big ideas, and maybe he won't succeed at his ultimate goal, but no one thought he could fly rockets into space, build an all-electric car or create a solar business either. Musk is not a yes man. He's perfected the art of sculpting no into whatever he chooses his future to be. He doesn't fear others, he fears not making the most of his time on Earth. He fears what is happening to the planet and he uses that fear to create alternative action.

The answer to people pleasing is in your imagination. Create alternatives that allow you to picture positive outcomes that benefit both of you. Find positive solutions that work for everyone. Use the word 'imagine'. Imagine if you pay me £25K more as a salary rise because I deserve it, and you get value for your money. Imagine if we share the chores, then we get to spend more fun time together. Imagine if instead of talking now when I need to get some sleep, we arrange to meet over coffee and I can tell you about my stuff too. Imagine if we create a non-hierarchical structure so that the whole team feels more engaged. Imagine if I let you know when I have finished what I am doing and then we go play.

And what do you gain, in the face of adverse reaction to your new no? You gain self-respect. You gain time. You gain rest and energy. You gain the ability to say yes to the things that you want to say yes to. You gain self-confidence. You gain the right to be direct and authentic. You gain space to breathe. You gain power over your own destiny. You gain inner strength. You gain the knowledge of what really matters to you. You gain the sense of pleasure and enjoyment.

You gain freedom from burden and liberty from obligation. You gain choice. You gain time to choose. You gain self-reliance. You gain fortitude. You stop allowing fear to dominate.

And all this gives you the ability to be more honest, creative, compassionate and driven by your core purpose.

⊨ CORE-WORK ⊨

Use your Nurturer to ask these types of questions and let your non-dominant hand answer.

1. What are you saying 'yes' to, when you want to say 'no'? What are you doing that is good for others but not for you? Have you asked for that pay rise? How can you put your foot down about your share of the chores? Devise some open questions around the people-pleasing issues you are running.

2. Ask yourself what is really important to you and what you stand for. When you are asked to make choices and decisions, use this as your benchmark. If you are called to take action outside of what you believe in, you will find yourself out of alignment. Your values are your guide and protector from the unreasonable demands of others. Stand by your values and you will gain respect from the people who matter.

3. Envision an 'imagine if' scenario with someone you tend to try and please in opposition to your own benefit. See if you can find a resolution that works for both of you (see chapter on Negotiation).

⊨——⊨

Compare and Despair

Life is a race of your two selves; no one else is in the running. Comparisons are not with others but in the balance between who you were yesterday against who you want to be tomorrow. Unfortunately, the world cultivates comparison and if we surrender to it, we succumb to our deepest fears of inadequacy.

The cult of comparison with others is a breeding ground for anguish, despair, fear and self-loathing. Academia and sports are honed at school on the sharp blade of competitive edge, but where does that leave the rest of the population who don't finish first? Look at the neurosis of Salieri when he compared himself to Mozart as depicted in the film *Amadeus*. He was a brilliant musician but his vision was blinded; all he could see was that he wasn't as good as Mozart. His passion for his music was destroyed by his fear of not being the best. Instead of looking to himself and drawing on his innate creative force, he let it wither in the shadows of jealousy.

Is that what we want to teach our children? Do we want to create little bundles crippled by fear of not being good enough; diminished by the comparison to others? There is even competition between mums at toddler groups. Who is crawling, talking, eating solids, out of nappies, gracing the potty or ditching the dummy first? It's crazy. Every child reaches their own milestones when they are ready. How many adults do you see in the street sucking a dummy and still in nappies? Growth and development happens in their own sweet time.

And then there is the pressure we put our kids under as they get older, forcing them to define themselves by how they rate against their peers. How we praise our children inflicts an emphasis on social comparison that they carry into adulthood. Praise is most beneficial when it acknowledges our effort towards personal development, not when it raises a fanfare for us being 'better' than other people. And who really wants to scan social media to check out the competition and be beaten down when what you see is a mirage of perceived greater beauty, smoother skin, skinnier limbs, more protruding hip bones, more upstanding boobs, more chiselled muscles, a longer string of A-star grades, double-firsts, gold medals and distinctions? We are becoming a neurotic generation. Rainforests are being decimated, but forests of measuring sticks are thriving.

Feelings of superiority are short-lived because being pumped up on the back of someone else's perceived failings is no basis for the building of rock-solid self-esteem and, soon enough, any ameliorated state starts to crumble. Comparison cramps our creativity.

Last year I exhibited as part of the Other Art Fair in East London. A couple of hundred artists exhibited side by side, displaying their wares to thousands of art-lovers. It could have been a hive of competitive jostling but instead, for the whole three days, there was a comradery and willingness to connect; to share ideas, to make friends, have a laugh, to commiserate when there was nearly but not quite a sale. Ego and its counterpart fear were absent from the proceedings. There was no comparing and despairing. We were each there on our own merits and we respected and valued one another for that. It's hard to sell your work, it feels personal, it's easy to feel rejected and isolated. But here we were, in it together. Each in our own lanes but cheering each other on at the same time.

So instead of comparing and competing, free yourself of fear and celebrate the lives and work of others, and look to them for inspiration. Creativity, innovation, invention and productivity thrive by building on what has gone before; but do your work while mindfully aware that your efforts and contribution are enough in their own right, free of evaluative and comparative judgment.

No Comparison Challenge

1. Know you are good enough, that you have all the ingredients to make the most of who you are. Update your 'This is Your Wonderful Life' book on a regular basis.
2. Be competitive with your own achievements. What challenges have you beaten? Where are you in comparison to this time last year? What are you working on to keep developing? Reading this book, for instance!
3. Construct your self-improvements from inspiration by others not jealousy. When you experience jealousy or envy, turn it into a call to action. It niggles you that someone else is doing better at that particular thing? What can you do to improve in that area if it matters so much?
4. Make growth and development your reward rather than being spurred on by fear of failing or falling behind other people.
5. Use your creative thinking skills, your ability to train your mind, body and imagination to take you from where you are now to where you want to be in the future.

⸝═ CORE-WORK ═⸜

Respond to your Nurturer using your Little You's non-dominant hand:

> Some possible Nurturer questions:
> - What areas are you feeling like you aren't doing as well as you might?
> - What are you afraid of?
> - What are you doing well at?
> - What can you use in your tool kit to help you improve?
> - How are you growing?
> - How are you doing with your goals and action steps?
> - How are you inspiring others?
> - What jealousies can you turn into inspirations or a call to arms?
> - How can I help you feel better about yourself?

Continue the dialogue on any one of these that starts to trigger you . . .

⸝═══⸜

No to Naysayers

So you're beating back the fears one by one. You're on a roll. And then once again you hear the words: 'Who do you think you are?' You need to get creative. Creative thinking will trick your deeply entrenched resistance into shedding the shackles of self-sabotage and naysaying.

How does it work? Well, it has its basis in anti-logic. The usual

rational solutions haven't done the trick, so you have to get even
more cunning. Resistance thinks 'can't' – creative thinking spins
your brain out of orbit and into a place where 'can' is actually possible. 'Yeah, but . . .' I hear you say . . .

The two words we coaches hear more often than anything are:
'Yeah, but . . .' When we hear them we know that person is wallow-
ing in the mudflats of miserable negativity and will bat you away
with the deftness of a hippopotamus's tail swatting flies. 'Yeah but
I'm not creative, yeah but I'm no good at that, yeah but I'm not
qualified, yeah but I'm a woman in a man's world, yeah but I'm too
old, yeah but I'm working class, yeah but I'm not clever enough,
yeah but I'm shy, yeah but I'm broke, yeah but that's too scary, yeah
but . . .' The yeah-butters are very creative in finding reasons to not
change or transform themselves even when they say they want to.
The yeah-butters put their energy into the treadmill of resistance.
What they are really saying is: 'I have decided it is not possible.'
What do you 'yeah but' about? What have you decided is not possible? What is scaring you?

There is very little that you can't get around somehow, if you
choose to. Beethoven had gone completely deaf when he wrote

his 9th Symphony. The great photorealist painter Chuck Close was paralysed so badly by a blood clot on the spine that he couldn't even pick up a paint brush. He had his brush strapped to his wrist and he developed a new technique in paintings. His work became even more successful than before. I bet no one heard either Beethoven or Close say 'Yeah but . . .' In fact, when you have suffered a setback or some kind of trauma you are more likely to become more creative and more able to say 'Yes, and not only am I not going to be held back by this, I am going to bounce back big time.' Look at those soldiers or victims of terror attacks who lose limbs then train for the Paralympics.

And then, when you've won the battle against yourself, you run headlong into the frontline of naysayers who hide behind the shields of 'we don't want to see you fail, we're only thinking of your best interests, we don't want you to get hurt, we're only trying to protect you, we don't want you to humiliate yourself'. The list goes on. They project their fear onto you. As if you haven't got enough of your own already! If they were people who had become immensely successful and happy on the back of this fearful approach then, by all means, it would be OK to listen to their concerns. But if they're not, don't. Do you think Richard Branson took any notice of naysayers proclaiming that setting up an airline was madness? I imagine the only voices he listened to were the ones saying, 'why not?' And now he owns an island in the Caribbean. I doubt those Naysayers are his neighbours.

When Elon Musk decided to use the relatively new internet to build an online bank he was told it couldn't be done. The regulations were too tight, fraud too much of a threat, the complexity of the banking system too intricate. One by one he worked through the problems. And true, the problems were huge. It was no walk in the park. But it wasn't as insurmountable as others imagined. What he co-created with other believers would eventually become PayPal.

Turn those blocks into rocks that will knock down walls that other people create to try and stop you achieving your dreams. Out-create them. Do what consistently excites you so that you can charge through the barriers of negativity put up to keep you 'in your place'. Your place is to show up and prove that whatever you believe is truly worth doing, can be done. And it is you who is going to do it.

If those negative voices are your own or someone else's put up a big STOP sign and work on some creative strategies to turn around the 'yeah but' and discard the naysayers. Use 'no' as a stepping stone to yes.

⊨ CORE-WORK ⊨

SEVEN WAYS TO YES!

Use your non-dominant hand to do these exercises.

1. For every 'yeah but' write down ten reasons it could work out.
2. Write down the consequences of staying the same.
3. Think of the people you admire who have achieved great things, imagine the naysayers they met along the way and what 'yeah but' things those naysayers would have said. Write them down and then do what your hero did and throw them away.

Now get even more creative:

4. Research five successful people and find out how many rejections they had along the way. Make a colourful collage of all the rejections you've received and turn it into a mandala for never giving up.
5. Spend the day pretending you are already doing the thing you want to do, or being the person you want to be.

6. Put yourself in a different context or with different people. It shifts your perspective.
7. Focus on what you love doing and are happy to apply yourself to, day-in and day-out. That is the only way to get good at something. Naysayers will have a hard time stopping you from doing what you love.

⊨==⊣

End of Week Two

⊨= CORE-WORK =⊣

Write the answers to these questions with your non-dominant hand

Nurturer:
- What tools have you learned in this week?
- How have you moved forward towards your goals?
- What action steps have you taken?
- How are you feeling about your fears right now?
- How can I support you this week?

⊨==⊣

Week Three

....

WHAT REALLY MATTERS

- SELF-LOVE: Putting a Spin On It, You are Not Alone, Learning to Love, Passion with Purpose, Cultivating Gratitude
- STICKING AT IT: Road to Resilience, 10,000 Hours to Mastery
- BEING FLEXIBLE: Embracing Change, Changing Places, The Power of Persuasion, The Art of Negotiation

....

Now you are going up a level with self-love, resilience, flexibility and going face to face with negotiation. Learning to spin bad into good, joining forces with others, driving forward on the back of your passion and purpose, and learning to love yourself first all push back the looming doom of fear. Finding ways to be grateful for what we have now subdues anxiety and fear for the future. Rising with resilience above every challenge builds stronger armour against fear.

Accepting with patience that nothing comes without consistent work and tenacity, and by taking the long view, we understand that, just because the results we want aren't happening now, it doesn't mean they will never happen. Rigidity and fear go hand in hand, the world becomes smaller if we try to grip it too hard. We must keep pushing back, bowing, flexing and evolving with every new circumstance and twist in the road. We can bend with change and we can create change, we can be a powerful force of persuasion and negotiation that stands before fear with an unflinching stare. Discover how amazing you can be.

N.B. READ each chapter. Anything that resonates for you, do the core-work around it. Not everything will be relevant to you at the time you are reading the book and doing the course. But later, even years down the line, something may arise that means you can come back to an area that does now strike a chord.

Self-Love

Putting a Spin On It

Spin has unsavoury connotations. We think political untruths and hidden agendas. But in fact, spin can do wonders to the way you see things.

Spin can turn the negative into the positive and it can bounce you away from fear and into a world of possibilities. Let's consider putting a spin on how we see stress. Generally, we think of stress as a swear word. It's not good for us. And indeed, prolonged stress with no let-up does take its toll. However, not all stress is harmful. If you see stress as the equivalent of lifting weights, of building strong emotional muscles, then when you face tougher challenges you know you can push through the burn.

Of course, chronic stress can make us sick, but instead of crumpling under the burden of anxiety, heart palpitations and emotional exhaustion, we can embrace what our bodies are telling us. We can listen to its message and take heed. Let's say, for instance, a large, egg-like fatty cyst is suddenly protruding out of your abdomen from under your right ribs. The doctor says it's nothing. But your body doesn't do things for no reason. What's the cause? What stress are you putting it under? What changes can you make, what can you learn from a situation, how can you creatively swing fear into fearing less? Challenges that are physical, mental or emotional make us stronger because our capabilities are under duress. If we ignore the stress indicators then we prolong the pressure and the more likely we are to become overwhelmed or sick. But with the right approach and attitude, that which makes us ill can equally make us stronger, more creative, compassionate and resilient.

When you transform stress into a steering wheel, you become more personally engaged in relationships and experiences and therefore feel happier and less fearful – if the stress is switched off on a regular basis. You can turbo-charge a car but you still have to stop and fill it with petrol from time to time. After you rise from a stressful situation, your brain rewires itself to grow and learn from it. Each stress makes you stronger and more resilient. Actually going through the experience is like giving yourself a vaccine. Next time, your brain recognises you survived the first time, so it knows it can do it again. This is how we learn to thrive.

NASA astronauts, emergency personnel, armed forces and elite athletes all deliberately practice under highly stressful conditions. They are given procedures to rehearse time and again. They practise and they prepare. They don't panic, they just do what they know until they reach a solution. Most of us don't have the advantage of having procedures in place but we may still have to deal with frightening, random or traumatic events. The sign on the side of a fire engine I saw the other day said, 'Know your escape route'. You never know how you will react in any given situation, but you can build resilience and feel better prepared for the bumps and cracks in the road ahead.

Stress and challenge don't have to be approached from a place of fear and anxiety, but instead we can create a way through by using self-compassion and mindfulness to combat the fear, anxiety, anger and frustration that fire unhelpful reactions to stress. First, we must understand that in order to put a positive spin on our feelings, we must embrace change. It is already happening, and we have no power to stop it, so we must learn to rise to it, accept it, change it, or learn from it. Challenges don't have to come in the form of a natural disaster or a manmade tragedy; they can simply be us trying to cling to the status quo even when it is causing us pain, whether that be a relationship, a job or our health.

See a way to spin life away from stress and towards a flexible and open-minded approach.

Develop a Spinning Mindset

1. Train under stress, so that when you hit a wall you are ready for it.
2. Use stress and fear as energy to power you in new and exciting directions.

3. Keep an adaptable, flexible, plastic approach to life's twists and turns.
4. Find alternative ways to see outcomes you might normally view as 'disastrous'.
5. Always look for ways to learn from any experience.
6. Listen rather than judge.
7. Take time to observe a situation before responding.
8. Gather all the evidence you can from every perspective before jumping to conclusions.
9. You don't always have to agree with others.
10. You can change your mind. Just because you believed something one way before doesn't mean that, with the benefit of hindsight, you can't see it another way now.

....

⊨ CORE-WORK ⊨

Draw out two columns. In the right-hand column, with your non-dominant hand, list the ten top things bugging you at the moment.

Then in the left-hand column, with your dominant hand, spin those bugs into butterflies. How can you see them with a positive slant?

⊨————⊨

You are Not Alone

If all this battling with fear has knocked you for six, and left you sitting on the pavement blubbing into the gutter, then rest assured, you are not alone. One of the hardest things in life is the ability to keep going in the face of obstacles, brick walls, blind alleys and dead ends. What helps people to keep on keeping on? Well, a bit of support from time to time doesn't go amiss.

It is no coincidence that the most successful are guided, cajoled, supported and encouraged by mentors.

The first step is to swallow your pride, silence your ego/fear and recognise that you will actually benefit from having a mentor. Trust that what their eyes have seen, ears have heard and their life has experienced may just give you an objectivity and insight that you can't get on your own. It is a flawed, foolhardy and lonely approach to attempt to take on the world alone. Mentoring isn't just for business folk. Everyone needs someone. Or many 'someones'. I have had mentors and coaches, as well as supportive, insightful and wise friends.

Everyone needs someone. Not just formally but informally too. At different stages of my film career director David Yates has acted as an informal mentor. He has willingly shared his experience, time, methods, encouragement and guidance. This includes (with the support of producers Yvonne Walcott and David Heyman) giving me the opportunity to shadow him on the set of *Fantastic Beasts* at Leavesden Studios. Observing the nuts and bolts of Hollywood movie making helped me to understand that success is scalable. With the right approach you can achieve, on a daily basis, the same ethos at a small level; you nurture relationships, respect the work and contribution of others, value teamwork, build in self-care, promote well-being for all and give space for creativity.

Every Friday night for the last thirteen years, a couple of friends and I have met in a local pub for an hour and half to meet and share the ups and downs of our week. We started when our children were little and we continued as, one by one, our children left home. There have been times when I have been alone all week working away in my 'cave', writing or painting, only to emerge like a new-born giraffe, into the light of day feeling unnerved and skitterish, unbound by too much solitude and silence. My friends have steadied me and grounded me. I refocus into normal life with a bit of banter and jollity. Later, I am unbent and reconnected.

My cousin Charlotte worked for Dell Computers in Austin, Texas and every year ran a conference for highly successful businesswomen and women entrepreneurs to come together from around the world. As part of this, some of them also mentor other women through the Cherie Blair Foundation.

Charlotte mentors a woman called Fundi Mazibuko in South Africa. The benefit seems mutual:

> I have never had a formal mentor before and having spent time with you makes me feel like I missed out on a lot of valuable insight. I also believe that for the mentor/mentee relationship to work, both parties need to be comfortable with each other. I am soooooo glad you were picked for me. I am continuously learning each time we have a meeting. The fact that you are in a different country also allows me

to learn new things that are not necessarily formal learning. The fact that we are both mothers, wives and working allows me to share my challenges with you without any fear of being judged. When I discuss my ambitions and growth ideas with you, I am confident that I am in a safe zone, where I will not be judged or belittled. That is the greatest benefit for me.

Her mentor, Charlotte, has this to say:

Becoming a mentor has added a new dimension to my working life. It gives me an added sense of purpose, knowing that my experience can be helpful to someone. I love the fact that Fundi is working in a different culture – sometimes the lights go out! But we have so much in common. Fundi already has many years of experience in business so it feels more like a peer conversation – I really try to help her with online resources and some tips around marketing, which is my background. What has struck me about the programme is that although we are separated by miles, we are both raising children, juggling busy lives and thinking deeply about our passions and purpose. We meet by Skype, which means that I have seen her family and she has seen mine. We are also connected on social media. We are excited to meet in person when my work will bring me to South Africa. It has been an enriching experience so far.

We are not solitary creatures, we need help to progress, and to get help we need to ask for it. We need to look to those who have gone before. The more support you have, the less fear you feel and the more creative and expansive you can be.

....

Find a Champion Challenge

1. Find a mentor in your field who knows more than you do, who will champion you and guide you, encourage and challenge you on the road ahead.
2. Be a mentor. We learn as much by teaching those that follow us, as by following those who are ahead.
3. Share your mentoring relationships in a blog so that others can learn from your experiences. Sharing also helps to distil what lessons you have learned and what skills you have gained.

....

⊨ CORE-WORK ⊨

Remember you always have your inner mentor in the form of your Nurturer. They are with you day and night, so use them. Keep that dual-handed dialogue going as a daily practice.

- What one question can Little You ask of your Nurturer today that will help you with your current niggly fear?

⊨——⊨

Learning to Love

It is one thing seeking out companionship, support, guidance and encouragement outside of your home life, it is another learning to receive and to give it within a relationship. It is a more delicate balance to negotiate, to check if there is too much leaning or neediness, or not enough listening or attempts to hear problems. We cannot be each other's counsellors but we can be partners in a fear-reducing alliance. When I worry about a health issue, my partner warns me off googling the imagined disease. He gets me past my fear of drowning and onto a boat to watch whales. I sit with him through a sleepless night when he fears his freelance work is drying up.

But what happens when the fear is about the relationship itself? You want a quiet life with your spouse; you don't want to ruffle feathers. So you keep schtum, when really you know you need to say that you are unhappy. You may be big and brave in business, but at home you slide into furrowed silences that sit heavily between the two of you.

And then, of course, you can't take any more. One flippant remark, one cutting side-sling too many, another evening of being ignored or taken for granted, and you break. Your tongue is spitting, your seething emotions tumble and trip over a tidal wave of words, your disappointment, despair, distress know no bounds. And then your partner takes this opportunity to counter-attack like there's no tomorrow. Of course, your hiccupping diatribe falls on deaf ears. Very little is accomplished in the outburst, and you both retreat to lick your respective wounds, with perfunctory promises of change and under-standing, compromise and commitment. Fear reasserts itself and you settle once again into silence broken only by the flickers of bickering and backbiting. Nothing is resolved and the big love you once shared slowly perishes under the paralysis of fear of rocking the boat.

Over time you pick up 'evidence' for your story, maybe your fear is that your spouse no longer loves you. So you store up your arsenal of their offenses and misdemeanours: he/she leaves their socks lying around, forgets to empty the bins, buy you flowers, make love to you or ignores you at a restaurant. Perhaps they are sullen when alone with you, but the life and soul of the party in others company. Nothing is said, instead they are all simply harboured in grief and projected with cataclysmic doom. Perhaps you fear saying anything because of potential violence. If violence is a very real threat then avoiding triggers is not a recipe for a peaceful relationship, it just delays the inevitable. Violence is never acceptable and you need to get support and help to leave.

Domestic violence aside, fear in relationships needs to be brought out into the open and dealt with honestly and openly between you. You have to understand what the fear is masking. Fear of rejection, abandonment, loss, of being alone, change, age, judgment, helplessness, neediness, commitment or lack of it, lack of control, of being controlled, of being bored or boring, of failing. Whether you're on the attack or on the defence, both of you will be hand-tied by your own fears and deaf to the needs or fears of the other. You need to work out which fear is being triggered and own it.

You also need to know when you have explored and tried everything. Know when it's time to call time on the husk of a relationship that has wizened in a desert of differing needs. Leaving is terrifying. There may be huge financial repercussions, you may never have been single before, you may have to find somewhere else to live, there may be children involved. If you know that staying has no potential for resolution then you also know you have no choice; but it doesn't lessen the mammoth challenge in front of you. Gather your supporters, look at your options and then make a concrete plan, broken into manageable steps. But first, if you can, honour the end, pay tribute to what has been and say your goodbyes.

Performance artist Marina Abramović took this to an extreme, but it is testament to the deep need to heal wounds and create closure before you can move forward. She and her partner were splitting up, but to give respect to the twelve years they had shared, they walked the Great Wall of China, starting from opposite ends and meeting in the middle. They said their goodbyes and parted forever.

When you have your life back on the straight and narrow, and you feel a bit more settled and secure, you may raise your head above the parapet and sniff the breeze for the faintest whiff of love.

How hard can it be? Just pull on your Sunday best and step out with a slash of lipstick or a slick of hair gel and off you go. Except of course you are paralysed with fear. Who wants an old has-been? Rejected once, rejected forever, no good at relationships, body not what it once was, if it ever was.

There is your date, waiting. And guess what, in the gloom of midday pick-ups, business attrition, and lonely leftovers, your date smiles nervously, the whites of their eyes flashing back at you. They're terrified too. Dating is scary, it may fizzle to nothing or end in fireworks but if you let fear keep your front door firmly bolted against the possibility of love, you'll never know.

So you take the plunge, and you find you're in deep. Love has swung its lasso and caught you good and proper. You're drowning and flying at the same time. Life tastes like expensive dripping chocolate and is lit with effervescent diamonds. You and your new love buddy are floating on cloud nine, lapping up each other's god and goddess-inspired gifts like kittens in buttermilk. You just can't get enough of each other. You devour each other's bodies, words, smiles, jokes, funny habits, lumpy bits, bulges and bumps. You see only perfection in their imperfection and you forget your own flaws in the forgiving mist of their adoration. Until that bit is over. And fear wiggles its way back in. The tortured texts of misunderstanding, that extra kiss missed off, the phone call that comes too late, that streetcar named Desire that is hurtling down the road off its tracks as your insecurities go haywire. Fear runs amok because you have something really special that you don't want to lose. It's the tricky part in a road of tricky parts. Another roadblock and crisis check point to navigate and negotiate.

'What happened?' you cry, 'Where's the romance, the passion, the endless nights of love-making and days glistening with the tears of joy?' Well . . . life, that's what. And new love transforms into solid love, if it's meant to. It's an animal thing. First the longing and lust that smashes you into each other, and then the normalisation that permits longitude (however long that may be). You find your way, you see each other's faults and fissures for what they are; not evidence of failing love, but the weathering of two people muscling along as best they can under the circumstances. Maybe there'll be kids, maybe there won't, maybe there'll be money, maybe there won't, maybe there'll be a long life together of health and happiness, and maybe there won't. Love's a lottery. It's scary and hard work, it has its rewards and sacrifices, its frustrations and absurdities, it sometimes works out and sometimes it doesn't. Fear and love go hand in hand, like Fred Astaire and Ginger Rogers. At any moment you can trip up and take a tumble but unless you take the risk you'll never get the chance to dance the light fandango.

Facing Love Fears

1. Don't over-analyse, ruminate and catastrophise.
2. Listen to understand.
3. Communicate in a state of calm.
4. Trust yourself and your other half. If they prove untrustworthy, move on; they are unlikely to change.
5. Take the rough with the smooth (not violence).
6. Understand what your fears are masking and find ways to heal yourself.
7. Your partner is not there to 'save' you. Only you can do that.
8. Kindness is key, on both sides.
9. Attack only meets with defence. Find another way to express your feelings.
10. Risk rejection and failure for love. It's worth it in the long run.

⊨ CORE-WORK ⊨

Of course, until you learn to love yourself, loving someone else will be a minefield of fear, anxiety, dread and jealousy. Core-work is essential if you are single, single but looking for love, in the first thrusts of love, in a disintegrating relationship, or decades in on a long marriage. Loving yourself first lays the groundwork for loving others.

Respond to your Nurturer using your Little You's non-dominant hand.

- How are you meeting your own needs?
- How are you standing by your values?
- How are you working on your goals and dreams?
- How are you rewarding your mini-successes?
- How are you acknowledging your achievements?
- How are you turning your fears into gratitude?
- How are you being your own champion?

⊨⊨

Passion with Purpose

You are working towards your big dream, but it's time to check in again now that you have more insight. Think again about your values and your mission statement. Remember this is the backbone to creating meaning and purpose in your life; giving you rock solid foundations with which you can withstand the fears that threaten you at every turn, whether that be in love, money, career, health, family, social life, environment or spirituality. We must always return to purpose.

Without purpose big dreams are like loose talk, all stuff and non-sense. Without substance with which to drive your dreams forward you will sink when the going gets tough. Having your purpose is like a rudder to guide you against the puff of ill-winds that blow to knock out your sails and have you drifting off course into fearful waters. Purpose and creative thinking are two of the most important things you can cultivate in order to have a meaningful and fear-busting life.

'Every being is intended to be on earth for a certain purpose.'
– Sa'di, twelfth-century Persian poet

Everyone deserves the chance to build fulfilling and meaningful lives by tapping into their own passions and talents, their ability to think creatively and their primal need to have a sense of purpose. But many struggle with trying to work out what that purpose is, and often don't even try to find out.

When I got a job for QTV and Channel 4 making the five-part documentary series *Death* that spoke to people with terminal illness, we filmed 12 people over a period of 3 years and it was an extraordinary journey. What we realised was that when people are dying they become very focused on what is important to them and how they want to spend the time they have left.

I also realised that I didn't want to wait until I was dying to work out what was important to me. I wanted to find out what would give my life purpose now. When the TV series went out, something amazing happened. One of the people we'd filmed who had chronic Crohn's disease received enough unsolicited financial donations from the viewing public that she could pay for the treatments she needed (and didn't have to access via postcode lottery), which allowed her a longer and pain-free life.

The indirect effect of the film impacting on someone's quality of life decided my purpose. Creativity that matters; be that Brave New Girl drawings, writing wellbeing books, making abstract paintings to meditate to, directing films about inspiring people facing adversity or coaching clients to help them find their own mojo. I am a creative mongrel. It took me a long time to find my 'why' but once I'd identified it, everything made sense, every decision was made easier, every course of action had direction. My fears took a back seat.

Why are we here? It's the big question. Eat, drink and be merry – or is there something more? Maybe there is a bigger force moving us round like pawns, or sitting back and observing us with wry humour, or maybe not. One thing is certain though; without our own sense of purpose we humans function below par.

Back in 1962, according to Daniel H. Pink in his book *Drive*, Clare Boothe Luce, one of the first women to serve in Congress, was worried that President Kennedy didn't have a clear purpose. People couldn't understand what exactly he was in office to accomplish. She told him that a man has one sentence. Abraham Lincoln preserved the union and freed slaves. Franklin Roosevelt lifted the US out of the great depression and helped the US win a war.

Each of us has a sentence that can define our direction and choices. Our mission statement. You looked at your core values and from them you can carve out your purpose. Having your 'sentence' makes getting up in the morning a lot easier. And at the end of the day you can look back and see if you have taken the right steps through small tasks to move you forward under your headline banner. Keep reminding yourself of your raison d'être. Reassess it every once in a while and make sure it still feels relevant. Does it need tweaking? Have other values moved to the fore? Are you living by them? If, say, 'kindness' is a value, then whether you are a road-sweeper or a king, it will inform how you live and how you apply yourself to your work.

Many people go through life with a deep sense of unidentifiable unease. They may serve as the head of the Bank of England, or they get by without causing too many waves on the Parents and Teachers Association. But they have a feeling that something is missing; they just can't put their finger on it. It's a sort of niggling despondency that no amount of diamonds, sports cars or beers in the pub at the end of the week can paper over. Those who reach their goals and achieve their own equivalent of Richard Branson's Necker Island expect to be greeted with the bells and whistles of nirvana. But with no sense of purpose they might as well have landed in an arid desert.

An article in the *Guardian* in 2010 by their science correspondent, Ian Sample, reported that a survey of 1,000 Americans found that happiness rose in line with salary, but only until people earned $75,000 a year (the equivalent of around £56,000). It's enough to waylay terrors of poverty, but after that something else has to happen to increase happiness. It goes back to having a purpose. Warren Buffet loved to make money for the sake of it. It fascinated him and drove him, but recently he gave most of it away for philanthropic purposes. Just having the money didn't interest him, doing something useful with it did. Bill and Melinda Gates set up their foundation to do the same.

Most of us, however, aren't going to find our purpose through pouring money into philanthropic causes. And you don't have to be Mother Theresa either. There are many ways to make meaning in our lives but you may well have to overcome fear to manifest it. If you want to campaign about climate change, but you are afraid of raising your head above the pulpit, then you are going to have to conquer your fear before you can deliver your message. Maybe start going to Toastmasters, where you can learn little by little to speak in public. If you want to do a one-woman walk along the Great Wall of China to raise money for charity, but you are scared of traveling alone, maybe you can start by doing long walks closer to home. How meaningful is your purpose? Is it enough to override your fears? Can you challenge those fears in small increments until you are ready to fulfil your purpose?

When we were in Gambia filming a project building schools and wells and vegetable gardens, we met an extraordinary woman at the hotel who agreed to take part in the film. She'd been having a week's break on her own between jobs until we muscled in. Her name was Ali Criado-Perez, and she was a humanitarian nurse committed to trying to make a difference in countries in conflict. She'd been thrown into a divorce after twenty years of marriage and found herself fearfully wondering what life was all about. Her anguish and anxiety was such that she had to seek professional help. After long months of terrible hopelessness, she picked up her courage to find a route out. She got a job as a nurse in A&E and was introduced to the charity Medecins Sans Frontieres (MSF), also known as Doctors Without Borders. She studied tropical medicine and, one step at a time, found her life mission and sense of purpose. Working for MSF means traveling to far-flung and war-torn countries to give medical assistance to those in terrible plight. She has been under gunfire and been exposed to the most highly dangerous and contagious of diseases. But with purpose you know what you're doing and why. It gives you courage and it makes you brave. Ali is in her sixties and shows no signs of stopping. Where she is needed she will go.

I interviewed her recently about the fears that she faces in her humanitarian work and how having a life purpose helps her get through those fears:

Scary things – like getting infected with Ebola while treating patients; or being bombed or killed by gunfire; or being kidnapped by guerrillas in Colombia – are always more frightening when you are thinking about them beforehand than when you are actually in the situation. Then, you are so concentrated on what you are doing that there is no time to be scared. Working with Ebola, for instance: it was frightening most evenings when you had to monitor your temperature, in case it was raised. But when you were actually tending to patients, all you could think about was how you could help them be more comfortable. The same with the Misrata evacuation: when men, women and even children were coming aboard with dreadful injuries, you just thought of what medical attention they needed. Fear for your own safety didn't even come into your mind.

Fear of the unknown. Fear of being unable to cope in a new and challenging situation where you are not sure what is entailed. The 'imposter syndrome'. This was especially so in the beginning of my work with MSF: how would I cope in such a remote environment, far from family and friends, in a war-torn country in the middle of Africa? Still now, with each new mission that is proposed to me, each one different, each one a new challenge, from working on a search-and-rescue boat in the Mediterranean rescuing refugees, to supervising programmes for providing health care inside Syria – I wonder if I am up to the task. But I continue to follow one of my mottos in life, that I only regret the things I haven't done, not the things I have done. And I know I will never forgive myself if I turn down a mission, where I have the opportunity to help people in great need, for fear of not being able to cope. I am learning, slowly, to have confidence in my inner strength.

I also asked her what has been her most scary moment, and how she got through it:

There have been many scary moments. Throwing myself to the ground under gunfire in the Central African Republic; being evacuated in the middle of the night from nearby shelling on the Syrian border; being stopped while in a small, unprotected canoe by armed guerrillas in Colombia. But maybe the most scary was coming by boat into Misrata, at the height of the Libyan conflict, to evacuate war-wounded from the overladen Libyan hospitals to treatment in Tunisia. Or, to be more accurate, reading the risk assessment document before agreeing to take part in the mission was actually more scary than the reality: the risk of being bombed by Gaddafi's forces in Misrata, or mistakenly by NATO planes. I became so aware of the danger that I wrote a letter to my children, to be given to them in case I didn't return, asking them to forgive me and to understand why I did what I did: my commitment to use my skills to help in a humanitarian cause. When we were actually coming into Misrata, my mind was 100% on what I had to do, in my position as medical team leader, to prepare for eighty or so severely war-wounded coming aboard.

Ali's situation is extreme, but having purpose over fear helps in subtler ways too.

When I worked with those people who were dying, their purpose became very simple. They wanted to get their affairs in order and then they wanted to spend time with their loved ones. Nothing grand. An overnight trip to Bournemouth. Sitting in the garden with friends. A birthday party. Listening to music. Once they had reached a level of acceptance that death was around the corner, they tuned in on what really matters. Sitting quietly with the gentle hum of a fan and its cooling breeze might be all that was needed for a morning. Looking through old photo albums and reflecting on a life well lived. In those close-focus ways, in the small meaningful details, fear abated. Life is a death sentence. It comes to us all, but mostly we live in a rush and panic to get things done in order to get more things done. We accumulate stuff and row over nothing. We pour oil on troubled waters. In the end what really matters? But let's not leave it to the end, let's work out what matters and live it right now.

Enjoy the meaningful moments, the imperfections and the nuances, the pitch and putt, the smile at a stranger, the food to a poorly friend, the run for a charity, the cuddle with your child, the smell of the garden that you've watered at the end of the day.

Defy your fears and focus in on the purpose and meaning in your life to achieve happiness, satisfaction and fulfilment. Everyone thrives when they live with passion and purpose. Know who you are inside and what motivates you. How do you want to spend the days you have left to live, be they many or few?

Ten Coaching Tips on Finding your Purpose

1. What are the things that make you smile?
2. What would make you leap out of bed in the morning?
3. Are you ever been 'pulled' towards something and you're not sure why? Trust your instincts and follow the trail.
4. What cause has made your throat tighten with emotion? Could you have a leaning towards helping them in some way?
5. Is there a theme in the books you read, in the films you watch? Maybe you are attracted to something that could inform a new direction?
6. Is there something that you lose yourself in? Where you lose all track of time, could do it all day and never be bored or tired of it? Why not incorporate it into other areas of your life?
7. Do you believe yourself to be 'successful' but actually feel hollow? Could you give some time to your community in someway that would give your life more meaning?
8. Tie your hobbies, gifts and talents with something that has significance to others. Being appreciated boosts our self-esteem and sense of self-worth.

9. What were your dreams when you were a child? Could you revisit some of those ideas, see if they still resonate with you?
10. **Values exercise:** Look at the values list again.

Values in order of importance:

1. ....
2. ....
3. ....
4. ....
5. ....
6. ....
7. ....
8. ....
9. ....
10. ....
....

⊨ CORE-WORK ⊨

Answer this question with your non-dominant hand. Just keep writing in a stream of consciousness for two sides of A4. Describe in full technicolour detail:

• If you only had a month left to live, what values become the most important and how would you live them?

Live with purpose!

⊨⊨

Cultivating Gratitude

When everything goes into a tailspin and you can't control the outcome, sometimes all you can do is bring your mind to the present moment and count your lucky stars for something, anything. Even in the darkest, bleakest, saddest times there is always a way to see things differently when we've learned to cultivate gratitude. It could mean we emotionally survive an event or set of circumstances or we don't.

Peace Activist Gill Hicks was a survivor of the 7/7 London Bombing that killed fifty-two innocent victims in 2005. In her talk for the ideas website TED called 'I survived a terrorist attack, here's what I learned' she describes how she was one of the commuters in the same carriage as the bomber. When he pressed the button he brought darkness down on many lives. Twenty-six people died on Gill Hick's carriage alone. Others were severely maimed. Gill lost her legs in the explosion. She nearly lost her life but for the courage and persistence of her rescuers. She could have come through the horror with the same hatred with which the terrorist blew up the train. But she didn't. What Gill Hicks experienced in those hours of hell, was the kindness and compassion of those who didn't care what colour she was, what faith, whether she was male or female, old or young, or what country she was from. The bomber didn't discriminate in his hatred but her rescuers didn't discriminate either. And she said that what she felt was the total and unconditional nature of their love. They held her hand, stroked her face, they got her out of the carnage, they saved her life. She decided that the terrorist's hatred stopped the moment he touched the button. It stopped with her, because what she took from the experience was the love of her fellow humans.

The gratitude she felt to her rescuers, her ability to see their love and not the terrorist's hatred, helped save her. It helped her find a way out of the psychological fallout and fears from being deliberately maimed. She has prosthetic limbs but she also came away with a solid conviction that what unites us is greater than anything that tries to divide us.

Before the 7/7 bombing, she says work was the most important thing to her. After her experience, her attention shifted. She wants us to feel our connection with each other; she has dedicated her life since the bombings to be an advocate for sustainable peace. She creates initiatives and projects that aim to deter people from following the path of violent extremism. She formed her not-for-profit organization M.A.D for Peace that connects people globally and encourages us to use the word 'peace' as a verb; one that cultivates gratitude as a way to 'do' peace.

How do you learn to do gratitude? The Americans do it once a year on Thanksgiving. Religious folk do it before they eat or sleep. But how can we build it into our lives so that we use gratitude to defeat our fears? If that terrorist felt gratitude and connection with the people in that train carriage would he have pushed the button? Who knows? Gill Hicks believes it is less likely to happen if we are grateful to our fellow humans, if we see what connects us rather than what divides us. If you see the world as a whole, and not as disparate factions, you are more likely to want to pull together, to embrace others, and to be in awe of the magnificence of the planet we live on.

I am always inspired by people who I hear about or meet who are raising the bar on living life, or helping others to do so. I once interviewed a human right's lawyer for my film *War Women*. She explained to me how she used to find it hard listening to people's everyday niggles and moans after coming back from working with rape victims in Bosnia or Darfur in Sudan. These women fight tooth and nail to reclaim their lives after some of the most horrific and terrifying of ordeals. They refuse to see themselves as victims. One day the lawyer was in the hairdressers when she overheard someone moaning about something trivial. The lawyer felt deeply angry: 'What on earth has this woman got to be moaning about; she doesn't know how lucky she is. She should live a day in the lives of those women in Darfur.' Then she stopped her silent tirade as another thought arose: 'No, actually that is what those women are fighting to achieve; the ability to have a day where the worst they have to worry about is what hairstyle they're going to choose.' This lawyer does dangerous, frightening work. She is witness to the worst and the best in what it is to be human. She gets to where she needs to be to help others rise up out of terrible situations, and because of that she finds it in herself to be grateful to a woman in the hairdressers who reminds her of the privilege of experiencing mundane pleasures. Being able to have a good old moan. Or a laugh. Or worry about what you're going to make for tea. Or the price of fish. An uneventful day is something to be thankful for.

Gratitude isn't just a one-day event in the year's calendar. It's the weapon of choice in combating fear and hatred, anger and violence, factions and exclusions. You don't have to go through a terrorist attack or have a religious awakening to see the importance of appreciating the positive. When you see a bee buzzing on a flower going about its daily business of honey making, you also see the survival of a whole ecosystem bound up in her busyness. When we're not grateful to bees, we stop remembering the importance of what they do. When we take them for granted we let commercialisation of honey making run the show. And whole colonies of bees start to disappear. Without gratitude for the simple honeybee we will allow them to be wiped out. Without them, most of our fruits, nuts, seeds and vegetables will disappear, leaving a bland choice of wind-pollinated grasses like rice, wheat or corn for our plates.

A sense of global responsibility can be enhanced with understanding and appreciation of what helps the world to keep ticking. But what about in your daily life, how can it help you combat your fears and concerns, your stresses and mental wellbeing?

Busy your brain with things to be grateful for and it has less time to dwell on its fearsome concerns.

Cultivate Gratitude

If you build up the habit of writing down three things you are grateful for at the end of each day (before you go to sleep) it forces you to acknowledge, through all the detritus of life, the small minutiae of things to be thankful for. But it's also more than that. The act of writing a gratitude journal activates your brain to start looking for things to be grateful for. So during the day your eyes open, you notice little events, achievements, relationships, acts of kindness and small wonders. Instead of racing through the hours, you do actually stop and smell the roses. You do look at the rainbow colours of the fruit and vegetables in your fridge, you do notice the bee buzzing on the flower outside your window. You allow all your senses to awaken, your field of vision opens, you feel the warmth of the sun more acutely on your back, the wind in your hair, the sand under your toes. You look at the faces on the metro, you see them as people like you, in all their colours, shapes and forms – you love them for their differences. You give off a vibe that makes them notice you too. Maybe you catch someone's eye and you smile. You've lifted their day and yours. You've created a connection between you and the world around you. With gratitude you make the world a more positive, vibrant and colourful place. You focus on the now, and on being present in the moment. And that is a powerful alternative to fear.

⊨ CORE-WORK ⊨

Using the double-hand dialogue technique, transform stress into **gratitude**. When you spin complaints into gratitude it forces your brain to be creative and solution-focused instead of fear-driven.

Think of something that is stressing you out right now. Say it out loud as a **complaint**. For example: *I'm always so broke.*

> NURTURER: *Not having enough money is very stressful. I understand that but complaining about it isn't helping you not be broke. How else can you think about it?*
> LITTLE YOU: *I don't know. If I knew I wouldn't be broke would I? (petulant toddler alert)*
> NURTURER: *Well, you can carry on complaining and carry on being broke if you like. Or you can put a spin on it, and give yourself a chance to not be broke and not live in fear about being broke. How does that sound?*

LITTLE YOU: *Unrealistic. (sulky voice)*

NURTURER: *Wow, you've got this bad.*

LITTLE YOU: *You try paying all the bills and the mortgage every month when you're this broke. (getting aggressive now)*

NURTURER: *Do you manage to pay the bills and the mortgage every month?*

LITTLE YOU: *Yes, but there's hardly anything left afterwards.*

NURTURER: *But you do manage to pay the bills and the mortgage?*

LITTLE YOU: *Yes. (reluctantly)*

NURTURER: *I am very impressed that as a freelancer, you do everything you possibly can to find different ways to earn money, so that you can pay the bills and the mortgage every month. You are incredibly creative at bringing in money from different sources. It really is an amazing feat.*

LITTLE YOU: *I hadn't thought of it like that.*

NURTURER: *You must feel incredibly proud of yourself. You do what you love and you manage to pay the bills. Not everyone can say that.*

LITTLE YOU: *I guess not.*

NURTURER: *How does that make you feel?*

LITTLE YOU: *Actually, it makes me feel grateful that I do a job I love and get paid for it. My time is my own and I am grateful for that freedom to be my own boss. I don't have much money but I do have lots of things to be grateful for.*

NURTURER: *I'm really happy to hear you say that. Gratitude is a much more creative way to think.*

LITTLE YOU: *It makes me feel less stressed and fearful. And I'm already thinking of other ways to bring in money or even of creating ways that I can earn money while I sleep.*

NURTURER: *Well done you!*

LITTLE YOU: *I am so grateful I have you watching my back and reminding me to think in more positive ways. Complaining really doesn't get me anywhere except a deep dark pit of despair. Instead I feel invigorated and inspired. Thank you!*

Now you try turning a complaint into a gratitude, or a fear into a blessing.

Sticking At It

- Resilience
- Mastery

Road to Resilience

How do you keep doggedly on from one fear-struck thought, action or event to another?

We hear remarkable stories of resilience and resourcefulness of ordinary people battling through extraordinary experiences. A Sudanese man whose whole family had been killed managed to escape Sudan, travelled across Europe, hid under the axel of a school coach through the Channel Tunnel, jumped off at a service station, turned up at a police station to seek asylum and ended up in Liverpool. Now he runs a humanitarian organisation to help people in war-torn Sudan. He displayed a resilient and creative approach to a terrible situation and came out the other side with a purpose.

Every day, those of us in less extreme situations find that we must dig deep into that well of resilience. It holds us strong through times of fear. What is that ability to tap into sustained effort against the all the odds? How do you keep on going when you want to give up?

Emotional resilience requires adaptability, ingenuity and innovation in tough times. It requires creativity, positive attitude, optimism and a determined proactive approach. But we build this attitude throughout life. Gary Hymns is a key grip in the film industry with James Bond, *Star Wars*, *The Golden Compass*, *Thor*, *Robin Hood*, *Captain America*, *Shackleton* and *Into the Woods* under his belt (to name but a few). All this from a lad who started out working as a post boy at London Weekend Television when he was sixteen.

Gary has a good analogy for resilience. He's still a runner at the age of fifty-nine, competing in races for the Serpentine Running Club: 'I always say to new runners who are exhausted or new people in the job, when they start the first mile and say 'I can't do this' – well, your body works like a gear change in a car, you set off and it's going, 'what's this, I was walking down the street and now I'm charging down the road, and it hurts'. But after about a mile it goes, 'Oh I know what we're doing, we're running', you keep going and it drops down a gear and suddenly it gets easier.

His job requires the same resilience and perseverance. Gripping is incredibly physical work, moving the camera like a choreographer, gliding it responsively with the actors, sometimes under supremely tough conditions. Often Gary and his team are standing up for thirteen hours, shifting heavy gear, physically tracking the camera, often in precarious locations, rehearsing one shot ten times, doing twenty takes and maybe running with Daniel Craig (OK it's not all bad) along rooftops, or on top of a moving train, or on location in fifty-two-degree heat pushing the camera all day.

So what keeps him going? Gary explains his motivation was always 'we wanted to save money so we didn't have such a big mortgage, having two children, we just got our heads down and did the work. But it's not for everyone, it's unsociable, you have to have a very understanding partner and you've got to be prepared to do the hours really . . . you've just got to continue, you've got to keep going. I've got eleven guys on my crew. If I my head drops or I think: "it's cold, I don't want to be working like this", you have to keep up your spirits, keep everybody motivated and break it up with humour, which we do all the time. Some might call it gallows humour, but it does work.'

Gary takes big, heavy-duty jobs now, not because he needs to but because he knows his men need to work. They are at the beginnings of their careers. They have young families, mortgages, bills to pay; they're freelance in a frighteningly fickle business. Gary fears for them and so, as someone at the top of his game, he leads by example. He takes the work, does the horrendous hours, grinds through impossible conditions, finds ways to make jokes when morale is low, and he gets all his team running to keep fit physically and mentally. On location he'll support and mentor his guys when they are feeling lonely and far from home, knackered and fearful that they won't get through the next gruelling day. He's been there, he understands, he's learned resilience and he passes it on. An inspiring career and resilient attitude; and it is people like Gary that can act as a guiding light to us all as we endeavour to carve our own way through the ups and downs of life. As ever, perseverance is the name of the game and being surrounded by people who support you, with a dash of humour thrown in.

But what about the time when hellfire and brimstone are hailing down on you and you want to plonk yourself down in the middle of the street and yell 'Alright already!' You don't of course, you trudge on through the mire of obstacles until you reach the other side. Does sticking it out through thick and thin come easily to you or could you do with a bit of help when you are faced with adversity? Indeed, is resilience something we can develop? Yes.

You use the tricks of the trade. You do your deep breathing, you practice your mindful meditation, you take aerobic exercise, you keep healthy. The more your body, mind and spirit are fed, watered and nurtured, the stronger your ability to face the stresses of life, the quicker you can adapt and recover, and the less you will be affected by surprises and negative throws of the dice. You will be able to forgive more easily, reducing the pain of resentment and bitterness when you have been hurt or let down. When the very worst happens, whether it be losing a loved one, or your home, or surviving a terrorist attack. Resilience is what helps you show your mettle and start over.

Scientifically, 'resilience' is defined as the ability of a material or an object to resume its natural form after it has had a disruption or a knock. For example, a building that settles back after an earthquake tremor. The more strength and flexibility that the engineers have built into its design, the more likely that it will resume its original shape without stress damage. Build your own strength and flexibility with the daily practices I set out in this book.

Using your creative thinking skills, you develop optimism. One of the ways is to seek out meaning and purpose even in terrible times. Victor Emil Frankl (1905–1997) was an Austrian neurologist, psychiatrist and Holocaust survivor, who devoted his life to studying, understanding and promoting 'meaning'.

His 1946 book *Man's Search for Meaning* offers profound lessons on being resilient in dire situations. Frankl says meaning and purpose is found in every moment of living; life never ceases to have meaning, even in suffering and death. This message is powerfully demonstrated in one notable passage of his book, where he recalls how a handful of men, in the concentration camps in which he lived, would give away their last piece of bread to others regardless of their own suffering. Despite having had seemingly everything taken away from them, their attitude and ability to choose how to behave, remained.

Resilience is not about being super human. When Frankl talks of withstanding the horrors of the concentration camps he argues that humans thrive on the fight and struggle for a cause and that it is the possibility of living with integrity and in congruence with one's own values that leads to resilience in the face of extreme adversity.

When we know why we are here, and that meaning is consistently entwined with our values, then we are able to keep going against the odds. Honing your creative thinking skills allows you to increase your competency levels for resilience in times of turbulence. As Albert Einstein said, 'Out of clutter, find simplicity. From discord, find harmony. In the middle of difficulty lies opportunity'. Finding opportunity takes imagination and the ability to reframe perspectives. Reframing is a creative thinking process at work. Creativity is a form of elastic thinking. It is looking at something with fresh eyes, from a different angle that allows us to see a way forward. Resilience is when we are able to be flexible, to improvise and reshape our circumstances or our response to unavoidable adversity, and keep going.

....

Learn to be resilient before you need it

1. Practise mindfulness.
2. Practise deep breathing techniques.
3. Keep working on your Vision Scrapbook or your Art Journal to keep your mind on the things that excite you, make you happy and are worth surviving and thriving for.
4. Practise daily gratitude.
5. Learn to forgive.
6. Deal with past baggage. Have psychotherapy if you feel you need it.
7. When you think you've gone as far as you can, go one step further.

....

⊱═ CORE-WORK ═⊰

Do this exercise from your Nurturer as Little You using your non-dominant hand:

1. What is the worst thing that has happened to you?
2. What did you do to come through it?
3. How could you see it as an opportunity for growth rather than something to make you more fearful and cautious in the future?

Now try this with your dialoguing.

1. Think of something that someone has done to you that you think you could never forgive.
2. Imagine you had done that to someone else.
3. Now imagine writing to that person and asking for forgiveness.
4. As that other person write a letter of forgiveness to you.
5. How do you feel being forgiven?
6. How does it feel forgiving someone?

We fear forgiving someone because we think it makes us look like a mug; tantamount to having 'kick me' tattooed across your forehead. But when you are able to forgive, you are freeing yourself from anger, bitterness and fear. It is not easy but it is vital to living a resilient life.

10,000 Hours to Mastery

Resilience is about not giving up or giving in. It is about keeping going in the face of adversity. It is what beats fear of failure, fear of success, fear of judgment, fear of losing out; or whatever fear you can name. When you keep showing up to tackle problems and face issues, your adaptability and flexibly evolve, and fear starts to take a back seat. You may not feel it for a while, but if you keep at it, no matter what, it is what gets you to mastery.

There's few artists, musicians, inventors, innovators or sports-people who don't understand the 10,000 Hour Rule. No matter how inherently talented they are, they know that to get better they have to keep applying what they know to the job at hand. Regularly, every day, forever. The same is true for the rest of us. Part of life

satisfaction comes from finding what we enjoy doing and then pushing ourselves, a little past our comfort zone, to keep trying to do it
better. Sometimes that includes the mundane, it is often hard and
always requires grit. Grit is defined as 'perseverance and passion for
long-term goals'. It's going hammer and tongs for about ten years
with focused effort to get even close to mastery. Of course, we never
reach absolute mastery or perfection, but it is the seductive allure
that keeps us going.

Some people think mastery is only for the talented. But mastery
is a choice, a mindset, a determination. A means to fight fear of
success or failure. We once believed that intelligence or talent
is hard-wired with a finite supply handed out only to the lucky
ones, leaving the rest of us scrabbling for the remaining crumbs.
However, now we know that the mind is like a muscle and needs
constant work to gradually pump it up.[21] We build intelligence, skill
and talent. Musicians know this to be fact. No matter what bright
little stars they were at five, they are not going to be walking the

boards towards the grand piano at Carnegie Hall until they have worked their fingers to the bone and perfected their musical muscles. And they will only do that if they have a passion for it.

Your 'thing' may not be to tinkle the keys of the *Moonlight Sonata*, but as long as your starting point is something that you could enjoy doing a lot, for a long period of time, then you can work towards mastery – and life satisfaction comes from being involved in that process. Choose something that will give you the opportunity to grow and develop ad infinitum. You will never regret it. The process of stretching that mastery mindset muscle is powerfully life enhancing. It doesn't require gongs, trophies, Oscars or big bucks to bring a sense of achievement. It delivers that on its own. It helps you FEAR LESS and be more.

When you are the wrong end of mastery; when you are at the foot of the mountain, it can be terrifying. You may want to give up at the thought of the gargantuan task ahead of you. As a novice runner at fifty-odd I get frustrated at my slow times and lack of endurance. I used to be a fast sprinter, I used to win races. This trudging through the miles feels wearisome; often it feels like hell. I feel disappointed in myself. When I push too hard, I injure myself. I put expectations on myself that I can't reach. YET. Yet is such a powerful word. It holds promise and hope. It silences the fear of not coming up trumps right now. If you keep going you will get better, stronger and more proficient. It's nature's law. And through the slog come glimmers of light. Last night I ran a shorter distance with the intention of picking up my speed. I ran my fastest mile yet. I am getting better bit by bit. My trainers have done 100 miles. At the rate I'm going, by the time you read this I will have done 1000 miles. If I do ten times that I will have run 10,000 miles. Maybe then I will be running like the wind.

In her TED Talk *The Power of Yet* and book *Mindest*, Carol S. Dweck describes her extensive work with children on the subject of gifted or learned ability. She devised studies with two groups of students. One who believed themselves to be naturally gifted, and another who were not burdened with this label. The tasks set were for children much older than the kids in either group, so essentially beyond the ability of any of the children selected. Dweck found that when the 'Naturally Gifted' group discovered they couldn't do the tasks, they feared failing or looking stupid, blamed the game and gave up. The other group, the 'Willing Learners', didn't blame anything or anyone. They knuckled down, enjoyed the challenge and kept persevering through the difficulties, trying different approaches until they had achieved a result. They weren't hampered by a belief in their own in-built ability, they simply knew they didn't know and set about learning how. The 'Naturally Gifted' group were held back by FEAR. The 'Willing Learners' group didn't allow fear to get in the way.

Mastery and Good Enough

Everyone has the ability to move mountains or build sandcastles; it's just done one clod at a time.

⊱═ CORE-WORK ═⊰

- Get five stones of different sizes. Using both dominant and non-dominant hand working together, place one on top of each other, until they are all balanced in a column

- Now rearrange them in a different order

- Do it five times in different ways

Is that harder? Did you give up? Did you get frustrated? Did you enjoy the challenge? Are you 'Naturally Gifted' at stone-piling or are you a 'Willing Learner'?

Do your dual-handed dialogue to answer these questions:

1. What are you scared of failing at?
2. What can you do to become a 'Willing Learner' around that fear?
3. What can you do today to start out on your learning curve?

⊨====⊣

Being Flexible

- Embracing Change
- Changing Places and Spaces
- The Power of Persuasion
- The Art of Negotiation

'Nothing is softer or more flexible than water, yet nothing can resist it.'

– Lao Tzu

Embracing Change

Q: *What have films and ego/fear got in common?*
A: *Resistance to change.*
At the Cannes Film Festival in 2015, I went to a seminar on film distribution with the British Film Institute's Head of Audiences,

and film distributors eOne and Icon. They were discussing the impending change in the viewing habits of film audiences. For years, theatres refused to budge on changing from 35mm projection to digital. They said the quality wouldn't be as good and audiences would turn away in droves. It took one film, *Avatar*, only distributed in 3D digital, to change all that. Whatever the story, the visual spectacle proved the point and the result was a box office phenomenon. The theatres were right to be afraid. Digital did change everything and perhaps the writing is on the wall for the physical experience of movie-watching in the way that we know it. But maybe the best is yet to come?

Humans are stubborn, but we'd still be living in caves if we didn't have that itch in the back of our brains that tells us we're more than the sum of a bearskin and two flints rubbed together. Not ones to rest on our laurels, we thought our cave walls were dull in plain rock and set about decorating them with fine drawings decanting tales of derring-dos. We had an instinct to tell stories and we acted on that urge to move from grunting to entertaining. We created the start of film in pictures with narrative. We could have been content with such raw cartoons, but we forged on through the centuries – never quite satisfied, we leapfrogged from one mode of visual storytelling to another, fuelled by our continuous unsatiated desire to disrupt the status quo.

So here we are on the edge of another visual revolution, virtual reality, where there are no screens but only immersive experiences. The world changes and we must change with it. We must harness our brain so that it can propel us forward.

In America, orthopaedic spine surgeons are performing over 600,000 back and neck fusions a year. It's big business. But one surgeon, Dr David Hanscom, author of *Back in Control*,[22] was getting frustrated. He realised that studies showed over and again that spine fusions were only 15–25% effective in stopping chronic back pain. He started to look deeper and discovered that acute pain is initially registered in the pain region of the brain but, after six months to a year, it leaves that area and settles in the emotional region of the brain as chronic pain. He realised that anxiety was setting off the adrenals and causing inflammation. It becomes a whole syndrome of the neurophysiological order, instead of just a physical one. He decided to change the way he'd worked the whole of his surgical career – he started to treat his patients' anxiety as well as their skeletons.

He now gets patients to do expressive writing about their negative thoughts, then asks them to immediately throw the paper away, without judging or analysing the content. Over time it helps to break the negative, anxious cycle. He focuses the patient on reprogramming, repetition and relaxing the body system. The programme also includes active meditation or mindfulness (awareness, detachment, and reprogramming), good nutrition, sleep, de-stressing, a positive outlook and body strengthening. It is a comprehensive retraining and it requires willingness and engagement on the part of the patient. If they are prepared to engage and change, then it works.

But most people are too scared to change their lifestyle – even when pain is their body's way of telling them that they need to change how they're living. Dr Hanscom says most would rather go under the knife, with its bleak outlook, than take responsibility and control of their own chronic pain treatment. A nutritionist friend of mine says that even trying to get people to start to drink more water is an uphill battle. And they have come to her for nutritional advice!

I have been lucky with my clients. They have had the courage to challenge their fears, to ask for coaching, to invest their money, to commit to the process and to do the work. But it's not easy for them. Change is like trying to ride a horse in the opposite direction to which it's heading. I was once on a horse that spooked. He bolted like a bat out of hell. I lost my stirrups, had to hold on by my knees, it careered towards a low hanging wire and I had to duck before I was garrotted. It was heading towards a six-foot high oil pipe leading to the sea, so I had to use all my might to steer it away. There was no way I would survive it jumping that pipe. But nothing was going to stop this beast beneath me until my two companions corralled it with their horses. When you face change are you like that bolting horse?

It takes a monumental effort to get people to the place where they are ready to do what it takes. It's all very well, lying on a beach in the sunshine, dreaming of how, on returning home after your holidays, you will resume your gym sessions, ditch the daily sugar hits, drink less, reduce the stress at work, spend quality time with the kids, find a hobby.

You put all your energy into creating change and, when the desired results aren't immediately forthcoming, you sink back into your own negative feedback: 'What's the point? It's never going to work, I'm useless, success isn't for me, people like us don't get rich anyway, I'm never going to get a six-pack, etc.'

You have to think differently, you have to do something differently. Change won't happen overnight. There will be mini-successes and major setbacks. It is important to understand the process and record the positive results. You will easily remember the failed attempts and forget the small achievements. You need to switch this around. The more you focus on each step forward, the more your brain will resolve to entrench its new-found successes. The brain is plastic; with enough repetition it will gradually build up new habits and, in so doing, change will arrive.

'I refuse to accept the view that mankind is so tragically bound to the starless midnight of racism and war that the bright daybreak of peace and brotherhood can never become a reality.'

– Martin Luther King, Jr

How to Change

1. Do a mind map of where you are now, where you want to be and what you need to do to get there. Make it very colourful and fill it with photographs and cut-out images representing the change you want to see.

2. Take consistent action; repetition in small steps will gradually 'change' your mind.

3. Refocus from the old ways of doing things, distract yourself with more interesting alternatives.

4. Reward yourself for each little change you succeed in making.

⊨ CORE-WORK ⊨

Daily brain dump. Let go of the past by consistently writing down your angers and frustrations on a piece of paper with your non-dominant hand and throwing it away. You are acknowledging what has happened, but you aren't tying yourself to it. The act of throwing away the paper releases you towards change.

⊨　　⊨

Changing places

In changing ourselves for the better we must also consider the envir-onment we inhabit: our homes, our schools, our work place or the public spaces we move through. We are hugely, if unconsciously, affected by our surroundings and if they are having a negative impact on our wellbeing we must make moves to change the spaces if we can.

Whether you're the guy that chooses to live in a citadel of cardboard boxes on a roundabout, or the gal who turned a truck container into a bijou pad, or the palace dweller, or social housing occupant, the space you create around you tells something of who you are. When hoarders hoard they bury their fears and anxieties in 'stuff'. When they are helped to clear the space, suddenly they feel clear-headed; ready to lose that weight, change jobs, ditch the loser boyfriend. Even for the rest of us, sorting out a cupboard or drawer makes us feel better, lighter and more ready for anything.

It is our antidote to the fear of an uncontrollable world. We can feel relatively safe and secure by creatively laying claim to our corner of the world. Even the Fourth Amendment of the US Constitution proclaims that:

> [T]he right of the people to be secure in their persons, houses, papers, and effects, against unreasonable searches and seizures, shall not be violated, and no Warrants shall issue, but upon probable cause, supported by Oath or affirmation, and particularly describing the place to be searched, and the persons or things to be seized.

We repeatedly lay claim to our safety zone. For example, when I was sitting in a windowless room with a bunch of actors waiting to go on the set of the TV show *Holby*, we displayed our fearful, animalistic and territorial instincts to mark our spots. From one day to the next each person returned to the same chair they had occupied the day before. There is something primitive about this behaviour, pre-ordained to assure we each have our slot of land to call our own. Which is why it is so distressing to see so many thousands of refugees, leaving war-torn homes, trekking across land and sea trying to find sanctuary and space in which to feel safe.

When we were filming in India, we travelled through acres of streets where the pavements were piled with rickety and rusty columns, two or three stories high, of open-sided boxes that contained whole families. One little boy wanted to take us to his home in the slums of Mumbai. He guided us along paths that meandered as rivers of mud across the municipal dump, along open sewers where people washed themselves and their clothes, made their daily ablutions, where children played, and on, into the corrugated hut he called home. His mother and father greeted us and we entered a single dark room, lit only by a small blue gas flame heating a huge, shiny metal pot of simmering onions. Other children played at his mother's feet. A dog sniffed the mud floor for scraps. There was one chair and a small table. And a mattress rolled up in the corner. Washing hung from the ceiling.

The whole place was no bigger than your garden shed, with an old pink sari strung up for a front door and the children's drawings stuck to the walls. The mother turned down the gas, with a deeply oil-scarred arm, and sat down with her son to help him with his reading homework. This family had created a home with the bits that they could scavenge, and made it a place for children to learn and grow. They created much from very little. Humanity's ability to think creatively can turn even squalor into a loving environment where people can thrive. Even when, every year, the monsoon rains come and sweep it all away, and they have to start again with what little they managed to cling on to, they do so; they rebuild the walls and the children make new drawings to decorate them. It is not ideal in any sense. No one wants anyone to live such a meagre existence. But with global population levels set to rise to 9.7 billion in 2050, and with the world in such fear-inducing political, economic, climactic, war-mongering turbulence, we need to start using our imaginations to find achievable humane solutions to escalating displacement, homelessness or impoverished housing.

Humans have evolved from the understanding that what we need is food, warmth and shelter. That fact that we stamp our mark on whatever space we inhabit tells of our further need for self-expression. Our creative juices flow out of us once we step up beyond basic survival. Our dream-palaces are individual, unique and may only consist of a mattress on the floor, a chair, a book and a freshly picked flower in a broken bottle on the windowsill. For someone, that is an inspiration. Van Gogh made art that fills major museums in cities across the world that depicted his home looking just like that.

My parents have recently downsized. They've given most of their possessions away and now have just what they need and love around them. They had the courage to let go of a lifetime's accumulation and enjoy a simpler, easier life. The Zen Buddhist monk lets go of pretty things and personal possessions because she strives to be enough, rather than to have enough. I don't propose you throw everything into a skip to show that you've knocked fear on the head, but perhaps as you take on the new habits outlined in this book, you won't need to bury yourself in 'stuff', but instead will slough off the slack and create places that reflect a simpler, streamlined, stronger, more resilient, self-contained and creative version of you.

Changing your Space

1. De-cluttering is symbolic of letting go of your fears.
2. Start with one room, one cupboard or one drawer at a time.
3. Have three boxes: chuck, cherish and charity. Throw away anything broken that you can't fix, anything you haven't used or enjoyed in years, anything that you just consider to be 'stuff'. Anything that is in good condition but you no longer love, donate to charity. Keep the things that you do love and want to cherish.

4. When you have worked through your home in this way you will feel a sense of freedom and liberation. You can make your space beautiful with the fewer items that you have chosen to keep, the things that give you pleasure when you look at them.

5. Simplify for peace of mind.

....

=== CORE-WORK ===

Answer the Nurturer's questions with your Little You's non-dominant hand:

NURTURER: *If your home was on fire and you could only take one thing (not your photos which the fireman saves for you) what would it be? Describe why it has meaning and significance for you. What makes it a talisman for your life? How would it help you to move forward and build a fresh start and new home? How does it symbolise change for you? How does it protect you from fear? What fears are they?*

LITTLE ME: *Mine would be a little stone Buddha head that I have. Somehow looking at him I feel that I would be able to find answers to my fears, to my way forward. I might find wisdom and inspiration in that stone head, maybe comfort in his eyes. I like to hold the stone in my hand, feel the contours, wonder at the age of the stone, who found it, who carved it, where they lived, what life they had, what they thought about when they carved the stone, the love they put into their handiwork. I think this piece of craft would help me start over.*

=====

The Power of Persuasion

You create your home as your sanctuary, as a place to step away from the world, a place to feel safe, secure and warm. But you can't hide there. The world awaits and if you don't step outside it will come and get you.

Sometimes you might have to stand on a platform before hundreds of others and speak publicly to persuade your audience of your argument. At other times, it might be that you have to persuade your boss, your boyfriend or your best friend to come around to your view. Persuasion takes courage.

Whether it's negotiating with an aggressor in a war zone or a child in a sweet shop, what you are *not* doing is trying to coerce them. It has to be to the benefit of them and you, not just you. Helping them to see why it is a benefit is the real art. Start by identifying those who will come around to your way of thinking pretty easily. They probably share a similar mindset and references. It won't take much to swing their vote. The others who are entrenched in their own persuasions will take longer. It takes time. And patience.

Think of segregation in America. Dr Martin Luther King was a great persuader. He was not afraid to speak out on a big scale. 'I have a dream . . .' He already had black people on side because they were suffering the degradation he was trying to change. Then he got the white folk who knew it was wrong and that it was time to do something about it. Then it was those who hadn't really thought about it, but recognised when confronted with it that it was wrong. And then those who felt guilty but went with the flow; afraid to rock the boat. Then those who found it inconvenient to change but saw they were beginning to stand out as the bad guys. And then the laws changed and the staunch resisters had to come on board. Dr Martin Luther King faced terrifying threats in his fight for equality for all. And he was eventually killed for his campaign. He knew he might be. He must have been scared, but it didn't stop him. In the end he won.

When you align yourself with your purpose, you and everyone else will be clear about who you are and where you are coming from. Approach people aggressively, or sneakily, and their shackles will rise and their defences will shift up a gear. Traditional selling methods leave a bad taste in our mouths. We are highly attuned to 'the pitch'. We know the pattern. But nevertheless we get drawn in, flirted with, flattered, then 'bam', here comes the left hook and their hand is in your wallet. That's not the ethics of persuasion we are interested in. You must believe that the other person will be better placed if they choose to take your proposal on board.

But you don't know if they will benefit unless you become consistently invested in them. Know what they like, be interested in what they do. Understand their FEAR. Help them climb over their hurdles. Let them challenge your convictions and beliefs. They must have evidence of your solidarity to your word. See how slowly persuasion grows in potency over time and context. Then, through persistence, you grow trust in those you wish to follow you. When you ask them to help you in return it touches their human need to reciprocate.

In the digital age, where so much is available for free, we must tap into the free exchange. It is easy to give free stuff. It helps people to like you and then when you have something to offer that they need, your levels of persuasion need only be gentle; if they are already with you in spirit they will pay because it suits them to. If you panic into high velocity persuasion tactics it turns people off, they think you are in it for the quick buck, not because you do what you do out of passion and conviction.

Consider Abraham Lincoln. He lost his mother, three sons, sister, girlfriend, he failed in business and lost eight separate elections before he was elected President of the United States. People voted for him because he believed in what he promised and he never swayed from his path, no matter what rocks were thrown at him.

When we lay out our table with what we can provide in a motivating, invigorating, refreshing and trustworthy way, we draw people to us. We validate them and honour them. We just have to stay consistently congruent to the path we have created, with their validation in our line of sight. When we transgress that silent agreement, we create a cesspit of calamity.

Look what happened to car manufacturer Volkswagen. They had generations of loyal followers, they stayed true to their purpose; they gave 'cars for the people'. And then they blew it by secretly tampering with the clean diesel regulation tests in the US. Decades of unbroken belief in the brand were brutally severed in an instant. They torched trust and time-honoured affection. They stepped off their path in pursuit of profit, and everything they built came tumbling down. It will take a very long time, and a lot of creative understanding, to gently persuade customers to come back into the fold. Betrayal is the enemy of persuasion.

Communication is key. Where there is conflict you must bring calm and conviction. Anger and armies must be the last resort, used when all else has failed and only in a short, sharp, shock treatment. Humanity owes it to itself to constantly fight for peaceful persuasion no matter how long it takes, no matter how scary the process.

The world will always be a land of negotiation, a place where we all jostle for scarce space, shelter, food, warmth, love. But the power of persuasion helps us interact, evolve and grow with and around each other, in the pursuit of creating better, less fearful lives.

....

Persuade with Passion

1. Know what you believe in and find people who second that belief.
2. Empathise with people so they feel you understand their point of view.
3. Face your fears about public speaking by starting in small ways: a one-minute pitch at a networking event, a speech at a family party, join a public speaking group or run workshops. Increase the size of your audience gradually.
4. Talk about what you know.
5. Prepare and practice.

....

⊨ CORE-WORK ⊨

Answer your Nurturer using your Little You's non-dominant hand:

Imagine you have been asked to do a talk for the ideas website TED. Talk about something that really matters to you – something you want to persuade others to care about. Base it around a fear that you have. For example:

'I am scared about climate change so I have decided to become vegan. Here are my reasons why I think you should care about climate change and how if you became vegan you could effect immediate change overnight . . .'

Write non-stop for ten minutes. Try it out on a friend. How convincing are you? Now ask them about themselves and their beliefs around your fear and solution to that fear. Really try to understand their point of view, even if you don't agree with them. Take it on board and then rewrite your persuasive talk. Is it more persuasive this time? Is your friend more open to your ideas now you have addressed their concerns?

Now imagine being in room with someone with extreme views that are the complete opposite to yours. In order to save lives, you have to be able to persuade them to come around to your way of thinking. Fear drives you to open up to them because you must. How differently do you listen and persuade now? How much more delicately do you proceed?

This is a hard task and I don't blame you for not trying it. But imagine those people who have to. For example, imagine taking part in the Paris Climate Change Summit and you fervently want to persuade an economic superpower not to leave. How do you use your passion to persuade someone who has diametrically opposed views to you?

The Art of Negotiation

OK, so not everything is going to go your way even when you've developed a mindset for peaceful persuasion. You are going to come to loggerheads with an obstreperous someone, somewhere along the way. You can just beat them over the head, cavewoman style, with a large club, or you can learn the art of negotiation. It's a dance, a piece of choreography between alternate ideas or offended parties. The creative thinking involved is intricate and balanced, it requires give and take, and it will test your deepest FEARS of rejection, of being wrong, of being rebuffed, or being ridiculed and of losing face.

Every morning I'm woken by the squawking of ducks, swans and geese fighting over territories. It's usually a right old barney and isn't over until one side is chased away by the other. Or a fox with sharp teeth has the last word. Fortunately, as humans, we have the choice to find another way. Global peace processes are, necessarily, defined by negotiation. But how do we learn the art of peaceful settlement in our personal and business lives?

The first step is not with the other side but within yourself. You are most likely feeling hard done by. You may feel emotionally hurt or misunderstood, unfairly criticised or judged. Fear of some kind is most certainly underlining it all. So how do you step aside from your ego in the spirit of bridging the divide and resolving the conflict? Imagine there is a gap between someone saying something that infuriates you and the moment that you respond. This space is filled with choice. You can choose to launch a counter-attack or you can choose to pause and reflect.

If you choose reflection then you can use that space to look at your values. Do they include peace, tranquillity, love, understanding, connection and friendship? If you understand your core values then you can plan your next steps not only with integrity for who you are, but with an open mind to the core values of others. You must also know your limits. Your healthy boundaries that keep your values protected. If not allowing other people's anger to intimidate you is one of your boundaries you will need to create a place of negotiation that keeps you safe from that intimidation. Now you are ready to open up the space for negotiation. Your role, as you stand before your 'opposition', is to extend the hand of trust. You make it clear that you will listen deeply to their views, feelings, emotions, hurts and you will seek to understand their position. But equally you express your wish for them to listen and seek to understand yours. When you listen, it is not just hearing their words, it is looking more deeply at the meaning behind them. What are they really saying and how can you help them to feel better about the underlying issues?

This is not the time to take what they are saying personally, even if you fear they are attacking you again. Ignore the sound of accusation and search for the layers of needs that aren't being met. Listen and repeat what they are saying so that they know you are hearing them correctly. Ask questions that take you to deeper level of understanding. People want to be heard, and when they feel they are being listened to, they become less defensive and will begin to be ready to hear what you have to say. When it is your turn to share your view, ensure that you remove all accusations and concentrate purely on how 'we' can find a solution so that everyone's needs may be met. It will be a two-way rotation of listening, understanding and acknowledging until the gap between you closes and the emotions subside.

It is in this space that both minds will open up to the creative process, and forward thinking and positive solutions will emerge. A successful negotiation is not one winning over the other, nor one appeasing the other, or a compromise in which neither feels satisfied. It is the middle way in which everyone feels understood, their values respected and their needs met.

You will have to tread lightly, you will have to think on your feet, you will have to artfully find a way to bring your 'enemy' to the table, and you will have to find creative ways to guide them to see why they should help deliver the outcome you desire. It will hopefully not be a life or death situation, but it might mean you can save a marriage, help a child out of a bullied situation, get a pay rise or nail a dispute at work. Whatever it is, if you have got to the point where negotiating is necessary, then a creative approach that stands fear to one side, will help you succeed.

Very often, as you may well have found working through this programme, the negotiation is between your inner selves. If you suffer chronic pain you will know this all too well. Fear makes pain worse, so there is a very good reason to negotiate with your fear on how to best manage it. I suffer from migraines, so my negotiation dialogue goes something like this:

NURTURER: *How are you feeling?*

LITTLE LOU: *I'm in agony, thanks for asking.*

NURTURER: *OK, so let's work through our pain coping strategies.*

LITTLE LOU: *Sod off and give me painkillers.*

NURTURER: *I can see that you want instant relief, but they are only going to make matters worse long term.*

LITTLE LOU: *I don't care about long term. I want the pain to go away NOW!*

NURTURER: *Yes, I can understand that. Let me work through the alternatives to painkillers so that you can get some relief now, but not endanger yourself long term. And I am also narrowing the field on the causes. There is evidence that gluten, caffeine and sugar can trigger migraine. How about we try taking that out of our diet for a month and see if that helps. If not, we'll look again at conventional therapies. How does that sound?*

LITTLE LOU: *One month? I guess it's worth a go. OK, but I can't take any more than that.*

NURTURER: *Great, that's a deal. And in the meantime, I am going to take care of you so you don't get stressed or dehydrated, and I will get delicious healthy foods to replace the sugar and gluten. Now forget about that deadline for now, lie down and do your deep breathing and I will get someone to massage those tight shoulders and neck muscles.*

LITTLE LOU: *Thank you* ☺

Negotiation is a delicate dance around our fears but if we put aside our ego and embrace our natural desire to find solutions, we will be able to find a middle way.

Ten Principles of Creative Negotiation

1. Remove the ego from the equation by understanding which of your fears is lurking.
2. Work from your core values.
3. Put healthy boundaries in place.
4. Find common areas of mutual interest.
5. Listen and seek to understand.
6. Respect given is likely to be to be reciprocated.
7. Be assertive not aggressive.
8. Engage fully with each other; name and acknowledge their emotions as you understand them.
9. Discuss how 'we' might find a solution.
10. Keep your eye on the end result: finding what works for both parties.

End of Week Three

⊨ CORE-WORK ⊨

Write the answers to these questions with your non-dominant hand

Nurturer:
- What tools have you learned in this week?
- How have you moved forward towards your goals?
- What action steps have you taken?
- How are you feeling about your fears right now?
- How can I support you this week?

⊨⊨

Week Four

....

SURVIVING and THRIVING
the hazards and hiccups

- THE BIG DIP: Catastrophising, When to Surrender
- LEARNING NOT FAILING: Learning to Fail, Rejoice in Rejection
- IT TAKES COURAGE: Being Brave, Slowing Down, Taking Time Out

....

You think you are making progress and then another hazard or hic-cup comes your way. You imagine disaster, and then it really does happen. You dread failure so you don't try. You're terrified of being rejected so you don't reach out. Fear holds you back and keeps you down. Maybe something huge and life-changing does happen, and forces you to take an alternative course of action. How do you find courage, how do you become brave? How can you survive and then go on to thrive despite bad things happening?

NOTE: *Not everything here will be relevant to you right now but read it all and do the core-work exercise for the areas that ring some bells for you.*

The Big Dip

- Catastrophising
- When to Surrender

So now fighting fear is feeling like a lot of hard work. You've got a job, commitments and not much time, and you're feeling over-whelmed and knackered. The results of your dreams and goal setting aren't coming fast enough, it's all going wrong and you're doubting whether doing this coaching malarkey is worth the hassle. Little You may be catastrophising big time . . .

Catastrophising

Do you excel at turning FEAR into Catastrophe? Do you imagine the very worst that can happen? Hollywood depicts the disaster movie, science fiction creates wild experiments gone awry, images of Hell hang in museums and yell out from religious texts. We scare ourselves witless with barbaric eventualities of doom if we step out of line from the status quo. Religion and the 'powers-that-be' have controlled the masses through history with tales of torture and everlasting punishment if we defy the rules.

Fear feeds the darkest recesses of our souls and **catastrophising** turns fear into something monstrous and uncontrollable. Especially for people who have experienced something traumatic and life-changing. On this matter, I am an 'expert'. I moved to Lockerbie in rural South-west Scotland from a road in London where people chased each other with machetes. I thought I had moved to a place where I could live and work peacefully, free of worry. Then Pan Am 103 was blown up by terrorists over the sky above us and all hell rained down. My worst nightmare had actually happened. For years afterwards I panicked and catastrophised. Sometimes I still do. But I know the tools that help bring me down and I try to put a distance between my horror-story tendencies and my ability to bring a more rational light to a situation.

Catastrophising has two parts:

Part 1: Predicting a negative outcome
Part 2: Jumping to the conclusion that if the negative outcome did in fact happen, it would be a catastrophe

It is hard when a plane blows up in the sky above you not to catastrophise that, when you are flying in a plane, it isn't going to blow up beneath you. Our imagination makes connections from what we know and creates the worst-case scenario. Fear and anxiety become terror if we don't try to rein it in. In the case of planes, I have learned to reassure myself with the knowledge that mostly planes get to their destinations without a hitch. If you have the ability to imagine the worst, then your brain can also be retrained to steer the great leaps of creative thinking away from disaster and toward positive possibilities.

Say something slightly unfortunate happened. You've spilt red wine over your white jeans. You'll probably be a bit upset that you've ruined your trousers. But if you catastrophise you are likely to jump to the next series of thoughts, which might be: 'I've been so clumsy recently, I might have some neurological disorder developing, I'm going to die.' You have gone from a wrecked pair of jeans to dying a slow painful death in which all your mental faculties agonisingly slip away from you. Until you have gathered evidence to the contrary it is safe to assume that the negative fallout can be ring-fenced to a dry-cleaning bill or, at worst, having to replace your jeans. But when you are in the habit of catastrophising it is hard to break the pattern. You ruminate and churn the disaster that is going to befall you. Instead you can transform the perceived disaster into something useful or something you can learn from. Perhaps you could invent an unstainable fabric? Or next time don't drink red wine when you are wearing white jeans.

When you create a gap in your mind between the imagined 'disaster' that looms and the reality you give yourself the opportunity to turn down your fear. My specialism in catastrophising is around health issues. For instance, I was convinced my migraines were a sign of a brain tumour. But I also know to create a gap between fantasy and reality. I take action. I went to my doctor, who ordered a brain scan, which was clear, but showed I needed physiotherapy for my neck. I don't try to deny my imagination its forlorn projections; I simply fill the gap with something practical. The physiotherapy didn't stop my migraines, so I keep up the investigations until I find the cause. I recently read the book *How Not to Die* by Michel Greger, MD. It is terrific reading for anyone who wants to take their health and healing into their own hands. Of course I'm going to die, and so are you at some point, but it's about delaying the inevitable, keeping fear at bay and embracing proactive wellness strategies so that while we live we are as energised and pain-free as possible. Calm the catastrophising with practical action, and get healthier as a result.

What makes you feel emotionally and physically secure isn't the belief that nothing bad could ever happen, but the knowledge that you will be able to find creative ways to get through it. You have learned about resilience, persuasion, negotiation, embracing change, mastery and asking for help. These are your tools in calming fear and allaying your tendency to catastrophise. You can also try the following creative de-catastrophising exercises.

⊨ CORE-WORK ⊨

DE-CATASTROPHISING CHALLENGE

1. You must get creative, and it has to be simple. Have a pad of paper with you and write down the incident when it happens. Draw two columns. In the right column acknowledge the 'catastrophic' future scenario with your non-dominant hand. In the left column write out a simple outcome with your Nurturing dominant hand e.g. 'I poured red wine over my trousers and so I can either try and get the red wine out, or failing that save up to get some new ones.' Score the 'truth' levels of each projected outcome out of ten. Draw a big black cross over the catastrophe and colour in the reasonable outcome in your favourite colour. Your brain will align itself with the colour and remind you to focus on a sensible response next time. Practise this daily for thirty days and you will regain control of your instinct to jump to wildly disproportionate conclusions.

2. Consider all the times you are not clumsy. Think of the myriad of physical and mental feats you manage to accomplish throughout the course of the day. Record your top three mini-triumphs every night before you go to sleep. This will embed your sense

of a capable self and raise your self-esteem. Even when bad things do happen, think about how you dig down, create a plan, work through what you need to do, and slowly get through the obstacle or challenge. You've done it before, you can do it again. Of course, it is natural to resist a change in the way we think. It's hard work. It's easier to leap up the spiralling whirlwind of panic, than to calmly work through a series of strategies to lower your emotional state and re-imagine an alternative narrative.

3. Equally, you can acknowledge your fears. Using your Nurturer/ Little You dialogue technique, ask them to do the 'And then what?' game. Little You states your imagined outcome, and Nurturer asks: 'And then what?', Little You expands and Nurturer repeats: 'And then what?' You keep this up until you have worked your way through to as far as you can go. You'll have looked at your projected situation in all its nuances. Talk about how you will feel at each stage. Who will be around to help and support you? What little strategies could help along the way, like breathing, writing down your worries, exercise, mindfulness? How long would each stage last? What would make a positive difference? What trail of help could you leave for others following in similar situations? You'll have dug around in the shadows for all your fears. You'll have dragged them out blinking into the cold sharp light of day and you can start to dismantle the likelihood they will happen, or work out what your strategies would be should they come true. Sharing the contents of the darker parts of your mind helps to lighten their heavy load, so find a buddy, mentor or coach to help you.

When to Surrender

Anything new carries with it a certain amount of fear. Fear of making a fool of yourself, fear of failing, fear of falling flat on your face. But allowing the fear to grow like a fungus on your aspirations and ambitions causes them to shrivel.

I am learning to be a new kind of mum. My 'offspring' are flying the nest and now they need un-mothering. When they lived at home, there was a sense you could control the dangers. Now they are out there on their own I have to relinquish control and support the choices my grown-up children make.

I must find creative ways to un-mother in the same way as a boss must find creative ways to allow her employees to try alternatives and fail at many of them. Nothing is learned if no risks are taken, no mistakes made. I realise this is the time to surrender to the unknown, not just for my children's sakes but for mine too.

We can't micro-manage the universe but we can appreciate the good and learn from the bad. We expend a lot of negative energy when we try to control anything outside our own choices. Our vision becomes narrow, our body starts pumping adrenalin, our heart pounds too fast. We are on danger alert. We don't change anything except our body state. When we surrender, we stop fighting and resisting, and we go with the flow. It immediately becomes easier, our breathing slows, we feel calm. We feel a peaceful sense of acceptance.

Paradoxically, by lowering expectations and creating a more relaxed approach we also attract better outcomes. If we stick to minding our own business and keeping our noses out of other people's, we remove the sources for discomfort. If it's not our concern then it's not for us to control. What if, instead of using up our energy in resistance and over-protection, we focus on filling our lives with things that make us feel excited, engaged, fulfilled and inspired? Then there is no space for our misplaced manipulation to creep in. We must fill as much of our time with what we can lose ourselves in.

'Ecstasy' in Greek means to stand to the side of something. You know that feeling when you are on the side of a mountain looking across a stunning view, or as you stand by the sea watching the sun set over the water? You surrender to the moment and you can feel a lifting of your spirit, the filling of your heart, a lightening of your limbs. It's a physical, mental and emotional hijacking of your attention as you willingly fall into the flush of captivation.

The runner releases herself into the movement of her limbs, the soles of her feet pushing away the ground, her breathing expanding in her chest, her mind slipping into the momentum of her pace as she falls trancelike into her stride. If she fights the sensation of surrender the whole run feels like agony, every step is torturous, jarring and juddering through her body. But when you do what you love, you let go and there is no fight, only flow.

What helps your body relax? When does time slip unnoticed as you involve yourself in some activity or other? Or, conversely, when do the clock's hands tick forward agonisingly slowly, making time feel like you're pushing an oil tanker through treacle? It's a good indicator that you aren't doing something you enjoy when it feels like this. Every moment has its own rhythm and when you allow yourself to slip into its ebb and flow you'll be fully present and you will experience life in its entirety.

Let go of fear and surrender to the unknown of future possibilities.

Surrendering Tips

1. Find what captures your imagination and do more of it while letting go of perfection.

2. Focus on the present by doing as much of what drives you, or answers a need in you, as possible. Enjoy the journey, don't wait to reach the destination.

3. Notice the sensations through your body when you see something captivating such as a sunset or a great band.

4. Keep a gratitude journal to record the moments in your day that you have surrendered to everything that you can find to be thankful for. Seek out the wonders of the world. Keep humble by looking for magnificence.

5. Try new things, it harnesses your brain as you learn; taking your attention away from fear and towards the excitement of stretching your abilities in new directions. Focus on growth, not on the satisfying of desires.

6. Boost your trust levels by building up your resilience muscle.

7. Let go of your need to control anything outside of yourself by practicing the art of 'loving detachment': letting small things slide and focusing on the bigger picture.

8. Increase your ability to achieve your full potential through creativity, independence, spontaneity and purpose.

9. Reduce unrealistic expectations by embracing the unknown and the ambiguous.

10. Accept yourself and your flaws by helping others. Of course you share deep relationships with a few close friends and family, but by lending a hand to those outside your own circle you increase your identification and affection towards the whole human race.

$\Longleftarrow$ CORE-WORK $\Longrightarrow$

Respond to your Nurturer using your Little You's non-dominant hand:

> NURTURER: *Sitting comfortably in a place that makes you feel calm, describe with pen and paper, in words or pictures, everything around you. Focus in on the sounds, the smells, the textures, colours, shapes, shadows, light, space and distance between things. Notice your fingers around your pen, your breathing, your skin, how your feet touch the floor, the shape of your spine, any aches or discomforts, your feelings, thoughts. This is you right now, in the moment.*

Whenever you start to feel anxious or fearful in life, tune into yourself and your environment. Take five minutes to run this exercise through, ideally with your non-dominant hand with pen on paper but if that is impractical do it in your head.

$\Longleftarrow$

Learning Not Failing

- Learning to Fail
- Rejoice in Rejection

Learning to Fail

Even with every effort, with every best intention, with all the right actions, we cannot prevent the inevitable times when our plans turn to pot. Failure feels like a gut wrenching, stomach curdling, humiliating experience.

And yet, within it lies a kernel of hope. Because if, after licking your wounds, you can bring yourself to look closely at the failure, to dig deeply and unravel its layers, you will find something that you can learn from.

The sooner you start failing the better. Before long you start to see it as a readjustment, a retuning, a pitstop for a wheel change.

I met a woman at a party who told me she was seeing a psychotherapist. She was terribly depressed after a major life event and her recovery had been knocked back again by something else that had happened to her recently, something that had shaken her to her core. She told me that for the first time in her life she had failed at something that she had always been brilliant at. I raised my glass: 'Congratulations!' She looked at me aghast.

I continued, 'I bet you have lived your life in terror of that happening?'

'I wasn't allowed to fail,' she replied.

'So, now you know that when you failed, the world didn't implode and you didn't die, that must be a relief?'

'But I musn't fail.'

'It happens to us all at some point.'

'Not me.'

'Even you.'

'Actually, I didn't work as hard as I could have. I just thought I'd nail it. It was just the next thing to do in my career. I hadn't realised I wanted it so much.'

'Where does that leave you now?'

'I'm going to take a bit of time out. Then focus on it properly, **give myself another chance**.'

In the space of a few minutes her perception of her failure had turned on its head. She was still disappointed but less angry with herself. She learned that she had taken success for granted and she realised she could learn from her failure. I could see she had taken a little step towards recovery. She was a little more fearless.

We have to make our own mistakes. You try something, see how it works, how it is received, find out the problems and mistakes, fix them, make adjustments, build up a little more, get feedback, adjust some more, push forward, assess, fine-tune, pivot, grow etc. It is a never-ending process.

There is no nirvana moment that you reach where you lie back and bask in the glory of success. The world is constantly changing and cantankerous. What worked yesterday won't necessarily work tomorrow. Failure calls for thought, observation, consideration, analysis and then reinvigorated energy and action.

When a relationship fails, there is the time for sorrow and then comes the time to pick up the pieces and start over. Unless you want a repeat failure in the next relationship you know you have to look back a little, learn a lot, and put on a new coat of determination and resolve to not make the same mistakes again. It is the same in all areas of our lives; it is our ability to honestly appraise ourselves that keeps us humans upwardly mobile.

Apparently most new businesses fail within the first four years. Even with blood, sweat and tears, they still fail. And this is **normal**. It is what happens. You may not have the *Dragon's Den* brigade shouting you out with their big thumbs-down but you know when the time-out bell rings. So, with the benefit of hindsight, you try something else and evolve.

If you believe in evolution, then you'll know why we are no longer apes. We have evolved **in spite of our fears**. There have been incremental shifts over long periods of time but, sure enough, most of us are able to walk tall, don't have to shave our entire bodies and have developed more delicate knuckles. We can also make decisions on what is good for us and what isn't, and we can act accordingly. Ditch the glue-sniffing and practice the piano more.

Learn to Fail and Learn from Failure

1. Court failure by taking risks. Risk-taking is telling your fears to take a hike. The more risks you take the more likely you will reach success.
2. Collect your failures and rejections like trophies. They are proof that you are trying, that you are moving forward.
3. Learn from your failures. In every failure, there is a nugget of learning to be had. Take it and use it. Each time you do this you become more resilient and more resourceful.
4. Never be alone with failure. Seek guidance and support when you need it.
5. Share your experience of failure with others. By giving voice to failure you lessen its blows and you build on what it has to teach you. Hearing about how other people have surmounted failure helps you clamber over yours.

⊨ CORE-WORK ⊨

Answer your Nurturer's questions with Little You's non-dominant hand.

1. What are you scared of failing at?
2. What's the worst that could happen?
3. What's the best that could happen if you did it anyway?

⊨ ⊨

Rejoice in Rejection

Rejection, along with failure, is an important part of the process of growing and beating back FEAR. It tells you you're not ready yet, or that you're looking in the wrong place for acceptance. Rejection is a signpost that says: 'keep going this way or that way, but keep going'. Most successful people have been rejected many times on the road to success. Collect your 'no's' on your way to a yes.

Last year I had the best rejection I've ever received to date. It wasn't the usual 'thanks but no thanks'. Or a resounding silence. It was over two pages of densely typed advice on how to improve the screenplay I'd written. I was thrilled. Finally, I'd created something someone felt strongly enough about to take the time to consider what wasn't right about it, and why. I could build on that, and I have done. Now it's nearly ready to send out again. David Yates, the director of the *Harry Potter* films, once said to me, 'Whatever you do, never, ever give up.' I hear those words every time another rejection pings into my inbox.

When you fear rejection it stops you taking risks. But in your pursuit to improve yourself, you must take the plunge. Of course the more you are rejected the harder it is to get back up your feet. You feel battered and bruised. The less successful people tell you at this point to call it a day. The most successful say that this is just the beginning, so get used to it. They wear their rejections like medals. Think of the second album syndrome. How many recording artists blow away the world with their first album, come back triumphantly with their second, only to find their audience rejects it? All they wanted was the first album repeated, not something new. If the artist believes in what they are doing, they'll persevere to album three, stick to their guns, and eventually they will attract the right fans.

Rejection keeps you on your toes. Not getting adulation and

success early on gives you much more time to experiment, play and try stuff out, away from the glare of public scrutiny. Early rejections force you to try harder but with a looseness not bound up in external expectation. We writers don't spend most of our time writing; we spend it re-writing. When I create an oil painting it doesn't all come together in the first layer. It is a built up of happy accidents and useful and less useful mistakes, layer upon layer that tells a narrative of imperfections and my own rejections.

In Michelle Obama's commencement speech she tells how, when she was dean of a university, she saw students with every privilege imaginable. They wanted for nothing, they scored high at every level. But when they received a bad grade they fell apart. They'd never experienced a knockback and so they didn't have the wherewithall to withstand the blow. On the other hand, Michelle saw students who had struggled to even get to university, from poor or deprived backgrounds, against a background of racism or sexism, who had built a resilience that ensured they were strong. They took rejection in their stride. They used it as fuel to drive forward.

So, next time a rejection comes knocking, put your ego/low self-esteem to one side, roll up your sleeves and get back down to business.

How to See Rejection

1. Rejection is not about you or your ego, it is about the work. Maybe now is not the right time for it, maybe it's not good enough yet, maybe you need to look at it another way?
2. Rejection encourages you to become more creative, to come at something with a different approach, to take the machine apart and rebuild it. What are the flaws? How can you iron them out or be more inventive?

3. Rejection is an invitation to improve, to make better work, to go the extra miles, to climb the higher mountain. Ultimately the view will be better.

....

⊨ CORE-WORK ⊨

Answer your Nurturer's question using Little You's non-dominant hand.

Nurturer:
1. What was your worst rejection?
2. What did you learn from it?
3. How can you do even better?

⊨⊨

It Takes Courage

- Being Brave
- Slowing Down
- Taking Time Out

Being Brave

Rebounding from rejection makes us braver and more resilient. When push comes to shove, the human race are a pretty brave bunch. We face down tempestuous storms, tsunamis, marauding terrorists, natural and man-made disasters. We help each other up, dust ourselves down and start all over again. Being brave means doing what you are afraid to do, and rising above the fear bubbling

away underneath. We may feel afraid but we must act with courage.
The definition of courage is: 'a voluntary action opposed to action
promoted by ongoing fear.'

    There has been a huge spike in levels of anxiety around the world
today, and it is created by our own fears and sense of inadequacy
foisted on us by external forces. For people with high levels of anxiety it is difficult to get up out of bed in the morning and face the
day. The fact that they continue to do so against their own crippling
negative internal voice shows tremendous courage and fortitude.
And for all of us, when we face our fears and take action against
them, the more courageous we become. The less we face our fears
the greater they grow.
    But we can take it gently, slowly breaking the fear into manage-
able chunks and overcoming it one crumb at a time. My client TL
was recently diagnosed with myeloma, an incurable blood cancer.
She doesn't know how long she's got and she doesn't want to know

too much about the disease itself. What she wants to know is how to help herself. How to keep strong in mind, body and spirit so that she has the fortitude to face whatever the future brings. I asked if she would find it helpful to write down her experience, to share with others, to give her a sense of having some purpose through it all. She wrote about her fears:

- Leaving my children behind at such a young age (makes me cry just thinking about it)
- Having to watch them watching me get sicker
- Not being around for S
- Wishing I had made more of a difference
- Wishing I had appreciated things more
- Making people sad
- Fear of the unknown – I don't know what to expect as I haven't read up on it
- Not being brave
- Failing at curing myself
- Acceptance of having it
- Pain

She thinks she's not brave but I tell her she is. She doesn't focus on the disease; she focuses on self-care. She's rebutted the blunt statement from her doctor, 'you won't get rid of it', with curiosity and courage about what wellness and wellbeing can look like in the wake of a seemingly poor prognosis. She says yes to trying different routes. She listens to people, to her heart, and to her body. She knows when she's overdoing it and promises herself rest. She is not afraid to experiment and open up to complementary therapies. She's taken up Tai Chi, Emotional Freedom Therapy and spiritual journeywork. She has a nutritionist and is following her advice along the lines of organic, mainly plant-based, healthy food and drink, as much as possible. She goes to an acupuncturist. She practices meditation and deep breathing. She is learning about other spiritual practices. She is prepared to learn and take what she needs and leave the rest. Her doctor's single piece of advice on drinking more water pales under the light of her own determination to upgrade her health and strengthen her body in any way she can.

She still slumps in her fearful moments. She wonders what her life is for:

> There have been times when I don't really want to get better as life can be pretty crap and the idea of living for a long time doesn't always appeal. I find it really difficult to tell people that I have it. I'm trying to get to everyone before the wedding as I don't want them to hear about it on the day, but that feels like I am making it into a bigger deal than it is! I sometimes struggle with 'why me?' as in 'why should I get better?' Not 'why have I got it?' I know why I have it: to make me stop and take stock. I needed the excuse to take time out, it has given it to me, I just need to take it! I don't feel like I have cancer, I feel like I have jumped on a cancer bandwagon that I don't belong to and that I will be found out to be a fraudster, only after some attention and sympathy!

She throws her toxic thoughts onto the page in the daily brain dump and then tears the paper up. She doesn't want to be defined by those fearful arrows. Interestingly, when I asked her to write about her fears and then write about what she does to overcome them, her fears amounted to a few lines and her self-care description was four pages. That's a good ratio for achieving courage and bravery. Beat back your fears with a practical plan of action and an open-minded spirit of curiosity, learning and hope. None of us can put off death when it comes, but we can do something about the life we have while we have it.

Becoming Brave

1. Face your fears, don't run from them.
2. Chunk down your fears into manageable, actionable tasks.
3. Work through them bit by bit with a workable structure.
4. Acknowledge when you have overcome a fear.
5. Next time, remember how you bravely beat back your fears and know that you can do that again.
6. Share your fears with people who will listen but not burden you with their own emotions around your fears.
7. Create a supportive team to help you through your challenges.
8. To create hope – focus on what you can do, not what you can't.
9. Acknowledge with gratitude when you feel like you've made progress.
10. Be patient and kind to yourself.

═══ CORE-WORK ═══

Do the following exercise as Nurturer/Little You dual-handed dialogue.

When the footsteps of fear echo down the corridor towards you, take a pen and paper and draw three columns. In the left column name the fear. In the middle column, write down the likelihood of it happening. In the third column write what positive outcome there could be. Really vamp it up, use your imagination and powers of visualisation, relish in the best scenario possible, describe it in minute detail.

If, on the other hand, what you fear comes to pass, again get your creative juices flowing. Brainstorm every which way that you can find to turn the situation around; what can help you to survive, learn and grow? How can you defeat what you have been through by channelling your pain into a force for good?

People do this all the time. They raise money for a cause, run for mental health, meet and forgive their enemy, work on developing a life-enhancing treatment, investigate the perpetrator of a crime, go into schools to educate children. People dig deep into their imaginations to find a way through, so that they may rise again and make life worth living.

Slowing Down

Getting past FEAR cannot be rushed, it requires time, delicacy and reflection. Fear flares in a rush, panic spikes at speed. When you need to achieve something important, you need to give it room to gestate and grow. Think of a garden; you don't plant a seed and expect to see a tree the next day. Think of genetically modified foods. They grow quickly and taste of nothing. In the film industry, we use the three-pronged model: quick, cheap, good. You can only have two of the three. Quick and cheap, but not good. Quick and good, but not cheap. Cheap and good, but not quick.

We are living life in a hurry, the ticking clock is like a terrifying time-bomb in our heads. We focus on the uber-list in front of us without a backwards glance at what we have already achieved. We get sick and the faster we have lived life, the longer it takes to recover. It is our body's way of telling us to take it easy, to go slow, to stretch away from our sound-bite culture and take the time to listen, to chew, to extract the juices from every second.

I learned the art of patience and slowing down in India. It is craziness on speed there and the only way to handle it is to take it easy. I learned the hard way. We were making a documentary on Indian classical music and had arranged to film at a yoga ashram. The journey to get there proved to be a challenge: a two-hour drive to Mughal Sarai station (the hub cap rolled off one of the wheels and down the highway), a seven-hour train journey to Kiul Junction, then a scrapheap jeep which bumped us along dirt tracks for five hours (passing little more than a shrouded body being laid out on an unlit pyre and a trail of water buffalo that lumbered across our path), until finally we arrived at the town of Mungar. A passer-by pointed out 'the best restaurant in town'. The restauranteur wiped down the dusty seats for us and removed the spittoon from the table. When we needed the toilet, he threw in a bucket of water first to clear the hole-in-the-ground of rats, who scuttled off every which way from the stinking pit.

We arrived at the gates of the yoga ashram and the mind numb-
ing cacophony of honking horns that accompanied us everywhere
in India melted away in the hum of insects, green trees and a
peaceful oasis of tranquillity. But despite our fourteen-hour journey to get there the Swamis now decided they weren't going to let
us film. We had documents but, no, they'd changed their minds.
British bureaucracy Indian style. They gave us a wooden slatted
bed for the night and a bowl of lentils that we had to eat with our
fingers. We fought off bird-size mosquitoes in the showers and
we had to adhere to the eight o'clock lights-out and total silence
code. Our passports were taken away and we were told that the
next day we were to be given an audience with the chief Swami
to present our case, hoping that we might be able to change his
mind. In the morning, we wandered amongst the white-clad
yogis and pretended to look calm, collected and at peace with
the world. In reality we were itching to get our filming done and
scared that after making this journey across the most dangerous
part of India, it was to be all in vain. We were forced to slow down
and be patient.

Three o'clock came and we queued up with the local villagers
armed with gifts and grovelling smiles. And gradually we edged up
the line on bended knees towards the chief Swami. We dutifully
kissed his feet and handed over our bribes. He looked down at me
and bestowed a knowing smile. He 'nodded' his head from side to
side before announcing that God had decreed that we would not
be allowed to film this time, but should we make the journey again
we could film then. All hope seemed dashed. But I held my nerve,
stood my ground, breathed very slowly. And something switched.
He bowed and said about as slowly as you can string one word to
another in a sentence; that in this instance God was willing to make
an exception. So after fourteen hours of travelling, and twenty-four
hours of waiting, we suddenly had ten minutes to film before racing

to catch the only train left that day for an eight-hour journey to Calcutta. Every minute of that footage made the film. Patience paid off.

It can be agonising but if you go with it and work incrementally towards your goal you gradually make progress.

You don't have to wait for the speed-bumps of stress or illness to be your wake-up call. If you slow down you don't become road-kill; you simply do things better. Eating, sleeping, making love, creating, inventing, designing all become better when slowness is your modus operandi. Understanding this has created the International Slow Movement, which started in Italy but has slowly spread around the world. 'Slow food' means growing and consuming in an organically sustainable way that celebrates pleasure and health. There is also slow sex and slow cities, where people slow down, smell the roses and connect with one another. Slowing traffic, putting in places for people to sit, read, take a breather and decompress, green spaces, art works for contemplation, poetry on the subway. It's all zen and the art of de-stressing.

The Scandinavian countries are showing that you don't need to work at the speed of light in order to have a kick-ass economy. They work reasonable hours and they are now among the top six most competitive nations on earth. They understand that to be more productive, people need to be able to work fewer hours, unplug, and sit in a quiet room and relax.

Increasingly, kids have stellar grades and super-charged extra-curricular interests, but they are fuelled on fear. Their ability to create, dream and explore ideas, has taken a back seat in the hot-house years of exam extortion and exhaustion. Young adults are being spat out into the world in a time-poor rush of adrenalin-induced neuroses.

Life is not a race with fear cracking the whip. The answer is to enjoy the ride, slowly savour the moments along the way, digest the hiccups and hurdles, mulch over the lessons and challenges, breathe in the ebb and flow, be patient and sacrifice the seduction of speed to the satisfaction of slowing down.

....

Five tips on taking time out

1. Breathe slowly.
2. Don't multi-task.
3. Stop for lunch and chew slowly.
4. Create empty spaces in your diary.
5. Unplug for an hour before bedtime.

....

⊨ CORE-WORK ⊨

Respond to your Nurturer using your Little You's non-dominant hand:

- Take five minutes to write out a three letter word. Slowly, slowly, slowly

- Take another five minutes to slowly decorate your word. Slowly, slowly, slowly

⊨

Taking Time Out

'There's no time to slow down' I hear you cry. I agree, time is a luxury. But why have wealth if you have no time to enjoy it? Why wait until you retire to get to dabble away at what you enjoy in the expanse that time affords you? Most people get two weeks a year to do as they choose and weekends if they are lucky. Many people are afraid of time, they fear what it will throw up, of what they may have to confront about themselves or about their job, their relationships, or their life in general. But getting creative with time brings a far greater satisfaction than fearfully filling up your diary. Everyone has twenty-four hours in their day. Richard Branson, Elon Musk, Adele, you. Time is a choice, fill it frenetically or engage with it creatively.

In Tim Ferriss's book *The 4-hour Work Week*, he seems to have found the answer, and in his wake thousands of people have followed. He is able to bring in plenty of money to live on, and still enjoy his life, by being incredibly efficient with the time he spends on 'work'. The rest of the time he travels, lies on beaches, and became a champion in both kick-boxing and tango. He values his time and will do anything within the rules to release as much of it for himself as possible.

He defied his fears and turned the creation of time and space into a fine art. He defends his time assiduously. He has got himself into the position where he owns his time and no one else gets a slice of it without his say-so. He wasn't born wealthy, says he's not particularly bright, but he is cunning. And, I would say, courageous. He taps into the creative thinking part of his brain to design his life. He worked out what he wanted to do with his time and he did what he had to, to achieve the results he was after. First, he knew what he wanted to do with his life in a way that would give it meaning, purpose, engagement and pleasure. Then he set about carving out his time to suit him, and creating ways he could have an automated income that allowed him not to have to work on it for any more than four hours a week, in any location he wanted to be around the world.

We can all do this. Most creative people understand the importance of empty space in their lives, time to mull, daydream, gaze. Clever organisations like Google and Pixar recognise their workforce is a lot more brilliant at coming up with new concepts or original solutions when they have places to go and play, think, snooze and loiter.

When you slow down and take time out from the hyper-frenzy, addictive, negative, fearful pace we are accustomed to, you find a calmer mind. Why not get creative with how you want to spend your time and learn to live less fearfully?

....

Learn to use time efficiently

1. Research ways to make money while you sleep.
2. Get up earlier.
3. Decide what is your most productive time of the day and do the hardest stuff then. You'll do it quicker, more effectively and get it out of the way.

4. Do the easy things first, fast.

5. Don't procrastinate, get things done and dusted. Try not to leave anything to the next day.

6. Do one thing at a time. You'll do it properly and quicker. The brain slows down when you try to multi-task.

7. Let go of the things that you don't enjoy, don't match your values, or are a waste of time and effort. Streamline.

8. Don't people-please or be with time wasters or energy wasters. I call these people 'drains'.

9. Learn to delegate.

10. Learn to not be afraid of spare time. Use it to do the things you love.

....

⊱══ CORE-WORK ══⊰

Respond to your Nurturer using Little You's non-dominant hand:

- Describe what spare time looks like to you
- Describe any fears that rise when you think of spare time
- What would it take for you to feel comfortable with spare time?
- If you won the lottery, which meant everything was taken care of and you were given a year to do what you liked, what would you do?

⊱══⊰

End of Week Four

⊨ CORE-WORK ⊨

Write the answers to these questions with your non-dominant hand.

Nurturer:
- What tools have you learned in this week?
- How have you moved forward towards your goals?
- What action steps have you taken?
- How are you feeling about your fears right now?
- How can I support you this week?

⊨⊨

Week Five

....

CHANGING YOUR MIND

- DIFFERENT MINDSET: New Minds, Impossibly Positive, Making Progress
- CREATIVE HEALING: Be Curious, Using Intuition, Serendipity
- KEEPING IT LIGHT: Game for a Laugh, Here's Hope

....

So it's week five of the Fear Less Creative Coaching Course. How are you feeling? Read back over the summaries you wrote at the end of each week. Can you see your progression? How has FEAR changed in your mind? In this penultimate week we are going to shift gear and elevate the mood. You are going to have the opportunity to evolve with new possibilities and potential. You are going to start really pushing your brain boundaries. Whether you are a self-professed creative or not, you can most certainly use the creative strategies to become less fearful and more happy, curious, positive and hopeful. You will learn how to make more progress and use intuition, laughter and serendipity to bring a hopeful future. Let's see what happens to fear when you create a non-toxic environment in which you really stretch your mind-muscles.

NOTE: *Not everything here will be relevant to you right now but read it all and do the core-work exercise for the areas that ring bells for you.*

Different Mindset

- New Minds
- Impossibly Positive
- Making Progress

New Minds

Explore
unknown territories with
an amateur mind.

When everyone around you is doing the same thing, it is easier for you to follow the tribe; do the daily commute, not stand up to the bully boss, sniff your wages up your nose. But what if it's not making you happy? What if you were to choose another path? People may criticise you or drop away. But when you stand up and stand out, make yourself master of your own universe, something amazing happens. Suddenly you start to attract new people who respect you for singing your own tune and you inspire others to have the courage to make their own changes and transformations.

I check-in with my clients, months after they finish their coaching with me, to see if it has had a lasting effect, whether with their new mindset they have launched themselves to greater heights. Do they keep hold of the tools they have learned and apply them to keep creating a better life?

Client J:
I reflect on the coaching a lot. I think the drawing and the developments from it is one of the best things that came out of it. And the arts management work I am doing now has all the ingredients that I love. But I feel like I am now on a transition course between the arts management and the drawing, as who'd of thought it, I am leading a few art journaling workshops now and have been invited back to do more. I am in a busy arts management spell right now but want to think ahead to Oct/Nov so am trying to set up opportunities and promo for more art journaling and leading other types of art workshops too. I enjoy it and it feels right. Thinking that in the long term I'd like to move and set up a studio of some sort. I'm doing it in a loose context of wellbeing and mental health – and of course promoting the idea of nurturing and releasing creativity because we know how important that is!

Client S:
I am well, moving house soon, new website is up. I have some print and display happening next week and I am about to embark on a big email campaign.

I move into my own home next week. Finally! So a lot of movement. Classes are going amazingly well. Getting people to bring friends. Happy and free!

Client Sa:

I was thinking about you the other day. I am really well and busy
working on [the feature film] at the moment. We start filming in a
week's time, so its crazy busy! I bought my dream kitchen yesterday
and the builders start at the beginning of September on the house.
I also have a wonderful man in my life. I have just started to option
a great book to make into a film as well, just talking to lawyers and
trying to settle on an option agreement . . . Life is great and I have
lots of things to be grateful for!!

The coaching tools you are learning are for life – if you allow
yourself the freedom to step out from the barriers of ego/fear and
self-defeatism, if you give yourself the chance to be bold, try new
things, explore and test your limits. If you don't feel adequate, test
where you think you're falling down. What's the gap between what
you think you know, and what you actually know? Fill in the gap
with knowledge. Ask questions, find someone who's a few steps
ahead of you. Learn from them. Dig into books, Google – the
world is a hotbed of knowledge for you to tap into. Practise, practise, practise; until you start to become the sum of your skills and
understanding.

Trust that if you fall you can pick yourself back up and try
another approach. Tesla took on the automotive industry and it had
to learn from the ground up. But it learned with fresh eyes, with
different questions. It took a Silicon Valley mentality, and applied it
to a debunked traditional industry and overhauled what a car could
be, not just an electric car. If it had allowed fear of its lack of old-
fashioned skills to hinder it, or to undermine it, then it would not
have evolved to be the revolution it is.

When we have the beginner's mind of an amateur or an enthu-
siast, we find we have an open mind. A font for new possibilities.

Building a New Mind

1. Try anything once.
2. Be as kind to yourself as you would to your best friend.
3. Gather around you people who like you just for who you are, warts and all.
4. Fill in the gaps of what you don't know with what you can learn.
5. Tell your ego to take a hike. If it's not with you it's against you and with friends like that, who needs enemies?

⊨ CORE-WORK ⊨

Respond to your Nurturer using your Little You's non-dominant hand:

- If there was nothing to stop you or hold you back, what one new thing would you change in your life for the better?
- What is stopping you?
- What could you do to make it really happen?
- Imagine a new you, a new life, a new way forward. What does it look and feel like?
- What one thing can you do today towards that?

Impossibly Positive

Positive thinking doesn't always come naturally. It is hard work and takes practice and creativity.

I once heard a Buddhist man give a talk. Buddhists have practiced positive thinking for thousands of years. It takes a lot of practise! He had suffered all his life with severe depression. He knew the depths his mind could spiral down to. After studying positive psychology and Buddhist philosophy he started to work on his mindset. He said that he learned to throw up a big mental STOP sign in his head the split second he started to motor down the road to negativity. He knew he couldn't afford the price of even one moment of unhelpful thinking. Not one second. So close was the edge of the cliff. He would get up, do something physical, distract himself in any way possible just to stop the internal negative chatter and inner knife twisting. For the first time ever, he felt that he was the one in control and not his thoughts. He could never be complacent though. The toads of mental torture are ready to jump in at any time; and he must continuously work to keep them at bay, or leap onto the back of one and point its energy in a more constructive direction. But practice is progression and he says most of the time he's the boss.

Positivity is not some mealy mouthed approach of the eternally sunshine minded. Far from it. Choosing to flip thinking from despair to self-determined direction and action comes from necessity. When you're not prepared to take the blows lying down, and you choose to make the commitment and superhuman effort to consistently and patiently overturn the boulders thrown at you, then a positive approach is the path to take.

Of course I don't believe that a lack of positivity is to blame for getting cancer, or for losing the battle against depression or for any other misfortune that may befall us. For some people life has its own agenda and no amount of positive thinking is going to change it. Still, we can attempt to stay on top while we can. *Channel 4 News* recently interviewed a mother dying of cancer. She said that she wanted to make the most of her last days. She was devastated to be leaving her children behind but she wanted to enjoy what little time she had left with them. In the face of tragedy she found the courage to look for whatever comfort she could find. Being positive was a last gift to herself and her family.

We can all choose to live a more hopeful and meaningful life, with whatever trials and tribulations we encounter. We can moan, complain and make ourselves feel worse. Or we can practice gratitude, hope, forgiveness, flow, generosity, kindness, compassion, love; and in so doing feel more optimistic and self-determining. It's not the big wins that bring you to a sense of positivity; it's the small wins, noted, over time, made with purpose, that make the difference. Fear looks pretty weak in the shadow of a proud, positive and progressive force.

....

How to be Positive

1. Identify your main strengths.
2. Apply them in a way that will fully engage you.
3. Learn to build your positive mindset through creating a meaningful life, full of purpose (see Find Your Purpose).
4. Look for the small wins and gradually you will realise you have made big progress, during which you will have incrementally elevated your positive mindset.
5. Please do also check with a health specialist that gluten, carbs and sugar aren't making your depression, anxiety or any other mind or health issues (such as brain fog, obsessive compulsive disorder, schizophrenia, or Alzheimer's) worse. This is according to Dr David Perlmutter in his book *Grain Drain*.

....

⊨ CORE-WORK ⊨

Respond to your Nurturer using your Little You's non-dominant hand:

- Think of something negative you have said or felt in the last week
- Flip it to the positive
- If neither are fact which would you choose to believe?
- What positive message can you project in this coming week?

⊨⊨

Making Progress

Celebrating success isn't about bragging, showing off, being self-obsessed or narcissistic. It's about quietly acknowledging to yourself every time you've done something well. It's about patting yourself on the back and building up your self-esteem. Goodness knows there are many failures, disappointments and setbacks; it is imperative that you counteract them with a healthy approach to your small successes. It makes you more self-reliant and less fearful; free of needing approbation from others.

In coaching, we break big goals down into smaller achievable chunks. But what is important is to celebrate each one of those little triumphs throughout the day. The mini-triumphs give a regular happiness-hit. I have my art journal out on the side in the kitchen, and every time I feel good about something I've done or eaten, I scribble a little picture or write a few words describing it. By the end of the day the page is popping with fun little outcomes. A cartoon collection of happy moments.

This is how Client H put it:

I felt for months in some ways I had failed as I have not achieved many of my goals discussed with you. However, I have achieved many other things – no TV or radio script but a children's play I wrote, directed and composed which parents at a local school performed for their children to great acclaim. Interesting that I forgot this achievement! And an awareness that I did not get in touch with you as I felt I had nothing to 'report' and yet I now have more private clients, have had a complete turnaround with challenging colleagues on my course who apologised and were able to have transformative dialogues with the rest of the course members. In fact, I was given a painted stone of a bird with the words: flying free.

I am still trying to tidy and sort 'my space' and have my vision board in a safe private place. And I'm aware how hard it is for me to create my private place externally.

I am noticing how trusted I am by others and my confidence in my private practice is growing. I have successes and great feedback which I am posting. I now need to grow my business and be disciplined on a different level than before. My tendencies are the same: to give more than receive and to doubt what I receive. And my yoga and meditation is helping me notice and shift.

My art is still not embedded, in fact I have been knitting cowls so perhaps I am needing to be practical!

My daughter sleeps in her own bed now and I am catching up with myself and my eldest is working successfully in art and drama and I will see her perform next month. My forty-ninth year began with depression and body challenges but familiar challenges and less anxiety. Determining my future based on what I really want is becoming clearer. I am going to study more in psychotherapy and body work and develop my intuitive self, which has astonished me of late.

Feeling like a champion isn't just for Olympians and Oscar-winners, each of us can shift our focus to tune in to our daily trophies of accomplishment. Start the day with what you can do easily and then move on to the more difficult tasks. I post my daily drawing and inspirational caption on social media first, then I set about doing my writing assignment. After that I tackle my admin and emails. I like to tick off my list as I go. It gives me a hit of 'I did that, now I can do this'.

My natural habitat is the pavements of London, so the slopes of mountains are daunting for me. But I take it step by step. I pause for breath. I look back at how far I have come. I treat

myself to some power balls and I plod on. Over and above other
mountain tops. A mirage of the summit beckons but as we reach
it another appears from behind. Undaunted, we push forwards.
Then the black crags of the summit rise up. A deep breath and
a final burst of energy and courage, and we clamber the final
ascent. The plateau is a moonscape of rock and we are draped
in mist, which leaves strings of water beads across our clothes.
Then a 55 miles per hour gust of wind and the clouds part like a
giant theatrical curtain and the valley below floods into view. This
is the reward for persistence, for forcing mind over body, determination over fear. This is the highest mountain I have climbed,
nearly 3000 feet. A lot for someone scared of heights. And how
did I do it? One step at a time, with little incentives and rewards
along the way.

Reviewing and writing down your accomplishments of the day,
however small, and reflecting how they made you feel, coupled with
a mini-plan for what you would like to achieve the next day, works
wonders on building your sense of purpose. I used to keep a journal
of everything that happened; the good, the bad and the ugly. All it
achieved was to highlight the bad and the ugly. I stopped that and
started to only write down the good. The way I felt about myself
dramatically lifted. Now if I experience bad feelings I just use the
daily brain dump to download the negative thoughts onto a single
piece of paper and then I ditch it. I keep the journals that plot my
positive progress.

There is comfort in knowing that with the right set of tools you
can make meaningful progress by acknowledging your progression
and letting go of the setbacks.

....

Monitor your Progress

1. Bring your attention to what you are doing, focus on one thing at a time, don't try and multi-task. Your brain is more efficient when it has one thing to concentrate on.
2. Make sure that what you are doing is part of the bigger vision for your life, part of your over-riding purpose.
3. Intend every day to move your vision forward with small steps.
4. Notice every time you accomplish each step.
5. At the end of the day, record your mini-successes in your journal. Give no attention to the mini-misses, except for what you can learn from them.

....

⊱═ CORE-WORK ═⊰

Respond to your Nurturer using your Little You's non-dominant hand:

- What have been your top three mini-successes this week?
- Imagine how you could reward yourself for those.
- Describe how it feels to receive those rewards.

⊱═⊰

Creative Healing

- Be Curious
- Using Intuition
- Serendipity

Be Curious

Creativity is thinking outside of the box. It's turning the box upside down. It's doing away with the box altogether. If you can form a question, then you have the ability to think creatively. Creativity is curiosity. Creative thinkers want to know why, how, where, when; they are archaeologists of knowledge, experience and ideas. The world is a fathomless dimension of exploration and discovery, and each of us has but a short time to make the most of what we've been given.

As a screenwriter, creating characters, I have to continually interrogate their very existence, their purpose, their motives, their behaviours, their thoughts, speech and interactions with others. But you can only go so far before you inevitably get stuck or get to the point where you think you've nailed your characters and story. At that point you need to ask for the opinions and comments of others. Even constructive criticism can feel like mind-acrobatics in free fall.

But if you keep curious and open to feedback, you'll improve your work (and your life).

Architect Frank Lloyd-Wright was self-taught. He questioned that buildings at that time *had* to be rectangular so he created the oval, arcs and circles of the Guggenheim Museum in New York. Steve Jobs bunked out of university, did a short course in calligraphy and created Apple. He didn't know that you *have* to go to, and stick at, university to get a good job or build a business. The art of not-knowing is like always having a beginner's mind; hungry and curious.

When we are curious about others we open ourselves up to different ideas and outcomes. Keith Johnson taught improvisation at London's Royal Court Theatre and wrote the classic book *Impro*. In it he explains the importance of stepping out of oneself and putting all focus on others. It is an incredible difference when one actor puts all their attention on the other actor; suddenly their own performance becomes fluid, natural and intense. When I was learning to direct actors, I was curious about the actors' process, so I enrolled in some courses to help me understand. I did a Meisner acting course, an improvisation course and a directing actors course. My curiosity about their work made me better at mine.

Leonardo Da Vinci, as the ultimate 'Renaissance man', is the poster boy for curiosity. His mind chased answers to problems and he acted on his findings. He was an artist but worked as a scientist, an inventor, a creator – his interests flowed between anatomy, geology, botany, hydraulics and flight. He set no boundaries or limits to the possible, he questioned everything and opened himself up to every experience.

Be fearless in your day, and question everything and everyone. Curiosity will get you out from behind your mind-blocks and fears, and it will break your imagination out into fresher pastures where you can experience new things and enjoy more innovative thinking and achieving.

Curiosity Challenges

1. Ask questions of people outside your network.
2. Read books on subject matters you wouldn't normally look at.
3. Take a class in a subject outside your experience.
4. Walk in nature with a botanical book and try to identify plants, flowers and trees that you don't know the names of.
5. Walk through an interesting piece of architecture and attempt to work out what makes it more innovative than the building next door.
6. Go to a new networking event or party where you won't know people and decide that in the spirit of curiosity you are going to meet and ask questions of three new people.
7. Wake up every morning with the question: 'What delights are in store for me today?'

⊨ CORE-WORK ⊨

Respond to your Nurturer using your Little You's non-dominant hand:

- Draw a big circle. Inside, write down ten things that you do regularly that are within your comfort zone. Outside the circle, write down ten things that are firmly outside your comfort zone. The circle represents fear. Curiosity expands your comfort zone by helping you to leap outside the circle of fear. Try one new thing a week

Using Intuition

Intuition is your body radar, picking up signals to give you inside knowledge on which to base decisions. It is an instinctive response, not an intellectual or logical one. It's a feeling. When you listen to and follow your gut, things usually turn out well. It is your animal instinct. Many of us leave it dormant.

Your creative nature responds to intuition, so the more open you are to the intuitive sense the more creative you can be. But you can only tap into it if you choose to stop and listen, for it is a subtle and delicate sense that can be easily drowned out by the hustle and bustle of everyday life.

Take time to pause, to notice moments of insight and flashes of inspiration. You notice avocados are pushed to the front of the shelves in the supermarket, then someone recommends avocado oil, then you read that avocados are a superfood. Your week starts to pop with avocados and before you know it you are eating them every day and putting avocado oil on your salad and making face masks from the flesh. It's how something slowly creeps onto your radar until it is multiplying across all your senses and you decide to act upon the flashing message in our brain: 'Avocados are good for you, eat more of them.'

The same thing happens when you start to become more positive in your life. You become more sensitive to negative people, the ones that drain your energy. Gradually you are so attuned that when you hear negative talk it feels like someone is running their nails down a blackboard at the back of your brain. Your intuition by now is so strong in that area that the moment you meet someone you instantly 'know' if they are good for you or not.

When an opportunity arises, your intuition responds first; a flutter of excitement or a sense of fear or dread. Then the best thing you can do is walk away, sleep on it, distract yourself with other projects. Your intuitive system takes over while your conscious analytical brain is distracted. It percolates the experience until it makes sense of it. Processed, it seeps its way to the surface of your consciousness and you are able to make your decision. Sleep helps the process, with dreams incubating and unravelling the issue, away from the meddling of your conscious mind, until the intuitive feelings become thoughts that can be acted on.

We feel intuition through a physical change in our bodies – sweaty palms, a tightening in our chest, a flutter in our stomach. When we feel a sense of foreboding about something we must pay attention to that sensation. When my grandmother started to lose her sight and her hearing, her other senses became more highly attuned. She said her dreams became more vivid. She always seemed to know how I was feeling. She herself said she had a 'nose' for things that only got stronger as her ordinary senses faded.

When Picasso started a drawing he would hold his pen above the blank page, not knowing what he was going to draw. Then he would touch the nib to paper and let his intuition guide his creativity and the drawing would flow from his hand. Writers find that just the act of showing up at our keyboard every day allows the words to pour from a place we can't intellectually tap into. But intuition doesn't just belong to the artistic. Intuition and creativity are an integral part of us all.

....

To develop our intuitive strength

1. Learn to become attuned to your intuitive sense, listening,
   paying attention to your physical body, to your feelings
   and to what your quiet inner voice is telling you.
   Meditating or doodling help you block out the external
   influences.
2. Learn to interpret what you tune in to. Are you responding
   out of fear, or conditioning, or from old habits and beliefs,
   or does this feeling correspond to you core values and mission statement? The more you work on the exercises in this
   book the better you will be able to differentiate between
   external forces and internal truths.
3. Learn to act on what you have connected to. When you
   know the right thing to do, take action. Do something,
   however small. Move gradually in that direction, one small
   action after another.

....

⊨ CORE-WORK ⊨

Respond to your Nurturer using your Little You's non-dominant hand:

- Put your hand on your belly, breathe deeply and abdominally
  three times
- Describe the flora/microbes in your belly as if they are little
  creatures in the Fear Evaluation Office. What do they look like,
  sound like, how do they run through their day?
- A message comes over the tannoy: 'Fear alert!' All the flora creatures stop to listen. They've been asked to make you draw an
  elephant. To your stations!

- The flora creatures tap away on their little machines and decide that even though you have little or no experience of drawing an elephant from your imagination, you will not die in the process. So they instruct you to proceed. Intuition says yes
- Draw an elephant from your imagination
- If, as predicted, you did not die in the process, describe how it felt to do something you haven't done before, just by trusting your gut and following the flow of your pencil
- It does not matter how the elephant turned out. It's the process of tuning in that counts

Serendipity

Serendipity is when stuff happens in beneficial ways by happy accident. In the creative process of life and business, serendipity is the currency of making good use of happenstance, of grabbing onto the shirttails of chances sweeping past, of hailing possibilities and wrestling potential to the touchline. It is taking advantage of the faintest whiff of something hot. Your creative radar must be on high alert at all times and you must grow antennae so as not to miss the slightest opportunity.

Mingling with strangers, listening and talking about what lights your fire is the fertilizer for finding connections and chances. It's about having the right attitude, and then attracting, approaching and interacting with people from all walks of life, so that you have more chance of meeting the ones that offer serendipitous opportunities.

Last month I had just been into a drugstore in San Francisco to buy some health supplements. When I got home I noticed to my

annoyance that 'somehow' a pot of l-Lysine had dropped into my
bag. I'd paid for something I didn't need. Back in the UK another
of my migraines kicked in and I was researching natural remedies.
L-Lysine popped up in my research as something that vegans are
sometimes lacking in. And, of course, I had some. Serendipity?
Because I have trained my brain to be on the lookout for these
opportunities I had kept the l-Lysine instead of returning it to the
shop and getting my money back. I'd thought, 'maybe there is a
reason it leapt into my bag'. And here it was, another aid for helping
my migraines.

So we must put ourselves in the way of things, keep showing
up, keep all our senses peeled, keep energised and curious and
every once in a while the serendipitous opportunity makes its quiet
entrance.

It's like searching the beach for pebbles. If you look for a stone
in the shape of a heart, look long enough and you will find it. Look

for a rusty nail or shard of glass and you will find those too. Look for disaster, slights and betrayals and you will find them. Don't let FEAR stop you listening and looking out for fortuitous occurrences. Pluck those strange serendipitous opportunities from wherever they present themselves and turn them into your good fortune.

Encourage Serendipity

1. Follow a hunch, change places, take time out, wallow in daydreams, scribble and doodle, go for a walk, let go of control.
2. Make space in the hustle and bustle of daily life and slow down.
3. Stop and smell the roses.
4. Drop everything that is routine in your life, find new encounters and discover new things.
5. Notice the small stuff.
6. Look up from your smart phone, take your headphones off, smile.
7. Do a random act of kindness.
8. Surf life for serendipity, paddle out and in the right moment catch the wave and there the magic happens.

'Chance favours the prepared mind.'

– *Louis Pasteur*

CORE-WORK

Respond to your Nurturer using your Little You's non-dominant hand. Use your imagination to create a story of serendipity.

- Write a paragraph in which you are travelling on a bus and something serendipitous happens to you e.g. a blank cheque flutters in through the window and lands in your lap
- How do you respond?
- What do you do with the opportunity?
- How does it change your life?

Keeping It Light

- Game for a Laugh
- Here's Hope

Game for a Laugh

In a life of hard-knocks, mini-misses and downright failures, it's vital to cultivate a sense of humour. I'm not suggesting you go into comedy, but let's imagine you try it once for a laugh. There you are, up on stage, in front of a room full of people who have paid good money for you to make them chortle. You've got nothing but you, your gags and maybe the odd prop to prevent you drowning in a sea of cynicism.

The audience is waiting for you give them a great night and they're ready to be pissed off if you don't. The opener is crucial to get them on side. If you've nailed that and got a few laughs under your belt you're onto your repertoire. On a good night the room is with you and you're riding the waves of twists and turns. Your fear of flopping turns into flying on fanfare.

Humour is about surprise, shifting perspective, throwing in the unexpected. It is creative thinking at work, the more creative, the better the laugh. An audience engages in a deeply subliminal way. It taps into their own fears at a subconscious level and triggers a sense of seeing something known, for the first time. You put surprising elements together and you create something new in someone else's brain. Their response is from the gut. It's compulsive and spontaneous.

When a gig's gone well a comedian will say, 'they were putty in my hands'. It's true, laughter is the great dis-inhibitor. People's barriers come down and their mind opens up. In enlightened corporations, laughter is encouraged. They do this by creating spaces where people don't feel judged, where anything goes. The leaders of these organisations recognise that people are more creative, innovative and solve more problems when they aren't afraid of criticism. Laughter frees people up. Give people a spacehopper and who knows how the day will pan out.

I love a comic strip. A good friend gave me a full set of all of *Calvin & Hobbes*. It is the story of a kid and his toy tiger taking life's pitfalls with an ingenuity, playfulness, energy and anarchy that unfailingly makes me laugh out loud. Ideas flow after I've had a good laugh. Nothing seems quite so scary when you approach it with humour. My character *Brave New Girl* came about because of my fears. When something frightens me, I'll respond by drawing her doing something ridiculous to combat the challenge, or overcome the fear. Now I've created *Brave Old Girl* and as a former wild child punk now in her golden oldies. Her antics are even more outrageous and 'out there'. Who says you have to be young to be brave?

Humour is ubiquitous. Babies giggle, children laugh a lot. As adults we laugh less, but we feel better when we do. Laughter is infectious. I saw a set-up of a guy standing on a railway platform. He started to laugh, quietly at first then gradually more loudly. Slowly one by one other passengers began laughing too, despite themselves. Even though they didn't know what they were laughing at, the more people laughed, the more catching it became. It connected everyone in ways they couldn't explain.

Martin A. Seligman, one of the founders of positive psychology, has identified humour as one of the twenty-four characteristics required for mental wellbeing and success in life. When we were filming with people who were dying, there was a lot of gallows humour, often precipitated by those who were terminally ill. In the three years that we were with those families there was a lot more laughter than there was tears, more light moments than dark. Fear muscled in through the cracks but time and again it was crushed underfoot by a wisecrack or a bad joke.

Humour and creativity are both about looking at your challenges in novel ways. Having creative confidence to meet life's inevitable obstacles and problems means you avoid feeling helpless. Fear is the foe, but laughter shields you from the full brunt of its force.

How to boost the humour in your life

1. Watch comedy on TV, go see live stand-up nights (preferably with friends), read comic strips.
2. Find the absurd side of a situation, imagine how it could be catastrophically worse than it actually is, go beyond ridiculous. Make yourself laugh.
3. Surround yourself with people who make you laugh. And people who laugh at your jokes, even when they're terrible.
4. When you see something funny happening in the street, write it down or draw it. Tell someone about it later to keep the memory of why it made you laugh alive.
5. Don't take yourself too seriously. It's bad for your health.
6. Don't take what others say too seriously. It's their words but your choice to respond without offence.
7. When someone you're scared of has it in for you (like your boss), imagine them on the toilet.
8. Combining laughter and movement is an excellent way to lift your mood. Before going into an interview or other scary situations, do a little jig in the bathroom with the biggest, widest grin on your face. It's a good way to get your blood pumping and your brain firing on all cylinders.
9. When you're in pain, find something to laugh at. The distraction of laughing takes your mind off the pain. Mid-migraine I sucked on frozen watermelon to give myself brain-freeze. The ridiculousness of the experiment made me chuckle.
10. Turn an embarrassing situation of yours into a good story for your mates. It's all good material.

Respond to your Nurturer using your Little You's non-dominant hand:

- Tell yourself a corny joke

⊨——⊨

Here's Hope

If ever there was a pioneer for positive mental attitude and taking a hopeful approach, it was Stanley Matthews. He was a footballer extraordinaire. 'Stan the Man'. Beloved 'Wizard of Dribble'. What was it about him that made him so successful and so popular? He was certainly single minded, his drive to win was as much a part of his DNA as his studs were part of his boots. But he was also generous of spirit, understood the importance of teamwork, celebrated the successes of his fellow players, and appreciated and learned from those on the opposition who aced him. He was a pioneer in healthy eating and training. It was the spirit of hard work and positivity that kept him on his toes throughout his career. And this spirit stayed with him past his retirement at fifty. It went into his global mission and campaigning work that focused on using football to help get kids off the streets and into lives that contained hope. He taught them to know what hope is made of. None of us knows what is in store for us, but hope is having a dream, making it our goal and training and preparing to make it happen.

Dr Shane Lopez, senior scientist at Gallup, is spearheading fascinating new research showing that not only is hope good for your wellbeing, but it's a measurable quality that can be increased with practise. His book, *Making Hope Happen*, discusses the science behind hope and describes practical ways to improve your wellbeing by nurturing a positive, active approach to life. He believes that by increasing the element of hope in your approach, you can lead a happier, less fearful and more productive and successful life.

Once again it is your creative brain that is harnessed to till the soil, ready to plant the seeds of hope. Without the proactive approach of constructive and creative endeavour, the belief that tomorrow will be better than today is merely an optimistic attitude. When we actually do something about making the future a better place to be, then you are living in the real definition of hope. Being hopeful also helps you achieve more and to do so more quickly. Dr Lopez's studies show that you are 14% more productive at work when you believe that you are going to be successful in your outcomes.

Hopeful people understand that they need to have no more than two or three meaningful goals to work towards. Trying to juggle a chaotic life makes it hard to focus so we need to edit down our goals to what we know to be achievable by making them clear, specific and easily imaginable. They must also reflect our purpose and the values that have meaning for us. They must make us feel excited and motivated. We have to decide what matters to us most and concentrate our efforts on that.

If ever there was a story of hope triumphing over adversity and fear, it is that of Malala Yousafzai, as described on her Malala Fund website. She was born on 12 July 1997 in Mingora, a town in the Swat District of north-west Pakistan. Her father, Ziauhddin, ran a school in Swat near the family home. Pakistan has the highest number of children out of school and in 2009 the Taliban's efforts to encourage this, by restricting education and attempting to stop girls going to school, were sharply increased. But Malala loved learning and going to school. She began writing a blog for the BBC Urdu service under a pseudonym, expressing fears that her school would be attacked and discussing the increasing military activity in Swat. Television and music were banned, women were prevented from going shopping and then Ziauddin was told that his school had to close.

But Malala and her father both continued to speak out for the right to education. In 2011, she received Pakistan's first National Youth Peace Prize and was nominated by Archbishop Desmond Tutu for the International Children's Peace Prize. Her public profile and popularity enraged the Taliban leaders and they voted to kill her. On 9 October 2012, as Malala and her friends were travelling home from school, a masked gunman entered their school bus and asked for Malala by name. She was shot with a single bullet which went through her head, neck and shoulder. Two of her friends were also injured in the attack.

Malala survived, but was critically injured. She was taken to Birmingham hospital in the UK and not released until January 2013, when she was joined by her family. The Taliban's attempt to kill Malala received worldwide condemnation and led to protests across

Pakistan. In the weeks after the attack, over 2 million people signed a 'right to education' petition, and the National Assembly swiftly ratified Pakistan's first Right to Free and Compulsory Education Bill.

Malala became a global advocate for the millions of girls being denied a formal education because of social, economic, legal and political factors. Malala accepted the Nobel Peace Prize in 2014 with Kailash Satyarthi. She started the Malala Fund to raise awareness about the social and economic impact of girls' education and to empower girls to speak out, to work to their potential, and to demand change. Throughout her trials Malala remained undefeated. She trusted in hope, she stood firm to her beliefs, she defied fear and those trying to stop her, and still today continues to use her voice to share hope with others. She transforms fear into fearlessness.

Even in our dying days we can create a hopeful legacy; we can pass on our approach, teach others to dream and to fulfil their potential. Nelson Mandela left us hope by living his life with courage, determination, wisdom and belief. He proved that when all else fails, hope triumphs. He never stopped working towards what he believed could happen, against all the odds. He dreamed and he made a difference.

CREATING A HOPEFUL FUTURE

Respond to your Nurturer using your Little You's non-dominant hand:

- What legacy do you want to leave for the next generation?
- What are your hopes for their future?
- What would you like to see as your hopes in the next five years?
- What one step can you take right now to help create that hope?

⊨ ⊨

End of Week Five

⊨ CORE-WORK ⊨

Write the answers to these questions with your non-dominant hand.

Nurturer:
- What tools have you learned this week?
- How have you moved forward towards your goals?
- What action steps have you taken?
- How are you feeling about your fears right now?
- How can I support you this week?

⊨ ⊨

Week Six

....

OPTIMISING YOUR CREATIVE BRAIN FOR A FEARLESS FUTURE

- BUILDING YOUR CREATIVE MUSCLE: Do a Doodle, Learning to Look, Connecting the Dots, Improvisation, Creative Compass
- BEYOND YOU: Creative leadership, Helping Others
- CONCLUSION

....

So here we are in the final week of your creative coaching programme. You have had the opportunity to dream big and identify your values in order to create your passion and purpose. You are beginning to meet your own needs and raise the bar towards self-actualisation. You know your heroes and heroines who can continue to inspire you and you have your mentor, your coach, or buddy to keep you accountable and encourage you and celebrate your triumphs with you.

You are continually monitoring and supporting yourself through your core-work, your journaling and your daily brain dumps. You have your emergency tool kit when your fears threaten to overcome you. You give yourself time to daydream, slow down, meditate and let your mind wander. You take regular time out to notice the small stuff and appreciate the fleeting yet memorable and life-enhancing moments.

You face challenges but you have the strategies to break them down into manageable chunks and you don't let your inner imposter sabotage your efforts or undermine your self-esteem and confidence. You incubate your ideas until you are ready but you don't dilly-dally or procrastinate once you've devised your plan of action. You enjoy the company of others but you don't allow negative people or naysayers to hold you back. You don't please them before you please yourself. You're no narcissist but you are no pushover either. You focus on your lane and don't worry about what others are doing in theirs. You no longer compare and you've let go of despair.

You're not alone on your journey but it is your self-love that protects you and nourishes you. When the tough times come you have a way to put a spin on it. You can view any situation with a healthy perspective and a sense of fortitude. You experience everything with gratitude and that helps you banish your fears and anxiety. You don't give up or give in because you know what is important to you, what you love and how you want to spend your life. You'll keep bashing away at it with mastery in mind but appreciate the progress you make as you go. You embrace change because it no longer scares you, you create your environment to reflect the new you, and when you come head to head with others who haven't got your vision or your wisdom, you know how to gently persuade and negotiate with them so that you all come out winning.

You recognise that life comes with its hazards, hiccups and pitfalls but you don't exaggerate the downturns by catastrophising doom and disaster. You know when to surrender and when to pick up the pieces. You use your intuition and your curiosity to capture every serendipitous opportunity and employ your humour and ability to create hope. The future is what you decide it's going to be.

Life can be anything and everything. You have already tapped into your creative mind to develop all these new skills and open mindset. Now you are going to optimise those muscles by learning to think like an artist. It gives you the power to take your opportunities from ordinary to extraordinary. It makes you even more resilient, more courageous, more curious, more intuitive, more appreciative, more abundant and more hopeful. You'll be doodling, learning to look, making connections, improvising, building your creative muscle, understanding how you can lead and helping yourself and others smell the sweet smell of success.

Let go of your fears, trust the process and give it your best shot.

NOTE: *Not everything here will be relevant to you right now but read it all and do the core-work exercise for the areas that ring some bells for you.*

Building Your Creative Muscle

- Do a Doodle
- Learning to Look
- Connecting the Dots
- Improvisation
- Creative Compass

Do a Doodle

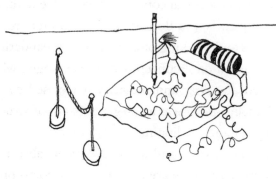

Let's jump straight in. I want you to get doodling. Doodling. DOODLING? 'You mean drawing?!' If you're not 'officially' an artist, these words may make you go into a cold sweat at the thought of making a fool of yourself. I'm simply saying, let your pen meander across a piece of paper and see what happens. Breathe, and let go. What's the worst that can happen?

When you absentmindedly scribble random marks while you think you increase your focus, grasp more clearly the concepts you're grappling with, and improve your memory. Maybe you think you can't draw, but who cares when the mere act of scribbling has such a powerful effect on your brain. Feeling nervous? Get your pen out and doodle.

A blank page and a pen is ripe territory for doodling. It concentrates your mind. It is a useful tool both at work and at school although, traditionally, getting caught at it would have got you into trouble. Now it is recognised as something to be encouraged; a way of aiding learning, processing, problem-solving, creative thinking and remembering.

Pre-mobile phones, people had landlines and very often a jotter pad next to the phone. You'd go to people's homes and see random marks on those jotters, sometimes even complicated scrawls, twirls and patterns. Visual abstract interpretations of a phone conversation. You could tell the emotional content by the dense dark, angry lines, or light flowery curls and flourishes. These jotters recorded the inner outpourings and working-outs of mental meanderings.

Recently I happened upon a concept called Zentangle, which is a form of combined doodling and meditation, devised by Maria Thomas and Rick Roberts in 2004 as an elegant system of structured patterns for zoning out and meditating.

Using deliberate pen strokes and a vocabulary of abstract patterns, artists and non-artists alike are equally able to focus on their marks with no pre-determined end result. Their attention shifts into a state of flow in which your anxious feelings abate and you open up your mind to let in new ideas and perspectives.

I practiced Zentangle for its meditative, anxiety reducing qualities, but it has also led me back to my love of drawing. Doodling seems to open up your natural urges and skills by tapping into your unconscious. Maybe the act of doodling will awaken the brain surgeon within you, or release the long-distance trucker desperate to get out on the open road. When you are trying to resolve a problem, take time out, pick up a pen and let it drift around the page. Try repeated circles, or lines, or geometrical shapes, dots, crosshatching, sweeping curves or angular marks. Place no judgment on what you do, there is no right or wrong. You may come up with a gorilla-headed flamingo surfing a rainstorm of samurai swords across a sea of platypus' feet on paper, but in your mind you may have just solved the conundrum to why, say, you are still in a job you should have left months ago.

The shapes, along with your hand movements, stimulate parts of the brain that allow you to make connections between things that you otherwise would likely have never come up with. It helps you tap into your memory, your emotions, your desires and your intellect. Sunni Brown, named one of the '100 Most Creative People in Business' and one of the '10 Most Creative People on Twitter' by *Fast Company*, is the leader of 'The Doodle Revolution', the purpose of which is to get people to think differently. Sunni Brown's design consultancy, Sunni Brown Ink, has worked with high-profile clients like LinkedIn, Zappos and Dell amongst others to improve organisation and planning by using doodles.

In decision-making, problem-solving and creative thinking we need to engage with at least two of the four learning processes: auditory, visual, reading/writing and kinetic. So in a lecture or in class or on the phone, where information density is high, doodling has the benefit of exploiting all four of the processes. Which is why it is so effective. As a visual person I have never liked using the phone. In fact it used to be one of my top fears. I felt like I was missing too much information, losing the subtleties and nuances of communication. When I started coaching I thought I would never be able to do it via phone. It really scared me! But I discovered by accident that if I sit with a pen and paper, and I draw in response to listening, that it becomes an incredibly powerful interaction. My fear subsided as I scribbled and I found I could hear even more deeply the essence of what my client is saying. I now also get them to draw as we talk; simple shapes, mind-maps or grids. Nothing tricky, but the act of doodling allows them to explore their thoughts, by placing words into the shapes and finding revealing patterns and constellations in the marks before them, which they are then able to describe to me. So simple but we reach profound solutions very quickly.

As humans we have the urge to make marks. We started daubing on cave walls and some of us still like to spray paint our inner primordial urges onto the sides of buildings. You can just pick up the nearest pen and the back of an envelope and scribble when you are feeling scared or trying to work out something that is troubling you. Who knows you may even end up shrieking 'Eureka!'

Start Scribbling

You need three essential items for this exercise:

1. A pen or pencil.
2. A blank piece of paper.
3. The willingness to surrender to wherever your pencil takes you.

That's it. Do it anywhere, at any time, but do it!

⊨ CORE-WORK ⊨

Respond to your Nurturer using your Little You non-dominant hand.

NURTURER: *Here are some patterns to get you started . . .*

What other patterns can you come with? Build your pattern alphabet until you have at least fifty. For inspiration, take photos of patterns when you are out and about. They are everywhere when you start to look.

Doodle these patterns in any design, as part of your FEAR LESS daily practice.

———

Learning to look

Imagine you are having problems with your boss at work. Normally a pretty congenial guy, as you've noticed over time, now suddenly he is flying off the handle at the slightest thing. Confused and nervous, but mindful of keeping your job, you don't fling back a plethora of pithy responses, but instead hold onto your hat, sit back to ride the storm and watch; trying to figure out what the hell is going on. You notice he's distracted, staring into his coffee cup, his fingers drumming the table, he fidgets, jumps up, paces. A female colleague walks in to ask a question on standards and ethics and he lets rip with a barrage of incomprehensible expletives. She backs out under the tsunami of abuse. He slumps in his chair. Then he turns the photo of his wife face down onto his desk. Bingo. Now you get what's going on. Noticing the subtle cues you can react to situations more subtly. You understand that he's going through his own private nightmare, and you become less judgmental, less fearful, more patient, and may even decide to offer a shoulder to cry on.

By taking the time to observe, without judgment, bias, preference, prejudice or fear, and by using your previous knowledge, you can notice changes. You can begin to unravel the mysterious, unlock problems and, with your creative and critical-thinking skills, you take the consequent correlations and connections, and begin to form understanding. And from there you can start to find solutions. Fear locks you down, observation opens you up.

How can you cultivate it?

Like any habit worth forming, the ability to observe and make deductions can be improved with deliberate practice. To writers, artists, scientists and private investigators, 'people-watching' is as important as practising scales is to a pianist. But who can't sit on the bus, tube or in a café and take a few minutes each day to focus outwardly at the world around them and learn from the inter-actions, the expressions, the movements, the textures and shades of human life?

There is no one way or right way to do it. Two people can visit an art gallery together; one will peer and investigate every picture in minute detail, the other will wander into each gallery space, scan the walls in a broad-brush fashion and only hone in on the work that jumps out at them. Then they approach the piece and exam-ine it with as much stealth as a scientist at her microscope. What are you looking for when you are drawn to a painting? You look at the brush strokes, the colours, the shapes, the composition, but you also search for the story, the emotion, the meaning. When you pull back and see the painting as a whole, it is as if you have 'felt' it, such is your deeper understanding of what you see. When you 'get' it, it resonates with you and somehow you feel better for it. Understanding calms the mind.

When my kids were little they went into the local post office to buy their Saturday-morning sweets. Their dad was waiting down the road in the car. My son Sol had to push the door to the shop quite hard and suddenly it gave way and they flew in. Intent on choosing which sweets they were going to have they went straight to the counter as the door closed with a bang behind them. Out of the corner of his eye, Sol noticed a guy standing in the middle of the small shop, wearing a tracksuit and trainers. The guy took one stride, pulled out a gun, pointed it at the post office clerk and yelled for her to hand over all the cash. But Sol had clocked that he was dodgy, grabbed his sister Ruby's hand, and they were already scrambling out the door and onto the street still clutching their unpaid-for sweets; no gunman was coming between them and their Saturday stash. The police were called and the man was eventually caught (and the sweet money paid). But the point was that Sol, even while distracted with the important task at hand, was observant enough to suss the situation and get his sister out. He'd observed enough that he was able to give the police a detailed description, even down to the logo on the gunman's trainers. The whole thing only lasted a few minutes. Of course they were terrified afterwards, as were we, at what could have happened, but his observation skills had shut down fear in the moment and he'd been able to take immediate, instinctive action. They both also gained a lot of confidence from knowing they had known what to do in a dangerous situation and had acted on their instincts. Observation and action had given them another rung on their resilience ladder.

Pump up your visual sense and your day becomes a brighter place. Look up from your smart phone, look out at the horizon, or zoom in on the nooks and crannies, climb to tallest building and look down at people scurrying like ants, or lie in the grass and watch the clouds turn into faces. Sit with a small child and see what they see, look through the glass into the gorilla enclosure and wonder what those intelligent eyes are conveying. Search out all the public art or graffiti in your area and stop for a while to contemplate what the artist was thinking when they made it. Take a walk through a forest and see how the branches twist and turn from one tree to the next, like scribbles in the sky. Tramp along a beach and see how many colours you can count in the pebbles or grains of sand. Peer out of the aeroplane window when you go on holiday and marvel at the patterns below, then look at the lines on the palms of your hands and see how the DNA of the planet and ourselves are interconnected. Keep a visual journal with you to scribble down what you see, in doodles or notes, and question the make-up of your observations. What more can you learn from what you have seen? The more you look outwards, learn to appreciate and be grateful for the wonders of the world, the less fear can intimate you. Keep looking and learning.

Creative challenge

1. Notice one thing today. Look at it in exquisite detail, run your fingers over it, take note of the many colours, shadows and tones. How warm or cold does it feel? Is it smooth, bumpy, scratchy, stiff, wobbly? What does it smell of? Imagine this object is new to the planet, how would you describe it to your relative who is now living on Mars?

⊨ CORE-WORK ⊨

Respond to your Nurturer using your Little You non-dominant hand.

NURTURER: *How many different ways could the object described above be used, other than it's intended function? Don't hold back on your imagination.*

Connecting the dots

The secret to creativity, intelligence, innovation and scientific thinking is the ability to make connections, to join the dots. In our heads we have a bunch of dots: memory, knowledge, thoughts. If we didn't connect them in some way to form coherent meaning then humanity would consist of amoebic lumps of jelly. And most of us aren't. When you see a new face, your eyes scan it for recognisable lumps. Ah yes, a nose, two eyes, a mouth. Good, yes it's definitely a face. Then your brain rifles through the memory bank to see if belongs to someone in your files. If it doesn't, then you search to see any features that resemble someone you know (the next best thing). If not, you check for traits you can identify with; kindness, intelligence, humour etc. All in a split second. If you reckon that the face is not going to bite, you probably put on a smile and say howdy. By connecting the dots of knowledge about faces you tap into your experience of people you know, trust, like and feel safe around.

So, besides avoiding being mauled by a hairy face with fangs, what use is connectivity? Presuming all the interconnecting wires of your brain are firing away merrily to allow you to function as you go about your business, how can you build on your ability to make connections? Highly creative people and scientists do it naturally. They are hunter-gatherers, particularly prone to investigate and question. Faced with a fact, they want to know why; uncovering a truth or a presumption is tantalising to them. They jump from one knowledge-image to the next, scavenging like jackdaws for shiny pieces of the puzzle, combining what they know with what they don't. They build bridges like a child uses Lego bricks, spanning one idea to the next. The work of creators and thinkers is a combinational force of found fragments. If anything could be called original it can only be in the way that anything new is simply a different pattern of elements or a combobulated combination of old facts or ideas. It's what lies behind problem-solving. And the better you are at that, the less fearful you feel in a changeable, uncontrollable world.

The police and anti-terror investigators are constantly making connections with each other, with other countries, with one suspect and another, with one atrocity or another. As they connect and evaluate, they see patterns emerge. They are able to assess, predict and gather evidence. The better the connections, and the understanding behind them, the safer we are; the freer we are to keep going about our daily business. We create our own connections around risk and danger. We use our experiences, our knowledge, our insights, our intuitions to make judgments on any situation and we calm our fears by understanding what is safe and what possibly isn't. Humanity is charged with curiosity and the need to connect, build and transform. Like a magnet, creativity repels us from fear and attracts us towards new solutions and ways of being and doing.

Elon Musk connects his companies; SolarCity provides the energy to charge the battery stations for his Tesla electric cars, which in turn cross-fertilise material and mechanical innovations with his SpaceX rockets. He anticipates an interplanetary population and he works out what dots he needs to connect to make that happen. He'll have to work out how to use methane to fuel his rockets to get to Mars, and he wants to create a space-internet to keep up communication between planets. Everything he does is to connect ideas and inventions in a trail towards his main goal of finding an alternative habitation when planet Earth is no longer sustainable. Fear of annihilation was the trigger; curiosity, creativity and connectivity are his way of repelling fear and attracting solutions. His mind and his methodology are an extreme example of how creative connectivity bounces vague dreams into unique and fantastical reality.

We can all be curious and fire up new connections, boosting

both our intelligence and our creativity; and find ways to transform our fears into something useful. The more we read, the more we expose ourselves to different experiences. The more we question, explore, challenge and investigate, the greater our ability to use our ever growing creative thinking skills. Perhaps you don't want to turn your unmade bed into a work of art or go down to the local butcher for a sheep's head to suspend in formaldehyde, but maybe you do want to find solutions to problems in your life. With enhanced creative connectivity (from recognising patterns of behaviour and how they interconnect) you won't find yourself going round and round in circles; you will mind-map your way to a greater level of understanding, illumination and insight about your life and how you can live and work in a more satisfying and less fearful way.

··

Connection Challenge

1. Think of your big dream or purpose in life. Draw lots of circles on a page. Write in each circle a piece of knowledge or resource you have that might help you with this dream. E.g. Musk wants a million people to inhabit Mars in the first instance. His resources and knowledge bank include: cheap and reusable rocket technology, solar energy understanding, the best minds in the business, the ability to tap into vast quantities of financial funding, a stubborn belief that he can make it happen and so on.

2. Draw lines between the circles with directional arrows. What resource enables what bit of knowledge to move forwards? What needs to happen, before something else can evolve? Who can help you? What knowledge or experience are you missing? What do you still need to learn? What

ideas fire up when you make these connections? What fears are driving you? What are the rewards for completion? What might trip you up along the way? What can you put in place as a firewall against this? What other questions do you need to ask?

3. Look at how your mind fires up when you make these connections. You start to think in a much more fluid four-dimensional way. When you visually see how your brain works you use its capacity to connect in much more ambitious and exciting terms. Our mind is like the universe, and the planets are dots or concepts. If you can draw the connections you can see more clearly the direction you need to go, what you need to have in your arsenal of resources, and what you are missing.

You can use this creative connecting technique on any problem, goal or fear. Having it on the page visualises your roadmap and without a map it's easy to get lost.

───

⊨ CORE-WORK ⊨

Respond to your Nurturer using your Little You non-dominant hand.

NURTURER: *Name a fear you have. What does life look like when you have overcome that fear? Now draw a road map of resources that you already have to help you combat that fear. What is the first step you are going to take today?*

⊨⊨

Improvisation

Life is one long improvisation. You plan something, then something else crops up and you have to think on your feet. But there is a difference between fire-fighting through your days and improvising. To live an improvised life is to live in the moment, acutely attuned and connected to your surroundings, to other people, listening, observing and responding spontaneously without preparation or pre-meditation. It makes everything feel alive, vivid and pin-sharp. There is no sluggishness or panic in this approach, it is quick, responsive and exciting. An improvised life is full of colour and laughter. Something troubling tips up; you improvise your way around it.

Showstoppers is an improvised musical show where the performers have a bunch of props and costumes, and the audience shouts out suggestions for a title, characters and story. The team then improvises a full-length musical, stopping every so often for updated plot points thrown in from the audience. It's an extraordinary, terrifying, edge-of-your-seat way to produce a show; as the audience you don't have the faintest idea what will happen next and neither do the performers. Much like life. And that's why it can feel so scary and out of control at times. Learning to think on your feet, to improvise, helps you surf the tidal wave and try to avoid the detritus coming your way.

The ability to improvise requires letting go of feeling self-conscious, of your known responses, of what's right. It uses gut instinct and the ability to act on intuition. It requires you to trust yourself and your abilities. Generally we learn to live in a very prescribed way, it feels safe on the well-worn path. We dampen down the voices that cry out to try something different, from fear of risk or of appearing foolish. Or, heaven forbid, from making mistakes. We tread carefully and we reduce the expanse of what life could be.

I learned to play the piano by reading sheet music. I could play Rachmaninov but not without the score in front of me. I was schooled in playing what I could read. I had no sense of music coming from within. I was a musical typist, as I was later told by a musical improv teacher. Harsh but true. I couldn't jam on the keys for toffee. I couldn't let go. The piece of paper with black notes in front of me kept me safe. Then I met a friend who improvises on the piano to silent films, on stage and in public. The horror! I asked how she could do such a thing without drowning in terror. She said simply that she parks her ego, sits at the keyboard, watches the film and responds to it. She allows the music to flow out of her.

I thought it was a good recipe that could be applied to other areas of my life. I wanted to be a better film director, to be able to work with actors, using their language. So I braced myself and enrolled in an improvisation class for directors with one of the *Showstoppers* performers. How excruciatingly uptight we all were to start with, our egos smarting with humiliation at the very thought of playing the fool. But slowly he punctured our self-conscious poses with exercises and games, thrusting us out of ourselves and our fear, until we could carouse around the room like kids on a sugar-spike. We were unburdened and limitless. We listened acutely, we responded to the moment; the other person being paramount in our attention. We were generous, we didn't block each other, our imaginations were set free, we played and experimented. We laughed, cried and howled to the moon. We performed, and our movements, reactions, exploits and intentions felt true, real and natural, because they were. We had learned to tap into the core of ourselves and to trust it.

So how do we free ourselves up from fear in everyday life? The art is to get outside of our heads, stop dwelling on the past, stop anticipating the future, focus on the moment, put your full attention on the other person and listen. Don't block them with 'No buts' but encourage with 'Yes and . . .' Roll with it, see where it takes you. Suddenly the world will come into sharp focus, you will notice details that blurred before, you will feel more energetic and enthusiastic. You will be less self-centred and self-censored. The more you do it, the easier it will become. You will park your ego and your fear. Life will feel more fun and spontaneous, and your relationships will improve because what are a few face-plants between friends?

Maybe it's no coincidence that improvisation is made of the word IMPROVE.

How to Improvise in Life

1. Do an improvisation class. It's terrifying but once you learn to get out of the way of logic and conditioning, you'll find your mind making giants leaps of thinking, you'll make connections you'd never normally make, and your party repertoire will improve dramatically.
2. Try the Cognitive Shuffle technique. Developed by cognitive scientist Luc Beaudoin to help people sleep, it's also called

Serial Diverse Imagining (SDI). It's a method designed to scramble your mind to take it away from your worries and stresses (which prevent you sleeping). When you use the technique, your brain thinks that the cortex isn't engaged in a dangerous situation or it would be focused on one thing, so it relaxes, and allows you to sleep. However, if you try it when you are up and about in the daytime, it acts like a creative exercise bike.

3. So, the idea is to think of one random image after another in rapid succession. It's easier if you decide on a letter and leap from word to word beginning with that letter: rhinoceros, Rastafarian, rolling pin, rental car, rhombus, retribution, rhinestones, regulatory systems, rhythm 'n' blues, rock star, revolution. Try it for five minutes a day to get your imagination leaping about and conjuring up different images. See how they connect and free-associate. Your visual and creative mind is like a muscle, so get it pumping. Also try this when you are feeling fearful or anxious; it works a treat in massaging your stress into calm.

⸙⸙

⊨ CORE-WORK ⊨

Respond to your Nurturer using your Little You non-dominant hand.

NURTURER: *Write out the letters F E A R L E S S. Underneath each letter write out all the positive words that come to mind beginning with that letter. Don't think, just write, as quickly as you can. Set a timer if you like.*

⊨⊨

Creative Compass

There is a seam of gold that runs deep in you and that is your creative compass. It builds on your intuition and helps you find ways out of danger, out of grief, out of fear, sorrow and loss. We strike out into the unknown with a map we've made ourselves, we learn from our mistakes and we choose a different path, we originate and innovate, we challenge ourselves out of our comfort zones, and we follow our imaginations to dream up exciting new futures.

If you had a serious health scare and, when in recovery, you were told you could only spend two hours a week doing what you wanted, what would it be? There is nothing like a bolt out of the blue to rock your world and force a sharp focus on what really matters. Any flabbiness in your life purpose gets whittled away pretty damned quick when your life depends on it. Even in the best-case scenario life is pretty fleeting, so it's best to get a sense of urgency on the matter.

When I directed the documentary on people with terminal illness, *Death*, for Channel 4, I was struck by the resourcefulness and passion that they took on once they'd passed the point of denial and had entered the period of acceptance. An energy and lust for life overtook them. They entered each day with a determination not to waste a single second. They got their affairs in order, they took care to make sure everything would be OK for the loved ones they were leaving behind; they designed their funerals and chose their coffins. They made a music playlist. The community nurse I interviewed, who cared for the terminally ill in their homes, said that those who made the most of their dying days were the ones most able to leave the world in a peaceful and less fearful, less painful way. The ones who clung to their anger and fear died in much more pain and with visible agony at having to depart. They say, we die as we have lived.

When I witnessed the elevated energy and creative flow of those who chose to live life to the full right up to the very end, I vowed not to wait until I had a terminal diagnosis to commit fully to life. Why wait? After all, life is terminal. My grandmother lived with a creative, loving, fun, positive spirit right to her final days. I sat with her when she was dying and the creative compass with which she lived her life held true to the end. Her passing made me less afraid of dying and more determined to live in her spirit. She was a huge inspiration in the creation of *Brave New Girl*.

I asked my daughter what, if anything, makes her fearful. Without hesitation she replied 'the future'. So, I asked what she does to reduce that fear and she told me that she makes little plans. She has a whole summer ahead of her before her next term at university. She wants to earn money, she wants to fill her time and not get bored or lonely, she wants to travel, she wants to get fit and she wants to do various work experience jobs related to her course. So she's planned her trips, applied for work and work experience placements, she goes to the gym and she sees her friends. I asked how her next few months look now. 'Not so scary,' she said. She had recognised her fears, and plotted what she could do about them and then she took action. Her fears subsided.

So if you only have two hours a week when you can do anything you want, what would you do? Watch your imagination jump about. Learning to fly, bungee-jumping, becoming a chess champion, swimming in the Danube, cordon-bleu cookery, ice-sculpting, stamp collecting, cave-dwelling, inventing an air-conditioning vest, finding a cure for meningitis, hanging out with friends, spending time with your children, reading your way through your local book shop? The options are dizzying . . .

We are essentially inquisitive, acquisitive, risk-taking and creative, we respond quickly to external rewards and punishments but we also get long-term gratification and satisfaction from being absorbed in a task we enjoy. When we are driven purely on the basis of curiosity, creativity and engagement we feel happier and we perform better, for much longer. Intrinsic reward follows as a natural outcome. Imagine how that knowledge can transform business, education and life choices.

Everyone has an inner compass they can use to transform their lives. When you feel stuck or scared, tap into your natural creative resources and use them to shift your thinking and find a better way forward. What sparks your attention, what fires you up, what did you dream of as a kid, what were your passions, what made your heart sing, what makes you jump for joy? Your inner creative compass is there to point you away from fear and towards what makes you happy. You already have everything you need within you to find the direction to get you to where you want to be.

Creative Challenge

1. Imagine you have six months left to live: how are you going to spend it, what are you going to do, who are you going to share your time with, what have you never tried but would love to? What have you never seen but have a deep yearning to visit? Get going on that bucket list.

2. Make a legacy box for someone you love. What messages, notes, little drawings, pressed flowers, photos, poems or favourite songs will you put in there? Imagine them at different stages of their life and the wisdom that you can impart, or experiences you've had, that you can share. Give the gift of your life in all its creative imaginings.

=== CORE-WORK ===

Respond to your Nurturer using your Little You non-dominant hand.

> NURTURER: *Imagine your funeral and, one by one, your friends and family stand up to give a speech about the things they loved about you. What would you like them to say? Are you living it now? How can you be more of what you'd like to be? Is anyone going to say, 'she/he spent way too much time in the office', or are they going to rejoice in the fun, innovative, explorative and curious way you led your life?*

=====

Beyond You

- Creative Leadership
- Helping Others

Creative Leadership

Humans thrive on sociability, on connecting and communicating; on following their creative and moral compass. Creative leadership is overtaking traditional leadership because it recognises this need and sees being a connector of people as paramount to its role. And connection starts with a creative approach, a willingness to connect the dots, to reach out, to be part of a network of people and ideas, to find a way through fear and beyond to where life-enhancing solutions may be found.

Creative leadership is for parents, teachers, bankers, office workers, astronauts, entrepreneurs; it's for anyone who works with more than one other person. It not leadership in the old sense, with the big cheese at the top of the pyramid; the creative leader guides from the middle, listens, looks out for connecting voices and thoughts and brings the right people together to encourage collaborative effort. Google and Pixar run their organisations like this (at Pixar every single employee is encouraged to give their feedback on the films) but effective schools do too. And it's also possible for families. Hierarchy is built on ego and fear. A flat structure is built on creativity and leading from within.

Imagine a creative leader (it could be a parent, CEO, film director, etc.) as a spider weaving a cobweb of invisible connections to other individuals around a central goal or interest. In the home, your connecting threads may stretch out to clusters of people you know at the gym, the children's friends, your friends, the school staff, the church group, the local pub. When your teenage offspring start looking for work experience, if you are a creative-thinking parent, you will talk to people in your cobweb of connections to find someone who can offer a work placement. Then your teenager is introduced to another cluster and their family and professional network is extended. It's less scary to reach out to someone when you have a mutual connection, however tenuous. With social media, the possibilities of connection are immeasurable.

If you work in an organisation that has a more segregated set-up it will be harder to have a dialogue with people in different departments. But even within that kind of scenario you can lead from within, no matter where you are on the traditional inflexible hierarchy. You can start to engage with others, make connections, communicate, form development think tanks made of people from all levels and across all divisions. It might be just to bring about a richer coffee bean in the coffee machine, or to introduce a book-lending rotation or to think up ways to give back to the community. But what you are starting to do is bring people and ideas together, and when you do that, you plant seeds of creativity that will send up shoots in many directions.

Connection is as vital as the air we breathe. When we filmed soldiers for our feature documentary *A Brutal Peace*, we discovered a critical part of their post-war survival is to meet regularly through the charity Combat Stress to help each other roll with the punches of post-traumatic stress disorder. They find each other when they leave the forces, they phone each other, they attend funerals together, they go to the Cenotaph on Remembrance Day together, they help each other find jobs, they organise events and fund-raising days. A private in the army becomes a creative leader in his ex-army community through his heavyweight determination to see his mates right. With imagination and understanding he rallies his ex-troops, leading from the middle and getting them through from one day to the next. Without the camaraderie of support and connection over shared stories and a pint by the bonfire, these men would fade into the recesses of unbearable memories, suffering and terror.

There was a report published recently by IBM called 'Capitalizing on Complexity'. It was based on a survey of 1,500 CEOs of for-profit companies, non-profits, social entrepreneurships, and public sectors from around the world asking what's on their minds. The CEOs said they had three overall priorities. The first priority was running organisations that can respond to **complexity,** because the world is getting more complex every day. Second was how to run organisations that are **adaptable** and resilient to these changes. But the top priority was how to promote **creativity** in organisations. The answer to these three priorities of complexity is to think differently about people and to reposition the role of leadership. That is, lead from the middle, to minimise the fear factor for others who feel they are at the bottom of the pile, or that their ideas are less significant. These priorities are a significant development from old, school leadership.

Hierarchy creates an atmosphere of fear. An integrated flat structure allows for creativity and connection. Try it at work, at home, in schools, hospitals, councils, governments, and see how everyone has the chance to become engaged, accountable, listened to, valued and creatively channelled.

....

Creative leadership challenge

1. Make connections that enable you to learn from and be supported by others.
2. Lead from the middle, to minimise the fear factor for others who feel they are at the bottom of the pile, or that their ideas are less significant.

3. Create a cellular structure instead of the old hierarchical one.

4. Hire people who share your 'purpose'.

5. Build a sense of community like a spider's web.

6. Don't let fear be your leader. Step away from your ego and join forces with others. Your employees are your compatriots who will contribute much more creatively and productively if you encourage them to.

7. Don't allow fear to hold back your teams. Let them take risks and learn from failure. Let them help each other to find ways out of problems, so that they aren't forced to competitively clamber over one another to receive your approval.

8. Be a guide and a supporter of other people's passions, proactive development, their growth and creative vision.

9. Lead by example. Experiment, explore, play, be audacious, listen, embrace change, be flexible, lean and compassionate. Drill down to the essentials and be driven by your bigger purpose. Know the power of collaboration, connection and community.

....

⊨ CORE-WORK ⊨

Respond to your Nurturer using your Little You non-dominant hand.

NURTURER: *Think of someone you care about who has a fear that is holding them back. From everything you have learned, what creative strategies would you share with them that you believe they would find the most valuable and why?*

⊨⊨

Helping others

Humanity thrives on co-operation, compassion, and creativity, keeping communities growing in a healthy and balanced way. The author of *Man's Search for Meaning*, Viktor Frankl, describes how he survived the concentration camps because he searched for meaning in the minute details of daily life and interaction with others, not because he trampled on his fellow inmates to beat them to the scraps of life hidden in the cracks between mass murder and destruction.

The situation with the huge numbers of refugees fleeing across Europe from their war-torn countries to seek safety, food, shelter, and a means to live, must yank the heart-strings of even the most narcissistic amongst us. Concerned citizens are digging into their creative-thinking skills to come up with ingenious way to contribute to the rescue of members of their wider community, suffering a nightmarish plight. Ever the pioneer in social responsibility, Bob Geldof, apparently offered his house to three Syrian families. A group of Scandinavians opened the back of their car to hand out collected supplies of food to refugees on the road. Young people donated their tents from the Reading festival to the people struggling to find shelter in Calais.

In times of crisis and fear we reach into ourselves to find ways that we can help others, our compassion awakened and called upon. But should we wait until catastrophe strikes before we are moved to think beyond 'I' to 'we'?

Occasionally we might perform a random act of kindness to someone in the street or put a few coins in the hat of a homeless person. But to live wholeheartedly on every level in a way which puts others' success and survival as paramount takes our abilities to be selfless into another dimension. The point where we unquestionably open our homes to strangers is where we reach our highest degree in humanity. A friend of mine's husband is a long-distance truck driver and, a few years ago, had a near fatal accident in Spain. My friend flew to be by his side, living every day in terror that he might not pull through. She knew no one and couldn't afford a hotel. A woman at the hospital, a complete stranger, invited my friend into her flat to stay through the long months of helping her husband back through a coma state and into recovery.

Going beyond yourself puts you out of ego's way. You may be dogged by fear, but lifting yourself to a place where you can shine your light so that others may find theirs, wrestles that fear out the way.

A seventeen-year-old young woman (Client Z) came to me for coaching only months after her mother had taken her own life. For the first time I was scared that coaching wouldn't be big and strong enough for what she needed. I knew on a deep level that I could help her, but I needed to trust myself and the process. I also needed to put my trust into the simple act of one human being helping another in a time of dire need.

My own daughter was Z's age. I made a silent promise to Z's

mother, wherever she was now, that I would help Z try to find a light through this very dark tunnel.

She had been seeing a psychotherapist but said it was making her more depressed, not less. She had found out about the coaching process and how it helps people move forward. She was about to do her A-levels and she had got a place at university. She wanted help getting through her exams and getting herself into an emotional place where she would feel ready to leave home in October. Her simple desire was that by then she wanted to feel 'normal'; like any other teenager heading off to university. We had about six months before she was due to go.

In our first session I talked to her about trying to find one positive thing a day, no matter how small, that she could write in a journal before she went to sleep. That one small task seemed mammoth, like trying to find a diamond in a mountain of black coal. But with huge courage she searched every day for that diamond.

Over a couple of sessions she felt more able to find up to three things a day she could say that she felt good about. Through the first few sessions we set about getting to know each other and building her trust and confidence in the process. We took time to really get to grips with what her core values were. She gradually started to carve out an idea for a mission statement, a 'why', and a 'purpose' that would give her strength to go on even when she felt she couldn't.

We spent time on her beliefs, both the ones helping her and the ones holding her back or bringing her down. She was particularly open about her mum around these and we were able to look at her feelings around her mum's decision to take her own life. Each step of the way Z was courageous and committed, never afraid to come face-to-face with her emotions and the difficulty of the situation she was in. Often we were able to laugh and find positive ways to move forward. At other times she was able to cry and be OK with that. We did lots of drawings and mind-maps to help visualise her feelings and thoughts. At first her 'needs' chart was very dense; when we redid it a few months later, she surprised herself to find how much less 'needy' she was.

We gradually built up a set of tools to help her through the times when she felt panicky, anxious, sad, lonely and scared. She learned to use her breathing, to build a gentle night-time routine, to keep journaling, to collect special mementos. She decided that one of her goals would be to ask everybody that knew her mum from around the world to send her photos and memories they had of her mum, and she created a memory book in chronological order of her life. She found it a profoundly therapeutic project and she proudly showed it to me when she had finished. It was her reward to herself for getting through her exams.

After a holiday break we met up again and she was so excited to tell me how happy she was feeling. She was excited about the future. Slowly she started to reclaim her life. Other times she would feel sad again but I was able to reassure her that bad days are normal and that she wasn't being thrown back to where she was at the beginning. Things were still up and down for her, but she was getting stronger all the time. Our coaching sessions became more organic, often led by her, as she gathered her toolbox of coaching and coping skills around her. Finally, she was ready to head off to university. She took with her the beautiful memory book she'd created of her mum's life. A book full of love.

If ever there is a Brave New Girl it is Z. She came through that dark tunnel and now with her huge smile and courageous energy she shines her light on all those around her.

Living beyond the straitjacket of the self makes us open our eyes to the possibilities of a more expansive way of living. Nourishing others gives you a sense of dignity and accomplishment, to live generously and kindly. By sharing our knowledge, our resources, our skills, our connections, our friendship, our empathy, our humanity, we extend ourselves past survival and fear and into a meaningful existence. When we see the picture from the International Space Station we look down on Earth and we see it as a whole. We don't see borders, boundaries, walls. We don't see different religions or cultures or skin colour. We see a mysterious ball of life that we are all part of and are all responsible for.

We should be afraid, our fear should be palpable and terrifying, when we think that we might destroy our planet through lack of care and disinterest. We should be afraid for our fellow citizens both human and animal. We should be afraid of division and inequality and violence and terror. We should be afraid of dictators and weapons and greed and arrogance. We should be afraid of the harm we do to our bodies, our minds and our hearts. When we are afraid, we are galvanised to take action. We hear our call to arms. We feel our values and our purpose and the threat to everything we care about. Let us be creative in our solutions and let us thrive beyond resilience and survival.

Let us help others and ourselves to fear less and fly high.

....

Creative Compassion Challenge

1. Be 'we' not 'I'. Practise for a week not using 'I' in a sentence, it feels amazingly liberating.
2. Perform a random act of kindness every day for a week. When you help others, you are less focused on your own fears and concerns.
3. Observe how concern and compassion change people's attitudes. What examples can you come up with of people whose lives are enhanced by the helping of others?
4. On social media what can you do 'for' others rather than

broadcasting 'about' yourself? Use social media as a tool for helping others.

5. At networking events go along thinking 'what can I do for others' rather than 'what can others do for me?'

Final summary for turning fear into fearlessness with creative strategies

1. Cultivate gratitude to promote healthy sleep patterns.
2. Find your meaning and purpose in life through your goals and values.
3. Learn to split the perpetrator/cause of your fear, from your reaction, and from you. Create a gap so that you are not your fear.
4. Maintain active mindfulness or daydreaming to stay in the present, to not catastrophise but to let your imagination gestate.
5. Take regular exercise, eat healthily for your mind, be mindful of your gut flora, and drink lots of water to keep your body and mind fit.
6. Do daily visual journaling or freewriting to dump your underlying fears and concerns, and re-programme your mind with a more positive outlook.
7. Learn forgiveness, take out the personal and the unenforceable rules, not to condone or forget, but in order to understand your hurt and to create boundaries.
8. Build healthy habits of mind and keep moving forward, one step at a time.
9. Use your imagination to solve problems instead of creating them.
10. And breathe . . .

⊨ CORE-WORK ⊨

Respond to your Nurturer using your Little You non-dominant hand.

Nurturer:
- Describe everything you have done for others in this last week that has made you feel good
- You have just won an OBE or the Nobel Peace Prize; imagine what you would have loved to have done in order to receive it
- How can you shift your life to align with your values more?

AND FINALLY

- Summarise where you were at the beginning of week one, the tools you have picked up along the way through the six weeks, where you are at with achieving your goals, and what changes have occurred to allow you to harness fear and use it to live more powerfully.

At this stage you may find you are writing more fluently with your non-dominant hand and that you are tapping into your core self much more easily. Don't stop now. Remember it is a tool for life. Practise through the good times so that when the going gets rocky you can call for help and your Nurturer will be right there for you.

⊨⊨

Conclusion

Congratulations on completing the FEAR LESS Creative Coaching Programme. It is a lot to absorb, so take your time to digest it. Go back and re-read sections that seem relevant for you now. In the future, other aspects might come to the fore. It's an ongoing process of learning, growing, getting stuck, and having to learn some more.

You conquer anxiety with action and use creative momentum to outrun self-doubt. You are working to continuously improve your life on all levels but in steps that feel manageable. You have an exciting vision for the future. You keep focused on the present moment, but you can also enjoy fond memories and past triumphs. You learn from your mistakes and you look for opportunity in every challenge, setback and adverse circumstance. Your purpose gives you your drive to reach higher and beyond yourself. Following your passion answers your deep call from your inner self to create and grow. There are no secrets to hide from, you live transparently, openly and you welcome those who share your values. That inner bully fear has slipped into the background because it knows that you have put yourself creatively in charge of your self-care. There are no guarantees in life, but this way at least you can make the most of what it has to offer, unhindered by fear and calm in the knowledge you have the tools to flex with the flow.

We started with fear and we end with finding creative ways to help others. Fearlessness is about hope for ourselves and for the next generation, it is about gratitude and appreciation, it's about understanding where we are vulnerable and how we can make ourselves stronger. It is using our creative skills to build on what's gone before, to evolve and grow. It includes failure and rejection and it uses our ability to pick ourselves up and keep moving forward, even if only slowly and incrementally. We know now we must rest and recharge our creative batteries, let our thoughts wander and our ideas gestate. We know it's about taking action when we need to, based on our intuition and authentic inner voice. We know it's about finding and pursuing our own unique mission in life. Fearlessness is fear used imaginatively as a force for good and as energy for making the world a better place. Cherish your creative powers, use them in every way you can to fulfil your own potential and to give every chance to others. Fear less and be more.

THE END

Appendix

CORE-WORK

DAILY JOURNAL

- How are you feeling today?
- What can I help you with?
- What fear-less strategies can we use?
- What action can we take today?
- How much do I love you?
- How are you being fearless and fabulous today?

References

1. Kaufman S. B, & Gregoire C. (2016). *Wired to Create*.
2. 'The Creative Brain: How Insight Works', *Horizon*, BBC Two, 2012–13.
3. Capacchione, L. (1991). *Recovery of your Inner Child*.
4. Greger, M. (2015). *How Not to Die*.
5. Mayer, E. (2016). *The Mind-Gut Connection*.
6. Greger, M. (2015). *How Not to Die* and Perlmutter, D. (2013). *Grain Brain*.
7. Singer, J. L. (1974). 'Daydreaming and the stream of thought', *American Scientist*, 62, 417–425.
8. Williams, M. & Penman, D. (2013). *Mindfulness*.
9. Kaufman S. B, & Gregoire C. (2016). *Wired to Create*.
10. Hawking, S. (2001). *On the Shoulders of Giants*.
11. Ordóñez, L. & Schweitzer, M.E. & Galinsky, A. D. & Bazerman, M. H. (2009). 'Goals Gone Wild: The Systematic Side Effects of Overprescribing Goal Setting', *Academy of Management Perspectives*, 23, 6–16.
12. Halvorsobn, H. G. (2011). 'The Science of Success: The If-Then Solution', *Psychology Today*. Available at: https://www.psychologytoday.com/articles/201101/the-science-success-the-if-then-solution
13. *Playboy*, February 1972, Buckminster Fuller interview.
14. Begley, S. (2009). *The Plastic Mind*.
15. Duhigg, C. (2012). *The Power of Habit*.

16. Duhigg, C. (2012). *The Power of Habit.*
17. First described by psychologists Suzanne Imes, PhD, and Pauline Rose Clance, PhD, in the 1970s.
18. Gilbert, E. (2016). *Big Magic.*
19. Cuddy, A. (2016). *Presence.*
20. Vance, A. (2015). *Elon Musk.*
21. Dweck, C. S. (2006). *Mindset.*
22. Hanscom, D. (2016). *Back in Control.*

Acknowledgments

To my mum and dad who have always supported and encouraged me to do what I believe in, to Pablo for his huge love, 100% belief and boundless cheerleading, to Tobe for his ever-lasting friendship and co-parenting partnership, to May for continuing to smile down on me from wherever she is now. To all my dear friends and family for being amazing human beings; compassionate, kind, courageous, outrageous, funny, anarchic, creative, caring, talented, inspiring, impulsive, intuitive, gutsy, ballsy, brave and unbreakable. To my mentors and collaborators, who have advised and supported me through thick and thin. To my coaching clients for their dedication, hard graft and commitment to the coaching process as well as their willingness to share their stories in this book. To my best buddies and soul mates Kit and Emma whose lives were cut too short but who stay alive in my heart. To Brave New Girl who pops out of my pencil every day and never fails to show me what fearlessness can be. To my passionate agent Clare Conville, who swept BNG off her feet and took me under her wing. To my wonderful publisher Amanda Harris, fabulous editors Lucy Haenlein, Amy Christian and Ru Merritt, and the whole team at Orion Spring who have been so creative in bringing this book to life. A big noisy Thank You to you all, from the bottom of my heart and the top of BNG's lungs. We wouldn't be here without you all.